The Fiction of Rushdie,
Barnes, Winterson
and Carter

The Fiction of Rushdie, Barnes, Winterson and Carter

Breaking Cultural and Literary Boundaries in the Work of Four Postmodernists

GREGORY J RUBINSON

McFarland & Company, Inc., Publishers
Jefferson, North Carolina, and London

ACKNOWLEDGMENTS

Extracts from *Midnight's Children* by Salman Rushdie © 1980 by Salman Rushdie. Reprinted with the permission of The Wylie Agency, Inc.

Extracts from *The Satanic Verses* by Salman Rushdie © 1988 by Salman Rushdie. Reprinted with the permission of The Wylie Agency, Inc.

Extracts from *Imaginary Homelands* by Salman Rushdie © 1981, 1982, 1983, 1984, 1985, 1986, 1987, 1988, 1989, 1990, 1991 by Salman Rushdie. Reprinted with the permission of The Wylie Agency, Inc.

Extracts from *A History of the World in 10½ Chapters* and *Flaubert's Parrot* by Julian Barnes used by permission of Peters, Fraser & Dunlop. Published in the United Kingdom by Picador and in the United States by Vintage.

Extracts from *A History of the World in 10½ Chapters* by Julian Barnes published by Jonathan Cape. Used by permission of The Random House Group Limited.

Extracts from *Flaubert's Parrot* by Julian Barnes published by Jonathan Cape. Used by permission of The Random House Group Limited.

Extracts from *Written on the Body* by Jeanette Winterson published by Jonathan Cape. Used by permission of The Random House Group Limited.

Extracts from *Written on the Body* by Jeanette Winterson. Copyright © 1993 by Jeanette Winterson. Reprinted by permission of William Morris Agency, Inc. on behalf of the Author.

Extracts from *The Passion of New Eve* by Angela Carter. Copyright © 1977 by Angela Carter. Reproduced by permission of the author c/o Rogers, Coleridge & White Ltd., 20 Powis Mews, London W11 1JN.

Extracts from *The Passion of New Eve* by Angela Carter. Copyright © 1977 by Angela Carter. Reproduced by permission of Time Warner Book Group UK.

Extracts from *The Sadeian Woman and the Ideology of Pornography* by Angela Carter. Reproduced by permission of Time Warner Book Group UK.

Extracts from *Heroes and Villains* by Angela Carter. Copyright © 1969, 1991 by Angela Carter. Published in London by Penguin Books in 1981. Reproduced by permission of Penguin Books Ltd.

Extracts from *Heroes and Villains* by Angela Carter. Copyright © 1991 by Angela Carter. Used by permission of Viking Penguin, a division of Penguin Group (USA) Inc.

LIBRARY OF CONGRESS CATALOGUING-IN-PUBLICATION DATA

Rubinson, Gregory J
    The fiction of Rushdie, Barnes, Winterson and Carter : breaking cultural and literary boundaries in the work of four postmodernists / Gregory J Rubinson.
        p.   cm.
    Includes bibliographical references and index.
    ISBN 0-7864-2287-4 (softcover : 50# alkaline paper) ∞
    1. English fiction—20th century—History and criticism.
    2. Postmodernism (Literature)—Great Britain.
    3. Winterson, Jeanette, 1959– —Criticism and interpretation.
    4. Carter, Angela, 1940– —Criticism and interpretation.
    5. Rushdie, Salman—Criticism and interpretation.
    6. Barnes, Julian—Criticism and interpretation.   I. Title.
    PR888.P69R83   2005   823'.91409113—dc22   2005012774

British Library cataloguing data are available

On the cover: Clint Griffin, *Guys in Red*, 2002, photograph and mixed media

Manufactured in the United States of America

McFarland & Company, Inc., Publishers
   Box 611, Jefferson, North Carolina 28640
   www.mcfarlandpub.com

For Frances Rubinson with love and gratitude
and in memory of Mitchell Rubinson

Table of Contents

Acknowledgments iv
Preface 1
A Note on Spelling and Abbreviations 5

INTRODUCTION. Genre and Postmodern Fiction 7

ONE. Salman Rushdie 29

TWO. Julian Barnes 77

INTERCHAPTER. The Gender Divide 110

THREE. Jeanette Winterson 112

FOUR. Angela Carter 147

FIVE. Failing to Observe Decorum 187

Chapter Notes 199
Works Cited 213
Index 223

Preface

This book explores the fiction of Salman Rushdie, Julian Barnes, Jeanette Winterson, and Angela Carter. I have chosen to concentrate on these four as their work broadly represents the major preoccupations of contemporary British literature; studied collectively, their work offers a comprehensive, aggregate critique of contemporary society, each aspect of which complements the others. Rushdie, Barnes, Winterson, and Carter focus their critique on a series of fundamentalisms—religious, political, racial, national, and sexual—that continue to foster social conditions in which disempowered groups are prevented from achieving full social, political, and cultural citizenship. By rewriting and directly challenging religious narratives, they desacralize religious legends, customs, and axioms of social behavior. Their critique extends to totalitarian political programs, world-wide androcentrism, and racism. These writers also portray some of the illusory foundations of the European Enlightenment and traditional Western approaches to subject matter in science and history.

The introduction provides an historical and theoretical context for the study of British postmodern fiction through its experiments with traditional genre conventions. Literary theorists such as Ralph Cohen, David Bleich, Mikhail Bakhtin, Thomas Beebee, and others have drawn attention to how literary and language genres have always been and continue to be in flux as they respond to social, historical, and cultural factors. Many contemporary British writers have been acting on this premise by changing received genres such as realism, fantasy, scripture, historiography, romance, fairy tale, the gothic, science fiction, and pornography to challenge traditional social values regarding issues such as gender, sexuality, religion, race, and nationality. Salman Rushdie, Julian Barnes, Jeanette Winterson, and Angela Carter are exemplary in this regard. They formulate their social critique through actions with genre. Because genre traits reflect the values of the social and historical scenes in which works of writing are produced, these postmodern writers mix, change, and self-consciously call attention to the conventions of genres in order to critique the traditional social values they carry and suggest newer, more egalitarian ways of responding to human differences.

Chapters One and Two discuss issues related to history, politics, race, nationality, and religion in the works of Salman Rushdie and Julian Barnes. Rushdie has been at the center of one of history's largest and most prolonged conflicts over issues of the sacred and the profane. As I discuss in Chapter One, the controversy surrounding the publication of *The Satanic Verses* raises important issues about religious and political fundamentalism, hegemony, and the social functions of art. Chapter One also focuses on Rushdie's use of magic realism (itself a mixed genre) and the grotesque to confront the political problems of post-independence India, race problems in contemporary Britain, and the ongoing conflict between faith and doubt on the global/political level and the individual/spiritual one. Chapter Two extends the historical and religious concerns of Chapter One, focusing on Barnes's use of a multitude of narrative genres to address problems of reliability in historical and religious sources of knowledge.

Rushdie and Barnes are incisive critics of religious and political manifestations of tyranny, but they are less aggressive in criticizing social injustices based on gender. As the beneficiaries of an androcentric world, Rushdie and Barnes are not as motivated to examine gender as they are other political and religious issues. But, as the primal form of human social division, gender inequality serves as a template for political and religious forms of oppression. In other words, as Virginia Woolf suggested in *Three Guineas*, political and religious oppression can be seen as extensions of gender-based expressions of inequality.

Contemporary women writers such as Jeanette Winterson and Angela Carter have attacked gender issues head-on, getting at the root of social inequalities. Chapters Three and Four, then, shift to questions of gender and sexuality. Winterson, whose work I discuss in Chapter Three, is one of the most popular figures in the younger generation of women writers influenced by Carter. Winterson self-consciously uses, parodies, and critiques the language and conventions of religious texts, romance, and scientific discourse to challenge some of the more conventionally restrictive ideas about gender and sexuality. Finally, although she did not precipitate the kind of global debate that Rushdie did, Angela Carter was one of the most profane voices in literature in the last decades of the twentieth century. Carter wasn't widely popular until later in her career, no doubt in part because self-consciously feminist literature has taken a long time (and struggles even now) to find a significant audience in an androcentric reading culture and publishing industry. Carter has grown in popularity in the last two decades and especially since her death in 1992. With some historical distance, it is now easier to see that she was a key early figure in Britain's literary renewal, and so Chapter Four discusses the fiction of her early and middle periods. Carter's experiments with genres like science fiction, gothic fiction, pornography, and fairy tales helped pave the way for a wider critique of gender and genre by writers like Margaret Atwood, Kathy Acker, Tanith Lee, Fay Weldon, Sara Maitland, Emma Tennant, and Jeanette Winterson.

While the majority of this study focuses on Carter, Winterson, Barnes, and Rushdie, it also makes comparisons to other British writers (past and present) who approach similar issues in similar ways. Chapter Five briefly considers some of the work by other genre-bending contemporary British writers such as Martin Amis, A. S. Byatt, Ian McEwan, Emma Tennant, D.M. Thomas, and Fay Weldon. These writers, too, insist that oppressive ideologies be met with vital resistance. They are all important figures in what seems to be a new boldness in contemporary British fiction. They and others like them protest long-standing social inequities through an aggressive artistic campaign of desacralizing received religious and pseudo-religious ideals. They challenge us to imagine and create a world order that will accommodate new peoples and new mores.

A Note on Spelling and Abbreviations

There are many British spellings within the quoted sections of this study. I have kept them in their original form.

Parenthetical citations to texts frequently referred to will use the following abbreviations accompanied by a page number. Specific details of each edition can be found in the Works Cited section.

AL   Jeanette Winterson, *Art and Lies*
AO   Jeanette Winterson, *Art Objects*
BB   Jeanette Winterson, *Boating for Beginners*
BC   Angela Carter, *The Bloody Chamber and Other Stories*
FP   Julian Barnes, *Flaubert's Parrot*
GS   Jeanette Winterson, *Gut Symmetries*
H   Julian Barnes, *A History of the World in 10½ Chapters*
HV   Angela Carter, *Heroes and Villains*
IH   Salman Rushdie, *Imaginary Homelands*
LL   Julian Barnes, *Letters From London*
MC   Salman Rushdie, *Midnight's Children*
PNE   Angela Carter, *The Passion of New Eve*
RF   Lisa Appignanesi and Sara Maitland, *The Rushdie File*
SV   Salman Rushdie, *The Satanic Verses*
SW   Angela Carter, *The Sadeian Woman*
T   Julian Barnes, *Talking It Over*
WB   Jeanette Winterson, *Written on the Body*

A poet's work.... To name the unnamable, to point at frauds,
to take sides, start arguments, shape the world
and stop it from going to sleep.
—Salman Rushdie, *The Satanic Verses*

Genre and Postmodern Fiction

Genre Play and Postwar British Fiction

At the very end of John Gay's 1728 play *The Beggar's Opera*, one of the players interrupts the progress of the story to confront the play's putative author about the proposed execution of Macheath, the polygamist thief:

> *Player.* [...] this is a downright tragedy. The catastrophe is manifestly wrong, for an opera must end happily.
> *Beggar.* Your objection, sir, is very just; and is easily removed. For you must allow that, in this kind of drama, 'tis no matter how absurdly things are brought about so you rabble there—run and cry a reprieve—let the prisoner be brought back to his wives in triumph.
> *Player.* All this we must do, to comply with the taste of the town.
> *Beggar.* Through the whole piece you may observe such a similitude of manners in high and low life, that it is difficult to determine whether (in the fashionable vices) the fine gentlemen imitate the gentlemen of the road, or the gentlemen of the road the fine gentlemen. Had the play remained as I at first intended, it would have carried a most excellent moral. 'Twould have shown that the lower sort of people have their vices in a degree as well as the rich: and that they are punished for them [Hampden 158–59].

The Player is upset, for Macheath's execution would defy the expectations of the genre. The ease with which the Beggar assents to and effects the Player's demands mocks the absurd lengths to which endings that result in marriage and general happiness are contrived in the operatic form. Similarly, the frequently facile morality of the genre is burlesqued by the ironic suggestion that "*lower-class*" morality can be as dubious as that of the upper-class. The title of the play in itself indicates a challenge to the formal aspects of opera, for opera, at this stage in history, was a form of elite theatre meant to deal exclusively with legendary characters through an elevated tone. It is not something to be scripted by a "beggar"; nor is it meant for the entertainment of the common populace (as is a form of theatre like pantomime); nor is it supposed to deal substantively with "commoners" and thieves as this play does.

This exchange is one of the most provocative in theatrical and literary history. It steps outside the realist frame of the theatre's conventions to mock and critique their complicity with problematic representations of class. It is also a signature moment of a vibrant eighteenth-century British anti-tradition characterized by unorthodox techniques including upsetting generic expectations and critiquing moral hypocrisy by satirizing and inverting dominant social values. Such irreverent practices were staple features of work by other eighteenth-century writers like Jonathan Swift, Henry Fielding, and Laurence Sterne, all of whom are frequently referred to today when discussing the traditions out of which "postmodern" writing has emerged. Just as Gay, Swift, Fielding, and Sterne turned a self-conscious eye to the genre conventions they were employing, today's "postmodern" writers have been working within and against the genre traditions which they have inherited.

There has been a long history of genre play in British literature. Much of the vitality of British cultural production stems from this tradition. British culture revels in ironic and irreverent rewritings of old stories, mixing genres to create new forms, and combining "high" and "low" culture. This is evident in British literature and other "high" arts as well as in popular British culture such as the television sketches and films of Monty Python and pantomime.

Pantomime, one of the most enduring forms of irreverent British art, is a farcical entertainment which began to develop in the early eighteenth century and was the immediate precursor to "ballad-operas" or "ballad-farces" like *The Beggar's Opera* (Nicoll 135–136). The pantomime remains a vital genre of theatre in Britain today, and one which refutes the stereotype of extreme British propriety. As Angela Carter has commented, "There's no other country in the world where you have pantomime with men dressed as women and women dressed as men, and everybody thinks this is perfectly suitable entertainment for children. It's part of the great tradition of British art, is all that 'smut' and transvestism and so on" (Sage, "Interview" 187). Julian Barnes describes pantomime as a form with a

> promiscuous permeability to modern culture, so that at any moment the stage is likely to be invaded by some two-minute television cult that the parents have barely caught on to. Darth Vader outfits jostle with TV magicians, old Empire racism with Green jokes, and all is resolved with much audience participation and a join-in-or-die singsong [*LL* 13].

In a pantomime I saw staged in Norwich in January 1998, Darth Vader was out and the Spice Girls were in. As Barnes sardonically remarks, "Perhaps, on reflection, it isn't too surprising that the panto hasn't caught on in other countries" (13).

Pantomime is generally considered to be a frivolous art form. Barnes says that by its very nature it is somewhat "debased—that's to say, various, eclectic, vulgar, referential, and topical" (13). But these and many of the other characteristics of pantomime—its self-consciousness, its mixing of forms and material in a playful, farcical, even bawdy way—are evident in much of the literature produced in Britain in the last thirty years or so. Perhaps by virtue of this dabbling with the "low," a common charge leveled at contemporary British fiction is that it has lacked scope and quality. Mostly this protest has been voiced by those who cling to literary traditions that reflected a grander, imperial England. Q. D. Leavis, for example, wrote in 1981 that

> The England that bore the classical English novel has gone forever, and we can't expect a country of high-rise flat dwellers, office workers and factory robots and unassimilated multi-racial minorities, with a suburbanized countryside, factory farming, sexual emancipation without responsibility, rising crime and violence, and the Trade Union mentality, to give rise to a literature comparable with the novel tradition of so different a past [qtd. in Connor 56].

On the contrary, it is exactly those less-privileged, formerly excluded voices who have breathed new life into the British novel. Leavis is certainly right that the old England is gone forever. Her lamentation of this fact is typical of the nostalgia for a putative golden age so prominent in the social imagination of the British elite and in the political discourses that characterized Thatcherism. Such nostalgic evocations of England's glorious past proved marketable enough to galvanize wide popular support for the Falklands War and the Tory government which instigated it and held power throughout the 1980s and half of the 1990s. Literary work of this era derived its energy and ingenuity in great part from adopting an oppositional stance towards that government and the values grounding its policies.

I agree with Lorna Sage who, in one commentary, remarked that British fiction in the 1980s was not, as is often thought, "insular, provincial, timid, inward-looking, and disappointing," but "bold, various, satiric, serious, funny and subtle" (qtd. in Massa and Stead 13). How else describe an era that gave us works as diverse and innovative as Salman Rushdie's *Midnight's Children* and *The Satanic Verses*, Martin Amis's *London Fields*, Angela Carter's *Nights at the Circus*, Jeanette Winterson's *The Passion*, Ian McEwan's *The Child In Time*, and Kazuo Ishiguro's *The Remains of the Day*? This era of literature is just as worthy of study and scholarly attention as the literature of the "great tradition" which Leavis and her husband admired with such enthusiasm.

British literature has gone through a number of phases where different sets of conventions have been dominant. Before the "postmodern" era of renewed experimentation, British literature of the twenty years or so after World War II returned to a predominantly realist mode. Though there have been some compelling scholarly attempts to defend the quality and importance of the writing of this era,[1] it is true that this was not the best time for British fiction. While America was giving us vibrant, experimental novels by writers like Thomas Pynchon, Joseph Heller, John Barth, and Kurt Vonnegut, British fiction, with few exceptions, was in an era of introspection and retrenchment.[2] It is as if the literature of the era was in a state of recoil, responding to the massive losses incurred during the war as well as postwar events and changes such as the loss of empire, the establishment and subsequent erosion of the Welfare State, and the Suez Canal crisis. Many writers turned away from the formal experiments of modernism and returned to more traditionally realist narratives. Steven Connor notes, for example, that writers like Margaret Drabble and Angus Wilson returned to a virtually nineteenth-century aesthetic (45). Though Drabble began publishing early in the 1960s, her sentiments seem typical of the dominant approach to art immediately following the war: "I don't want to write an experimental novel to be read by people in fifty years who will say, ah, well, she foresaw what was coming ... I'd rather be at the end of a dying tradition, which I admire, than at the beginning of a tradition which I deplore" (qtd. in Connor 45).

Jeanette Winterson has written in opposition to this kind of nostalgic approach: "The 1940s and the 1950s seem to me to be a dead time, in my terms because the anti-art response, Realism, bounced back again in a new outfit but wearing the same smug expression" (*AO* 42). Winterson dislikes realism—even to the extent of proclaiming it "anti-art"—because for her reality defies encapsulation: "Reality is continuous, multiple, simultaneous, complex, abundant and partly invisible. The imagination alone can fathom this and it reveals its fathomings through art" (151). For Winterson, art is by definition a "heightened" or imaginative representation of reality, an aesthetic philosophy reflected in her own work and in that of many of her contemporaries.

But the fact that Drabble, Wilson, and others like Graham Greene, Iris Murdoch, Muriel Spark, and Kingsley Amis returned to a realist style in this period does not mean that this literature was unimportant. Winterson is in part responding to what she sees as a betrayal of the experimental spirit of modernism. The social realists of the 1940s and 1950s were less daring in style than the modernists, but Winterson's comments are perhaps tainted by a misapprehension of realism as an unchanging genre of representation. As Andrzej Gasiorek points out in his study of postwar British fiction, the dominant understanding of what realism is does not account for the variety of styles which have been categorized as realist: "realism should be seen as a complex phenomenon, which takes a variety of forms in different historical periods" (181). Gasiorek's study demonstrates that realism itself is a genre or a collection of narrative conventions which have varied in subtle but important ways throughout literary history and, further, that the twin claims that realism is "fundamentally conservative" and experimental forms of writing are "inherently radical" are misconceptions (181).

Although the formal experiments of modernism receded following the war, British writing continued to respond to many of the same problems and themes of modernism, including a focus on representations of the world and the individual in a state of decline and loss. Henry Scobie, the protagonist of Graham Greene's *The Heart of the Matter* (1948), replies to an inquiry about the Catholic conception of Hell by saying "They tell us it may be a permanent state of loss" (194). Hell, according to this definition, is his life for he is overwhelmed by the loss of his child and, with her, his youth, vitality, and the capacity to do something new. He is condemned to follow a pre-scripted path of banal interactions with his wife and mistress. Writing to his mistress, he laments the banalities and clichés which he considers himself and everyone else trapped into continuously reenacting:

> *I love you more than myself, more than my wife. I am trying very hard to tell the truth. I want more than anything in the world to make you happy* ... The banality of the phrases saddened him; they seemed to have no truth personal to herself: they had been used too often. If I were young, he thought, I would be able to find the right words, the new words, but all this has happened to me before [181].

In the end, the clichés and the pain they cause drive Scobie to suicide, a literary cliché in itself.

The sentiments that Scobie expresses and the themes of the novel— the overwhelming sense of loss, impotence, and nostalgia in a world facing its twilight—along with the representation of subjective experience are common features of modernist literature; but the story-telling is in a very traditional mode, unwilling or unable to "do" something new, as if the very clichés that Scobie laments constrict the potential of the novel form. It is this sense of entrapment in old, recognizable forms that Winterson regrets. For the next generation of British writers, however—writers like Angela Carter, Salman Rushdie, Kazuo Ishiguro, Ian McEwan, Martin Amis, Graham Swift, Julian Barnes, Will Self, and Jeanette Winterson herself—contemporary reality may be dominated by previously scripted clichés, but those clichés can be appropriated and rewritten for a critical effect. They do not, in other words, have to be passively accepted as they are, for example, by Greene's Scobie.

Postmodern Profanity

British writing slowly began to regain a sense of innovation in the 1960s, a decade which saw the publication of key unconventional works like Anthony Burgess' *A Clockwork Orange* (1962) and John Fowles's *The French Lieutenant's Woman* (1969). Even some of the writers at the forefront of Britain's new social realism such as Spark, Murdoch, and Wilson began to turn to more experimental, self-conscious forms, albeit in much less dramatic ways than more contemporary writers. Part of this renaissance was no doubt indebted to the rebellious spirit of the sixties which was crucial to the formation of a new critical consciousness in British society (and elsewhere) and helped shape a newly re-energized literature. The 1960s saw significant domestic tensions around issues such as race, class, gender, sexual orientation, and political enfranchisement—topics that remain volatile throughout the world today. In a well-known appraisal of that era's social significance, Angela Carter wrote that "there was a brief period of public philosophical awareness that occurs only very occasionally in human history; when, truly, it felt like Year One, that all that was holy was in the process of being profaned" ("Notes" 70). Among other things, Carter attributes this "profane" spirit of the sixties with inspiring her to begin questioning how the "social fiction of [her] 'femininity' was created" (70). That same profane spirit is at the core of a great deal of British writing since then, especially of the four writers I give special attention to in this study: Salman Rushdie, Julian Barnes, Jeanette Winterson, and Angela Carter herself.

Rushdie, Barnes, Winterson, and Carter (as well as others such as Graham Swift, Ian McEwan, Martin Amis, and Fay Weldon) are often referred to as exemplary writers of postmodern fiction. The frequently unorthodox conventions of postmodern fiction include, among others, any combination of the following: genre mixing and self-consciousness about genre conventions; an explicit attention to the construction and constitution of cultural sign-systems; intertextual references; re-readings and re-writings of old texts including literature, myth, and scripture; meta-fictional authorial intrusions; a de-personalized, analytical tone; parody; satire; and a denial of realist conventions including narrative closure. Post-modern fiction's experimentation with traditional literary forms and self-conscious transgression of genre boundaries mirrors a prominent irreverence towards social conventions.

It is a critical commonplace nowadays to say that postmodern fiction is subversive or critical of dominant ideologies or master-narratives. As Linda Hutcheon has influentially proposed, postmodern writing is char-acterized by a "de-naturalizing" critique of various dominant ideologies (*Politics* 3); it attempts to overturn hierarchies and give voice to previously marginalized, oppressed, or suppressed groups and individuals. The issue of profanity which Carter raises expresses more or less the same idea, but it puts a specifically religious emphasis on the process. Profanity automat-ically invokes the concept of the "sacred," a category these and other post-modern writers are clearly out to challenge. In the most obvious sense of the word "sacred," each of the four writers I discuss in this study respond irreverently to values, knowledge, and expectations that are the product of religions and religious texts. In general, these writers view religion as a fraud engineered partly to control and limit human action and choices. By rewriting and directly challenging religious narratives, they desacralize the origins of religious ideologies. But there are other kinds of ideologi-cal "fraud" these writers are out to desacralize or at least debunk, whether they derive from political programs, culturally pervasive androcentrism and racism, philosophical movements such as the Enlightenment, or tra-ditional approaches to disciplinary study of subjects such as science and history. All of these are sources of values that are deeply rooted in human society and often seen as authoritative or unchallengeable. But, as the epi-graph to this study suggests, it is the work of writers to "name the unnam-able, to point at frauds, to take sides, start arguments, shape the world and stop it from going to sleep." Rushdie, Barnes, Winterson, and Carter take this stance.

Throughout this study I will be discussing how these writers formulate their social critique through actions with genre. Like John Gay in *The Beggar's Opera*, they mix, revise, and self-consciously draw attention to the traditional conventions of the various genres with which they work. These kinds of innovations with genre, I will be suggesting, are integral to their project of desacralization and "pointing at frauds." However, traditional ideas of genre are not broad enough for fully understanding their work.

New Considerations about Genre

According to Aristotle, Plato, Longinus, and Horace, genre refers to a fixed set of characteristics which classify literary forms. Classical, New Critical, and structuralist theories further sought to define rules and boundaries for different generic forms. Alastair Fowler comments that "Until now, genre theory has largely consisted of empirical listing of generic repertoires, or (more superficially still) of structuralism's aprioristic dichotomies" (296). For example, Northrop Frye sought in *Anatomy of Criticism* to establish a scientific study of literary form, attributing unvarying characteristics to specific genres in opposition to one another. The history of art and literature tells us something different—that genres interact, blend, and evolve in response to a variety of social and historical factors including technology, ethics, market forces, and politics. Genres come to prominence, reach a point of regular use, fade away, and then later re-emerge in different and combined forms.

In the broadest of senses, genre is what enables us to distinguish between primary formal categories such as novel, drama, and poetry. Even on this fundamental structural level, however, these forms are not discrete. Most British drama up until the nineteenth-century was composed in part or entirely of poetic verse; a poem can employ a number of conventions from drama, as is the case with a great deal of Robert Browning's poetry, for example; and novels can have whole sections presented in the form of drama (e.g. Joyce's *Ulysses*) or poetry (e.g. D. M. Thomas' *The White Hotel*). Nevertheless, most imaginative literature can still be said to fit primarily into one of three categories: novel, drama, and poetry.

Mikhail Bakhtin has suggested that the reason for the novel's overwhelming popularity is that it is capacious enough to include other genres. For Bakhtin, the novel as a genre is still developing, a form which insists on generic dialogue and a mix of language and voices (*Dialogic* 3–40). While this theory of the novel as a hybrid of forms is an essential contribution to our present conception of genre, Bakhtin's elevation of the novel at the expense of the other genres is problematic. Drama and poetry are not the "dead" or fixed forms he proclaims them to be, though perhaps their relegation to the elite margins of literary interest is cause for concern.[3] It is important to recognize, however, that Bakhtin uses the designation "novel" in a more global sense to denote an impulse in literary history commensurate with those features of the "novel" he recognizes as central: namely, its dialogism and heteroglossia.

The novel form has led to a popular reconception of what genre is. The most common use of genre now is as a category to describe and market the thematic contents of prose fiction: a text is considered science fiction if it concerns the future, technological innovations, space travel, and aliens; a western if it tells the story of a heroic individual fighting against the odds in the old West; pornography or erotica if it features explicit descriptions of sex primarily for the purpose of titillating the reader; and so on.[4] Genre tells us what we can expect from the book we are going to read. Thus, another defining feature of genres is the communities of readers that develop around them. In *Reading the Romance*, Janice Radway took the innovative approach of investigating the readership of mass-market romance novels. Her study demonstrates that a genre is in part defined by the needs of those readers attracted to it. The romance genre, Radway determined, compensates for a lack of emotional gratification in its primarily female readership (95–96). Thomas Beebee calls this function the genre's "use-value" (4), a use-value which is catered to by the publishing industry. Similar use-values could presumably be found for all genres. Though one can't expect that each reader of a particular genre would share the same use-values, a degree of consensus could be obtained for many. As Beebee claims, however, "use values are shifting rather than fixed — which is why generic systems are shifting, rather than fixed" (279). In general, then, the use-value of a specific genre will vary at different points in history, particularly in response to changes in dominant social ideologies. And as use-values change, so too will literary genres.

This is the major idea behind current versions of genre theory. Criticism that delimits literary genres disregards the diversity of literature which defies generic boundaries. Not until relatively recently have there been attempts to think of genre as a heterogeneous set of recognizable formal and thematic conventions which evolve and mix. Ralph Cohen has argued that all genres are inevitably mixed and that they evolve in response to specific social, cultural, and historical processes. Cohen observes that "genre concepts in theory and practice arise, change, and decline for historical reasons. And since each genre is composed of texts that accrue, the grouping is a process, not a determinate category. Genres are open categories"; genre groupings, he asserts, "arise at particular historical moments, and as they include more and more members, they are subject to repeated redefinitions or abandonment" ("History and Genre" 204, 210). Thus, a very old genre like fantasy has given birth to the science fiction genre which itself has diversified into recognizable genre categories such as feminist science fiction and cyberpunk—two genres which developed out of specific modern historical situations, namely women's liberation and the "information revolution." Another way of thinking about the evolution of genre is as generic transformation. As genres develop, continuity between two examples of a particular genre can be perceived, yet changes are also inevitable. According to Cohen, examples of such generic transformation "might be revisions or alterations that result in modifying a genre or in providing it with a different concept" ("Afterword" 275). Angela Carter's use of pornography and fairy tales (see Chapter Four) to critique rather than (as is traditional with these genres) perpetuate sexist and gender-essentializing social values is an excellent example of genres being modified to convey unconventional concepts. Cohen's contribution to genre theory, then, is his recognition that genres are not fixed formal rubrics but categories that mix and evolve with historical and cultural changes.

Speech or oral genres should be viewed in terms similar to those used for written genres. In his essay "The Problem of Speech Genres," Bakhtin suggests that all language, oral and written, is communicated through a variety of "speech genres" which include:

> short rejoinders of daily dialogue (and these are extremely varied
> depending on the subject matter, situation, and participants), everyday
> narration, writing (in all its various forms), the brief standard military
> command, the elaborate and detailed order, the fairly variegated reper-
> toire of business documents [...] the diverse world of commentary (in
> the broad sense of the word: social, political) [...] the diverse forms of
> scientific statements and all literary genres (from the proverb to the mul-
> tivolume novel) [60–61].

It is a diverse catalogue, but Bakhtin claims that any language use participates in a specific set of conventions. For example, business documents such as memos, law documents such as briefs, or scientific writing such as lab reports will all tend to conform to a set of conventions or expectations that affiliate them with other examples of the same genre.

Further, dialects themselves exist in different genres. In *Know and Tell*, a study of genre, language use, and writing pedagogy, David Bleich discusses how languages such as Black English, Yiddish, and "Spanglish" are variants and mixtures of other "standard" languages like white English, German, and Spanish (40–41). Bleich suggests that people are bound to each other in communities through their own genres of language. Naturally, these languages reflect aspects of the particular community's social and cultural situation: "Spanglish" is spoken by those who are geographically and culturally on the border of Latin-American and North American society; Yiddish reflects the separation and mixing of Jews and Europeans, especially Germans; and the very structure of Black English, according to June Jordan, reflects an opposition to the dominant values of white American society (see Jordan, "Willie Jordan").

In literary texts, paying attention to the language idiom used by a particular writer can aid in classifying and understanding a text's genre. Take, for example, Kazuo Ishiguro's novel *The Remains of the Day* which recounts the exploits of a model English butler in an aristocratic house both before and after World War II. Ishiguro's novel is a revision of the genre of comic novel centering on the stereotype of the taciturn, wry, nonplussed, and endlessly resourceful English butler as found in P. G. Wodehouse's numerous Jeeves novels.[5] A crucial distinguishing feature of *The Remains of the Day* is the idiosyncratically staid diction of the butler-protagonist, Stevens. Here is a sample from the novel's first paragraph:

> It seems increasingly likely that I really will undertake the expedition that has been preoccupying my imagination now for some days. An expedition, I should say, which I will undertake alone, in the comfort of Mr. Farraday's Ford; an expedition which, as I foresee it, will take me through much of the finest countryside of England to the West Country, and may keep me away from Darlington Hall for as much as five or six days. The idea of such a journey came about, I should point out, from a most kind suggestion put to me by Mr. Farraday himself one afternoon almost a fortnight ago. In fact, as I recall, I was up on the step-ladder dusting the portrait of Viscount Wetherby when my employer had entered carrying a few volumes which he presumably wished returned to the shelves. On seeing my person, he took the opportunity to inform me [...] [3].

Nearly each sentence contains a modifying clause such as "I should say," "as I foresee it," "I should point out," and "as I recall." There is an element of linguistic excess in these phrases and other aspects of the diction which comes off as a compulsive attempt to control language and the potential for misunderstanding just as he attempts to control every aspect of the affairs of Darlington Hall. In conjunction with the generally "stuffy" and pretentious tone of the language, Stevens' diction reflects the controlling compulsiveness of the butler role he takes pride in playing to the fullest.

This idiom, which Ishiguro sustains throughout *The Remains of the Day*, is one of the characterizing features of the novel's genre for it places the novel in the tradition of "butler fiction" popularized by Wodehouse. In typical postmodern fashion, however, *The Remains of the Day* departs from the tradition it participates in. Wodehouse's Jeeves is a master of witty "bantering" and he demonstrates his resourcefulness time and again by engineering plans to get his master, Bertie Wooster, out of trouble. Stevens, on the other hand, is utterly unfamiliar with the "bantering" speech genre his contemporary American master expects from him, and he is unable to prevent his former master, Lord Darlington, from becoming a Nazi dupe and facing national shame. This failure plagues him for the rest of his life and is reflected in the restrained language he employs to attempt to re-assert control over his domain.

Language and idiom, then, contribute to the generic make-up of literary texts. This is particularly evident in postmodern fiction (like Ishiguro's) as one of the more common conventions of postmodern writing is to draw attention to and exaggerate language characteristics. The aggressively hyperbolic diction or the highly theorized jargon of some of Angela Carter's writing, and the "Indianized" English idiom of Salman Rushdie are examples of this, as I will discuss in greater detail later in this study.

The word "genre" comes from the Latin root *genus* which means "kind," "sort," "species," or "class." It is only through academic tradition that genre has come to be used in limited ways. The term itself invites us to develop categories for grouping texts according to any recognizable affinities. As I have attempted to demonstrate, genre represents a variety of ways of categorizing texts: by readership, primary formal structures, literary themes and milieu, narrative conventions which cater to a particular use-value of readers, aesthetic philosophies, historical trends, and language dialects and styles. Discussing genre, then, is a complex task because one can be referring to any combination of the above categories and/or others. Further, every text participates in a number of genres simultaneously—a text has its marketing, historical, thematic, formal, and idiomatic categories all at once. Often, texts participate in a number of genres in a single genre category. Thus, a text can be simultaneously science fiction and thriller; novel and short-story collection; naturalistic and self-reflexive; fantastical and realist; realist and postmodernist; written in "standard" English and Black English. Ralph Cohen writes that a text is a hierarchical network, a system that is linked with other texts in a larger system to form a generic hierarchy. Thus some forms, like tragedy, or epic, or satire, or lyric, are dominant at one time and recessive or subordinate at others ["Afterword" 266].

My discussion of genre in relation to contemporary British literature, then, requires a much more broadened conception of genre than is traditional. The dominant conventions or traits of a text's genres are often continually in flux, especially so in much postmodern literature. The specific mix of genres in a text requires study in relation to its social, cultural, and historical scene—what David Bleich calls "its existential locus" (36).

The Ideologies of Genres

Like many others, Ralph Cohen has noticed a strong similarity between postmodern literature and the anti-traditional literature of eighteenth-century writers like Swift, Fielding, and Sterne: "Fielding's self-conscious addresses to the reader [...] his use of inset stories and thus of multiple narrators who result in making the primary characters become secondary while some of the trivial characters become, for the inset story, the primary narrators" are "practices [...] analogous to some in postmodern genres" ("Postmodern Genres" 18). Similarly, Sterne's *Tristam Shandy* is frequently referred to as exemplifying metafictional self-consciousness, generic flux or play, parody, and open-endedness—all traits commonly associated with postmodern fiction. Cohen recommends that a "generic history will not merely point to [such] recurrences, but suggest that these are tied to social and cultural no less than literary phenomena" (19). But what are these social and cultural phenomena? Fielding, Gay, Swift, Sterne, and others turned to such unorthodox methods in order to register their protest against prescribed social values and their propagation through the dominant literary conventions of the era.

Fielding himself was effectively prevented from pursuing his ambitions as a dramatist by the Stage Licensing Act of 1737, which was passed partly in response to the production of his plays *Pasquin* and *The Historical Register*, both of which satirized Sir Robert Walpole and his government. In the wake of that legislation, the theatre became a place purely for the articulation of conservative moral standards (Hampden xviii–xix). The novel and the stage had both become dominated by conservative ideological interests. Thus, Fielding and others turned to a satirical and self-conscious use of these genres to protest conservative values and hypocrisy. With *Shamela* and *Tom Jones*, Fielding approached novel writing in a highly self-conscious manner to satirize and critique the morality expressed by his ideological rival, Samuel Richardson, in *Pamela* and *Clarissa*. As I've already suggested, today's postmodern writing—which also self-consciously reworks the conventions of specific genres—is often motivated by similar ideological protests.

Not all critics, however, are convinced that "postmodern" writing has anything distinctive to tell us. Notably, Fredric Jameson laments the loss of the distinctive, individual voice of modernism, arguing that postmodernism has devolved into "blank parody" or a toothless recycling of once vital forms of expression (*Postmodernism* 16–17). His argument is based on the mistaken belief that distinctiveness cannot arise out of mixtures of genres and styles. To spend any time reading someone like Salman Rushdie is to know that he has a very distinctive voice indeed, even if it is (or, rather, *because* it is) a "mongrel" one. And is this literature toothless, as Jameson implies? We only have to look at the events surrounding the publication of Rushdie's *The Satanic Verses* to feel its bite. But books don't have to spark an international conflict for them to be political. Following Linda Hutcheon's lead, most scholars tend to view postmodern literature as critical of status quo political, social, and cultural values.

The self-conscious or metafictional aspect of the genre mixing and manipulation in postmodern literature plays a strong role in creating this political edge. Much of the theory and criticism of postmodern literature talks about how metafiction draws attention to the text's status as an artifact in order to raise questions about the relation between reality and fiction (see, for example, Waugh). But, more specifically, the metafictional features of postmodern literature often call attention to the conventions of various literary and non-literary genres and their ideological underpinnings. Since genres are informed by and instill social values, the hyperconscious foregrounding of genre in postmodern writing urges us to consider its ideological messages.[6] As Thomas Beebee argues, genres are related to prevailing ideologies; writers who self-consciously challenge or deviate from the conventions and limits of specific genres may well be engaged in ideological projects (19).

Beebee further suggests that a fruitful path for the critical study of literature is in examining the tensions between contradictory generic features within texts. Linda Hutcheon's naming and analysis of "historiographic metafiction"—novels which integrate historical or "true" events and personages into a self-consciously fictional or artificial frame—is one of the most influential examples of this kind of generic criticism (*Politics*;

Poetics). But historiographic metafiction is just one prominent trend in contemporary genre mixing. As Susan Suleiman notes, there are a great variety of other mixings:

> The appropriation, misappropriation, montage, collage, hybridization, and general mixing-up of visual and verbal texts and discourses, from all periods of the past as well as from the multiple social and linguistic fields of the present, is probably the most characteristic feature of what is called the "postmodern style" [191].

In addition, the mixing of genres, self-consciousness about genre conventions, and other kinds of innovation with genre are principal strategies by which postmodern writers like Rushdie, Barnes, Winterson, and Carter register a social protest. This study will discuss historiographic metafiction and a variety of other such combinations and revisions of genre to explore how Rushdie, Barnes, Winterson, and Carter critique received values about gender, politics, race, history, and religion.

For some scholars, genre mixing poses potential difficulties for studying postmodern literature. Many have suggested that generic boundaries which were once believed to be secure have dissolved and therefore that it is difficult or even impossible to talk about genre in clear terms. Linda Hutcheon, for example, points to texts by Alice Munro, Michael Ondaatje, Maxine Hong Kingston, Salman Rushdie, and John Banville to declare that

> The borders between literary genres have become fluid: who can tell anymore what the limits are between the novel and the short story collection [...] the novel and the long poem [...] the novel and autobiography [...] the novel and history [...] the novel and biography? [*Poetics* 9].

Does this mean that genres can no longer be identified and used as critical guides? In her introduction to a recent anthology of essays on "postmodern genres," Marjorie Perloff asks about the relevance of genre in a postmodern era of "openness, inclusiveness, and flexibility" (5). And Ralph Cohen, in his contribution to that collection, asks a similar question in titling his article: "Do Postmodern Genres Exist?" The answer is of course they do; we simply need to move away from the idea that genre borders have ever been discrete. If anything, genre has become *more* relevant to literary study than ever before. Perloff suggests that despite the emphasized dissolution of traditional generic boundaries in postmodernism, it is impossible both to talk about texts without reference to generic features and to read texts without a particular set of generic expectations:

however "irrelevant" generic taxonomies may seem in the face of the post-modern *interdisciplinarity* of the arts [...] however pointless it may seem to classify and label texts that refuse to fit into the established categories, practically speaking, it is virtually impossible to read a given new "text" without bringing to it a particular set of generic expectations. For how, in the first place, does one decide what to read or hear or look at? [4]

Postmodern writing, then, does not eliminate genres. It changes them, putting old genres to new uses. Aesthetic forms or genres are continually being revised to find incisive and meaningful ways of speaking to contemporary and/or past reality. These new uses of genre need to be looked at in detail to understand what postmodern writers are saying about previous uses of individual genres; how contemporary social and cultural values are expressed and challenged through genre; and how generic innovations might interest and challenge readers.

An important purpose of generic classification and criticism now is to aid us in understanding how a text is participating in and responding to specific literary/discursive traditions and their ideologies. Toni Morrison's *Beloved*, for example, revises the genre of the nineteenth-century slave narrative. In most cases, slave narratives were transcribed, edited, and otherwise mediated by white abolitionists for a white audience. The abolitionists who recorded the stories of the slaves "doctored" them to give superficial group depictions and downplay the violence of slavery so as not to repel their potential audience. In *Beloved*, Morrison imaginatively reconstructs the slave narrative genre to include things that were generally left out and especially to portray with some depth the inner life or psychology of individual former slaves like Sethe and Paul D. Morrison's revision of the slave narrative genre corrects for the ideologies which effaced the subjectivity of the individuals whose lives these narratives portrayed.

Ralph Cohen notes that such conceptual changes in genre are often signaled by "parody of a norm or form" ("Afterword" 278–79), a strategy that is evident in the work of the writers discussed in this study as well as most writers who are considered postmodern (including Morrison). One of Cohen's more salient examples of this is William Blake's use of a hymn form in "London": "the violence of the diction and the synaesthetic imagery undermines the form and converts it from a peaceful support of social and religious values to a violent attack on them" (279). Formally, "London" remains a hymn, but the changes Blake effects in the language and imagery gives it a new social function which is antithetical to the traditional one.

Although, as Ralph Cohen notes, "no particular genre is essentialistically connected to a particular ideology" ("History and Genre" 209), individual genres such as the slave narrative have served specific ideological functions at various points in history. The dominant "use-value" of literary fairy tales and fables throughout the eighteenth-century, for example, was as a means to instill socially-sanctioned models of behavior in children. Similarly, eighteenth-century "conduct books" (including the incorporation of this genre in novels such as Richardson's *Clarissa* and *Pamela*) sought to instill male-authored behavioral models in women. Along with the case of the slave narrative, such examples are clear enough. But it is true that the ideological messages of some genres can be a matter of serious contention. Pornography, for example: is it an expression of androcentric sexism, a celebration of human liberties, or a protest against puritan values? One reasonable answer is that it has been and still is all of these things: the answer will change depending on the individual circumstance of the work and of its reception. A genre's ideological function varies with history and according to what the reader brings to a text (Cohen 209).

Despite these variables, the way a text makes use of its constituent genres can tell us a great deal about the ideological histories of those genres and its own historical scene. As Jameson writes: "Generic affiliations and deviations from them provide clues that lead us back to the concrete historical situation of the individual text itself, and allow us to read its structure as ideology, as a socially symbolic act, as a proto-political response to a historical dilemma" ("Magical Narratives" 157). Cohen suggests something similar when he advocates for a generic criticism that would examine how genre and generic transformations are arising out of and responding to specific historical, cultural, and social circumstances ("History and Genre"). Cohen gives a few examples of what such a criticism might entail. It might, for example, examine the different genres one writer employs; relate generic changes to changes in the writing of history; analyze reasons for the neglect of certain genres; examine a single narrative's generic transformations over time to explore how the process of selection and emphasis in rewriting involves an ideological foregrounding; and identify popular and polite functions and statuses of genres (214). This study is in part an attempt to bring some of these methodologies to bear on the work of Rushdie, Barnes, Winterson, and Carter. These writers mix genres and explicitly call attention to the fact that they are doing so; because of this, a detailed discussion of the generic features of their work is especially warranted.

"British" Fiction?

Although generic innovation and the mixing of "literary" and "non-literary" genres is a common characteristic of literature throughout history, it has become an especially popular approach for writers on the margins of "mainstream" society and dominant social values. In *An Alchemy of Genres*, for example, Diane Freedman calls attention to the recent rise to prominence of an "associative, nonhierarchical, personal, and open-ended" (3) style of writing embraced especially by feminist poet-critics such as Marge Piercy and Audre Lorde. These writers, Freedman argues, self-consciously mix genres to give voice to the experiences of previously silenced women. Similarly, Angela Carter and Jeanette Winterson mix and revise genres for a specifically feminist agenda. However, this strategy of writing is in wide practice among writers of many backgrounds, not necessarily feminist.

Since the late 1960s, British fiction has become increasingly daring in its themes, experimental in form, and global in outlook. Recently, an important factor in this development has been the immense success of the Booker Prize as a means of marketing literature in English. A list of the Booker winners and authors included on the shortlist quickly reveals that the makeup of British literature is not necessarily "British" anymore. It is telling that Q. D. Leavis laments the passing of a specifically "English" tradition, for perhaps the most important development of contemporary literature in English is, as Richard Todd puts it in his informative study of the Booker Prize's effect on Britain's literary culture, that "'the novel in Britain' [...] now includes fiction from Australia, New Zealand, Canada, South Africa, Nigeria, the Caribbean, and many other areas of the English-speaking world which is published in Britain" (8).

From 1980 to 1997 there were eleven out of eighteen non–British or immigrant winners of the Booker Prize (Todd 79–80).[7] A new generic classification—"Commonwealth literature"—has emerged in part to take account of this phenomenon, but this category, as Salman Rushdie notes in his essay "'Commonwealth Literature' Does Not Exist," is misleading and dangerous for it proposes a ghetto-ized notion of literature in English not written by white Britons or Americans: "It would never do to include English literature, the great sacred thing itself, with this bunch of upstarts, huddling together under this new and badly made umbrella" (*IH* 62). Rushdie identifies "Commonwealth literature" as a genre category whose chief purpose is to separate this new literature from the putatively "pure" English literary tradition. Adding to this concern, Aijaz Ahmad has argued in *In Theory* that "It is in the metropolitan country [...] that a literary text is first designated a Third World text, leveled into an archive of other such texts, and then globally redistributed with that aura attached to it" (45). For Rushdie, the result of this process is that such literature can be perceived by "academic institutions, publishers, critics and even readers" as inferior or marginal to the English literary tradition (*IH* 66); for Ahmad, it means that Commonwealth or "Third World" literature can become yet another exoticized product for Western exploitation.

Here are Rushdie's speculations on what would be made possible if the genre category of "Commonwealth literature" did not exist:

> If it did not, we could appreciate writers for what they are, whether in English or not; we could discuss literature in terms of its real groupings, which may well be national, which may well be linguistic, but which may also be international, and based on imaginative affinities; and as far as Eng. Lit. [sic] itself is concerned, I think that if *all* English literatures could be studied together, a shape would emerge which would truly reflect the new shape of the language in the world, and we could see that Eng. Lit. has never been in better shape, because the world language now also possesses a world literature, which is proliferating in every conceivable direction [*IH* 70].

By including Rushdie in the category of "British" fiction, I want to demonstrate my support of this vision. Rushdie and countless other "commonwealth" writers are now part of the British/Anglophone literary tradition rather than exiled to a ghetto category of their own. Since 1983 when Rushdie wrote the passage above, the Booker Prize, for all its faults,[8] has helped facilitate this. Despite Ahmad's very justified suspicion of Western market forces, the Booker Prize has helped readers in Britain and elsewhere cross national boundaries in their literary taste. After all, isn't the important thing that more people than ever are reading literature in English produced by writers of diverse backgrounds? Whether or not they open a window on the experience of the "Third World" or that of the metropole, such literature is changing the way we look at the world, making us—in the East and West alike—more global in perspective.

As I have already suggested, one of the most important effects of this change in orientation is that we are having to revise our notion of just what "British literature" is. Since the Booker is identified as a *British* prize, inclusion in the Booker shortlist or actually winning the Booker renders a work a part of the British literary tradition. At the same time, the market success of non–British Booker winners like *The God of Small Things* (Arundhati Roy 1997), *Paddy Clarke Ha Ha Ha* (Roddy Doyle 1993), *The English Patient* (Michael Ondaatje 1992), *The Famished Road* (Ben Okri

1991), *The Remains of the Day* (Kazuo Ishiguro 1989), *The Bone People* (Keri Hulme 1985), and *Midnight's Children* (Salman Rushdie 1981) has meant that the canon of "British literature" is itself changing—becoming a more global, pluralistic construct. Rushdie is certainly the foremost figure in this new internationalized literature in English, and his work reflects the diversity of that new category, mixing, as it does, generic conventions from both Eastern and Western literary traditions. As Richard Todd suggests, "Rushdie's 1981 success [with *Midnight's Children*] created a precedent that enabled commentators to conceive of the Booker as a prize administered in Britain but offering English-speaking readers a panoramic, international and intensely *current* view of 'fiction in Britain'" (82).

The Booker-led success of "non–British" writers has led to some criticisms of racial tokenism.[9] Perhaps there has been a bias in frequent years for non–British writers, but even if that is so, it is hardly something to be lamented. Judging any such prize is of course an extremely subjective task, and the Booker panels have been notorious for rendering uneven judgments.[10] Because of such controversies, the Booker Prize has enjoyed a relatively large amount of attention in the media, attention which has fed an annual hype over who will win. Not only has this public exposure helped re-define what "British literature" is, but, according to Richard Todd, it has led to "a new public awareness of Britain as a pluralist society" (83). That may well be the case, but it is also true that cultural mixing remains a source of immense tension in Britain, as is evident in fictions like Rushdie's *The Satanic Verses*, Hanif Kureishi's *The Buddha of Suburbia* and *The Black Album*, and Timothy Mo's *Sour Sweet*, all of which thematically treat the difficulties posed by this new "pluralist" Britain. Indeed, the redefinition of British literature as a more pluralist, global category mirrors the postcolonial restructuring of British society. Large waves of immigration have re-defined the racial and cultural make-up of British society and called into question a number of previously held sureties about the essence of national identity. Britain is more diverse than ever, especially in its metropolitan areas, and writers like Rushdie have, like Freedman's "feminist poet-critics," turned to self-conscious genre mixing to convey a sense of what it is to be on the margins of or excluded from the dominant culture.

My choice to discuss Julian Barnes may seem somewhat out of place in this respect, but it is not my intention to suggest that only "disempowered" groups like women and postcolonial "Others" have been producing exciting literature in Britain, though Britain's literary scene has been greatly enriched by them. Barnes is one of many excellent contemporary British writers who have been writing unconventional novels for quite some time. Were there enough space in this project, I should have also liked to have given detailed attention to writers like Martin Amis, Ian McEwan, Kazuo Ishiguro, Will Self, Penelope Lively, A. S. Byatt, and Graham Swift, all of whom have been adventurous and often controversial in their craft. One of the reasons I am including a detailed discussion of Barnes is that, by doing so, I hope to show that one's national heritage does not pigeon-hole one's art. Rushdie has a great deal more in common with Barnes than he has with, say, V. S. Naipaul.

The shape of contemporary "British" literature, then, is truly an international one and it has, in these last thirty years, taken on an increasingly global subject matter. Not only is the canon of British literature becoming more diverse, but so is the literature itself. The new internationalization of literature in English has contributed to the increasing generic diversity of the novel as an art form. Because of this, the study of genre becomes all the more important for understanding how contemporary works are responding to the many narrative traditions they draw upon.

CHAPTER ONE

Salman Rushdie

Genre, Cultural Purity, and Postcolonialism

Salman Rushdie employs a multitude of genres including myth, satire, comic epic, autobiography, historiography, *Bildungsroman*, magic realism, oral story-telling, religious allegory, fable, fairy tale, the grotesque, and the picaresque. Rushdie's mix of genres is so variegated that it frequently appears to have Joycean dimensions.[1] That some or many of the genres Rushdie uses are prominent at any given moment makes his fiction particularly difficult to talk about, but it is also a reflection of Rushdie's project of portraying the experience of individuals and nations in the postcolonial era. In drawing from both Eastern and Western narrative traditions,[2] Rushdie crosses cultural lines not just in theme and content but in form.

In her discussion of genre in Anglo-Indian writing, Fawzia Afzal-Khan suggests that Rushdie blends genres "to mirror the state of confusion and alienation that defines postcolonial societies and individuals" (143). The "state of confusion and alienation" Afzal-Khan refers to is the legacy of colonialism. Decolonization precipitated seemingly innumerable struggles for defining the identity and character of newly liberated nations. When Britain left India, for example, a country was to form where none had previously existed as an autonomous unit. How were the people of this nation to reconcile the immense differences in the values, traditions, cultures, religions, and languages of its peoples? Benedict Anderson, in his influential analysis of nation-formation entitled *Imagined Communities*, argues that a nation is an "imagined political community" (6)—that is, there is no "essence" to a nation or to one's national identity. The nation is "imagined" through a network of discourses or genres—slogans, political speeches, patriotic anthems, national holidays, history texts, news media, literature, elections, and a plethora of others—that knit national unity by portraying the nation as united despite its ostensible heterogeneity. Anderson implies that the image of unity disseminated through such discourses hides the disunified actuality. A relatively recent example of this would be the numerous discourses proliferated by the British government to foster support for the Falklands War which re-invigorated the stagnating ideal of Britain as a united nation which once dominated the world.

The absence of the British empire as a unifying force in post-independence India resulted in the speedy disintegration of the sub-continent into three countries: India, Pakistan, and Bangladesh. This political division reflects a wider scene of social and individual fragmentation, as Rushdie suggests in an interview: "One of the things that has happened in the twentieth century is a colossal fragmentation of reality" (qtd. in Afzal-Khan 154). Afzal-Khan suggests that this perspective helps us to understand the often chaotic mixture of genres Rushdie uses:

> the mode or genre equal to dealing with the exigencies of political fragmentation must perforce be equally fragmented. In fact, the narrative must be a mishmash of conflicting genres and modes, a narrative in which the comic and the tragic, the real, the surreal, and the mythic all "defuse" one another, so no one genre can predominate and "unify" the others [154].

Interestingly, Afzal-Khan implies that for a single genre to predominate would be the formal equivalent or expression of totalitarianism, and it is against the ideology and practices of totalitarianism and fundamentalism that Rushdie's major novels are in large part directed.

For Rushdie, India's modern history has been dominated by forces which have sought to repress and homogenize its diversity: the British, the dynastic Nehru family, and the numerous communalist movements. The communalists in particular have sought to "purify" India as a nation by expelling or disempowering those with different beliefs. Rushdie was and is quite right to be concerned about such things. Hindu nationalism has been recently popular in India, leading to elections that made the fundamentalist Bharatiya Janata Party (BJP) the majority party in India's government for a brief period in June of 1996 and then again from March 1998 to April 1999. The institutionalization of such extremists has led to an extremely dangerous and frightening new expression of an age-old conflict: in May and June of 1998, India and Pakistan each exploded a series of "test" nuclear bombs underground, threatening a new cold war or, worse, an actual nuclear war.

It is an often uncompromising adherence to ideologies of national, racial, religious, and cultural purity that have led to this state of affairs in modern India and Pakistan. Discussing the danger of ideas about social and cultural purity in a lecture he gave in Denmark, Rushdie declared that

> the Indian tradition has always been, and still is, a mixed tradition. The idea that there is such a thing as a pure Indian tradition is a kind of fallacy, the nature of Indian culture has always been multiplicity and plurality and mingling. [...] [T]he people who these days talk most violently about purism in Indian culture tend to be Hindu religious extremists, and in Pakistan, similarly, the people who talk about a pure culture tend to be Muslim religious extremists. I think that the idea of a pure culture is something which in India is [...] important to resist ["*Midnight's Children* and *Shame*" 11].

Midnight's Children, Rushdie's enormously successful 1981 novel, resists "the idea of a pure culture" and portrays the recent history of the drive for cultural purity which has contributed to the current crisis in India and Pakistan.

Midnight's Children employs a variety of genres as a general strategy for depicting modern India and the postcolonial experience in general. It is difficult to single out individual genres for discussion but the genre category that best captures the prevailing conventions of the novel, and the genre most relevant to the kinds of historical and social conditions Rushdie portrays, is magic realism. The mix of fantasy and realism characteristic of this genre appears in *Midnight's Children* as a response to specific social, historical, and cultural exigencies: namely, the failure of India's democracy and the splintering of the country in the decades after independence, culminating in the totalitarian regime of Indira Gandhi. Rushdie uses magic realist conventions to highlight the damage wrought by totalitarian forces in India's modern history and to present a utopian, if doomed, alternative to those forces. But to understand how Rushdie's use of magic realism responds to colonialism and its legacy, nationalism, and totalitarianism, it is important to first understand something of the history of the genre.

Magic Realism

Magic realism is a good example of Ralph Cohen's principle that genres need to be examined in relation to their historical, social, and cultural scenes of appearance ("History and Genre," "Postmodern Genres," "Afterword"). Though today it is most often associated with postcolonial writing, the conventions of the genre we now recognize as magic realism—the mixing of realism and fantasy—are at least as old as classic literary texts such as *A Thousand and One Nights* and *Don Quixote*.[3] In terms of its conventions, then, magic realism is similar to other subgenres of the fantastic including fantasy, fairy tale, myth, fable, etc. But a variety of twentieth-century texts have been recognized as "magic realist" by virtue of their conventional mixing of fantasy and realism combined with the historical and political contexts in which they have been produced. As Lois Zamora and Wendy Faris observe, the diversity of texts considered magic realist reminds us that "a literary genre is both a formal and a historical category" (5). Partly because of its departure from Western realist traditions, magic realism is often viewed as a genre well-suited to representing the experience and concerns of marginalized and disempowered individuals and groups. It is frequently used to describe a trend in combining realism with fantasy in the fiction of South and Central American writers such as Jorge Luis Borges, Ariel Dorfman, Laura Esquival, and, most prominently, Gabriel Garcia Marquez.[4]

Though the term was coined by Franz Roh in 1925 to describe a particular trend in post–Expressionist painting,[5] magic realism came to prominence as a literary genre in South American fiction in part as a way to express the experience of individuals suffering under totalitarian, dictatorial forces. Interestingly, the mixture of reality and fantasy typical of magic realism has prominent twentieth-century antecedents in the works of Eastern European writers such as Bruno Schulz, Franz Kafka, and Milan Kundera.[6] These writers also were often writing under various conditions of persecution and oppression. In Kafka's *The Metamorphosis*, for example, an outrageously fantastic thing occurs amid a scene of otherwise classical realism: Gregor Samsa transforms into a gigantic insect and, just as in more contemporary works of magic realism, the impossibility of this magical event is never really discussed. Gregor's magical transformation physically manifests his intolerably oppressive familial, labor, and ethnic situation. Women writers such as Angela Carter, Jeanette Winterson, and Toni Morrison have made use of the genre for similar reasons, and it also has been an extremely popular genre for writers with a postcolonial background such as Ben Okri, Michael Ondaatje, Wilson Harris, and, of course, Salman Rushdie.[7]

The popularity of the genre among postcolonial, women, and Eastern European writers suggests that there is something particularly attractive about the genre for representing political protests. Lois Zamora and Wendy Faris propose that

> Magical realism's assault on [the] basic structures of rationalism and
> realism has inevitable ideological impact. [...] Magical realist texts are
> subversive: their in-betweenness, their all-at-onceness encourages resist-
> ance to monologic political and cultural structures, a feature that has
> made the mode particularly useful to writers in postcolonial cultures and,
> increasingly, to women. Hallucinatory scenes and events, fantastic/phan-
> tasmagoric characters are used [...] to indict recent political and cultural
> perversions [6].

Though it is by no means used exclusively as a politically charged genre,
political concerns are prominent in a majority of literature considered
magic realist. This is not surprising considering the fact that magic realism is closely related to fantasy, a genre Rosemary Jackson influentially
described as "the literature of subversion." Fantasy, Jackson observes,
attempts to "make visible that which is culturally invisible" (69). In other
words, fantasy brings to the surface the dominant but often unconscious
ideologies of society. So in Angela Carter's *The Passion of New Eve*, as I
will discuss in Chapter Four, the normally invisible androcentric assumptions about womanhood are made visible through the process of Evelyn's
transformation into Eve. Or, to return to the example of Kafka's *The Metamorphosis*, the magical transformation of Gregor Samsa into a giant insect
makes visible the "invisible" oppressiveness of being a Jew, a son, and a
bureaucrat in Czech-German society. Similarly, in the "Circe" chapter of
Joyce's *Ulysses*, Leopold Bloom's transformation into a pig literalizes what
it is to be a marginalized Jewish immigrant in Irish society. Such transformations and other magical events which are conventional of numerous fantasy genres have been given renewed prominence in contemporary
magic realist literature, especially Salman Rushdie's.

"Remember the wild profusion of my inheritance"

Like Kafka's Gregor, Joyce's Bloom, or Carter's Evelyn, Saleem Sinai,
the narrator of Rushdie's *Midnight's Children* undergoes fantastic transformations. Saleem believes, quite sincerely, that he is "handcuffed to history" (*MC* 9) by virtue of the timing of his birth—the exact moment of
India's independence from Britain. In this and Rushdie's other novels, we
are urged to accept this kind of metaphor as literal reality. Thus, when
something significant happens to the country, whether it is partition, war,
communal violence, language riots, etc., Saleem develops a physical symp-
tom which parallels the national situation. Or, from Saleem's perspective,
what happens to *him*, happens to the country. This conflation of the literal

and the metaphorical is the novel's primary magic realist trope, one which suggests that reality is never as straight-forward as it appears.

By the time Saleem starts writing down his story, his body is cracking:

> Please believe that I am falling apart.
>   I am not speaking metaphorically [...] I have begun to crack all over like an old jug—that my poor body, singular, unlovely, buffeted by too much history, subjected to drainage above and drainage below, mutilated by doors, brained by spittoons, has started coming apart at the seams. In short, I am literally disintegrating [...] I shall eventually crumble into (approximately) six hundred and thirty million particles of anonymous, and necessarily oblivious dust [37].

In magical realist fashion, metaphorical and symbolic elements of the narrative come to form the fabric of the milieu's literal reality.[8] The implication here is that the social and political body of India (which he personifies) is cracking as a result of having been "buffeted by too much history." Although his reliability as a narrator becomes increasingly questionable, Saleem repeatedly insists that we accept the literalness of what he tells us, an insistence which, because we know his experience is the fabrication of a fiction writer, asks us to suspend our distinction between literal and metaphorical perceptions of reality to emphasize the gravity of metaphorical portrayals.

Saleem further literally/metaphorically embodies India in his complex heritage. Putatively the child of Ahmed and Amina Sinai, Saleem was switched at birth with another child and is in fact the biological offspring of an adulterous affair between the Englishman William Methwold and Vanita, the wife of the street singer and accordionist Wee Willie Winkie. Saleem's heritage is so mixed up that it is impossible to separate the backgrounds that constitute him. In this sense he is truly a mirror of Indian society: within him vie the experience of colonizer and colonized, rich and poor, Hindu, Christian, and Muslim.

Saleem believes himself brought into the world to reconcile this diversity of heritages. One of one thousand and one "midnight's children" born in the first hour of independence who possess magical powers ranging from the potent to the merely whimsical, Saleem is a telepath and hears voices from all over India: "the inner monologues of all the so-called teeming millions, of masses and classes alike, jostled for space within my head" (168). He is at first faced with the problem of understanding these voices which speak in all the diverse languages of the subcontinent, but he soon discovers that he can probe "below the surface transmissions" to a place where "language faded away, and was replaced by universally intelligible thought-forms which far transcended words" (168). The real potential of Saleem's magic, then, is this utopian notion of a place where different languages and cultural traditions do not inhibit communication; where diversity does not divide but connects; where "masses" and "classes" freely mix.

With the awakening of this power, Saleem commits himself to transforming his head into a kind of "parliament" or "Midnight Children's Conference" (the MCC) for all of the children of midnight to meet and discuss their purpose. The MCC starts out as a kind of democratic utopia, embodying the promise of a free, independent, and truly democratic Indian nation empowered rather than fragmented by its multitude of ethnicities, races, languages, and religions. If the mutual intolerance of differing class, religious, and political ideologies could be overcome, the novel implies, then totalitarian and fundamentalist univocality could be resisted. Unfortunately, the MCC splinters according to class, religious, and ideological differences after Shiva, Saleem's alter ego with whom he was switched at birth, encourages dissent. The MCC fragments without having ever tapped its potential, just as India's development was quickly enfeebled by political divisiveness after independence. Pessimistically, this failure suggests that the only way unity can be arrived at is through totalitarianism—the enforcement of unity by an authoritarian leader.

In the novel, Rushdie pinpoints Indira Gandhi as the source of such a totalitarian project. Saleem, who refers to Gandhi as the "Widow," perceives her as a direct threat to his existence and the existence of what he feels he represents. He portrays her as a self-created absolute totalitarian ruler: "When the Constitution was altered to give the Prime Minister well-nigh-absolute powers, I smelled the ghosts of ancient empires in the air [...] the sharp aroma of despotism" (424). During the State of Emergency she imposed after being convicted of election fraud in the 1971 general election, Gandhi suspended civil liberties, arrested thousands of political opponents, and pursued a program of forced birth control. These historical events become focal points for the narrative of the novel. Rushdie attributes a fundamentalist desire for a pure tradition and homogenized populace to Mrs. Gandhi's administration in which a new, all-encompassing narrative of Indian unity was written: "Indira is India and India is Indira." Confirming Saleem's suspicion, this slogan attempts to replicate the structure of imperialism which unified and controlled disparate parts of the world under the monolithic symbol of the monarch. In other words, Indira Gandhi adopted one of the primary strategies of imperialism, which was to figure the monarch, in all the discourses of nationhood and empire, as the inviolable essence of the nation. The slogan is an obvious example of what Benedict Anderson refers to as a discourse aimed at generating an "imagined political community," and Rushdie draws attention to the narcissism of this particular slogan to criticize the monolithic ideology it announces. The idea that "Indira is India and India is Indira" is a myth engineered to conceal the complexities of India's modern heritage.[9]

In his essay "Imaginary Homelands," Rushdie argues that *Midnight's Children* exemplifies how there are virtually an infinite number of versions of a nation: "my India was just that: 'my' India, a version and no more than one version of all the hundreds of millions of possible variations. I tried to make it as imaginatively true as I could, but imaginative truth is simultaneously honourable and suspect" (*IH* 10). Indeed, with Saleem's ridiculous ego-centrism—believing himself directly or indirectly responsible for nearly every major event in modern Indian history—it is certain that Rushdie wants to foreground just how suspect "imaginative truth" can be.[10] In a sense, Saleem makes the same mistake as Indira Gandhi in posing himself as an alternative embodiment of India as a nation. But at least in the principles he advocates and the diversity he embodies, Saleem stands for plurality and democracy whereas the "Widow" stands for forced unity. And although Saleem's narrative of Indian history is unreliably ego-centric, it is an important one in that it dramatizes a power struggle between who will narrate India's history. In an interview, Rushdie commented that "a country which has so many people in it also has a very large number of versions of the truth in it" (Chaudhuri 40). It is the suppression of these other "versions of the truth" that is essential to the "imagining" of a nation, while at the same time it is a form of extreme violence to a nation's populace.

With its irreverent disregard for the conventions of realist narrative, magic realism is the ideal form for portraying how there is always more than one "version of the truth." The State of Emergency, Saleem suspects, is explicitly motivated by the desire to suppress voices of dissent through "the smashing, the pulverizing, the irreversible discombobulation of the children of midnight" (*MC* 427) who, in the text, represent a multitude of fantastic or magic realist alternative versions of the truth to the monolithic one—the "imagined political community" and its discourses of origin—posed by Indira Gandhi. To Saleem, the children represent the immanent potential of Indian independence, and he revels in his perception of them as a "many-headed monster [...] the very essence of multiplicity" (229); but to the government they represent a subversive threat: they are "the grotesque aberrational monsters of independence, for whom a modern nation-state could have neither time nor compassion" (434).

The grotesque—as manifested in Saleem, the midnight's children, and other figures in the novel—is interlinked with the magic realist framework of the novel and is a politically motivated genre of representation. In *Orientalism*, Edward Said's discussion of Western representations of non–Westerners, Said demonstrates that colonial narratives have a long history of portraying African and Asian individuals in grotesque ways, reifying the Western fear of and repugnance for non–Westerners by ascribing inhuman, animalistic attributes to their physicality. Said, Rushdie comments, "makes clear that the purpose of such false portraits was to provide moral, cultural, and artistic justification for imperialism and for its underpinning ideology, that of the racial superiority of the Caucasian over the Asiatic" (*IH* 88–89). Reflecting on Rudyard Kipling's story, "On the City Wall," for example, Rushdie notes that "Kipling's treatment of Wali Dad is, by any standards, pretty appalling. He [...] is transformed into a sort of savage—'His nostrils were distended, his eyes were fixed, and he was smiting himself softly on the breast' [...] the meaning is clear: Western civilization has been no more than a veneer; a native remains a native beneath his European jackets and ties. Blood will out" (*IH* 79).

There are similar depictions in key colonial texts such as Joseph Conrad's *Heart of Darkness* and H. Rider Haggard's *King Solomon's Mines*. For example, Marlow, the narrator of Conrad's *Heart of Darkness*, is utterly incapable of viewing any of the African natives as "whole" beings. Whenever he sees them, they are described in the most fragmented terms: "a whirl of black limbs, a mass of hands clapping [...] feet stamping [...] bodies swaying [...] eyes rolling" (59); and their very humanity is denied by Marlow's horrified realization that they are "not inhuman" (59).[11] Perhaps more odious, H. Rider Haggard's Gagool, the native witch-guide in *King Solomon's Mines*, is described in purely demonic terms: she is "wizened, monkey-like. [...] It crept on all fours"; her face is "shrunken" to the size of a "year-old child"; her mouth is a "sunken slit"; she has no nose; "the whole countenance might have been taken for that of a sun-dried corpse had it not been for a pair of large black eyes [...] like jewels in a charnal-house"; the skull's "wrinkled scalp moved and contracted like the hood of a cobra" (320–1). Drawing on Edward Said's *Orientalism* and Fredric Jameson's "Modernism and Imperialism," Fawzia Afzal-Khan suggests that such representations of non–Europeans function as "strategies of containment" (2). As Said explains: in Western discourse,

> the Oriental is depicted as something one judges (as in a court of law), something one studies and depicts (as in a curriculum), something one disciplines (as in a school or prison), something one illustrates (as in a

zoological manual). The point is that in each of these cases, the oriental is *contained* and *represented* by dominating frameworks[12] [*Orientalism* 40].

Non-Westerners are similarly degraded by grotesque representations such as Kipling's Wali Dad, Conrad's Africans, and Haggard's Gagool. Such figures represent a danger to the "purity" of the Western world, threatening "infection" if they prove to be too similar to Westerners[13]; but at the same time the effect of such descriptions is that the native remains forever grotesque and dehumanized, unable to share in the "wholeness" and "wholesomeness" attributed to Western individuals: their "threat" is "contained."

Rushdie's use of the grotesque makes what Ralph Cohen calls a "conceptual change" ("Afterword" 278) in the genre: he uses the genre's conventions, but he does so in a way that parodies the Orientalist tradition. Similar to early modern European writers such as Swift and Rabelais, Rushdie uses the grotesque as a form of political and social satire which calls attention to the ills people have suffered under colonialism, neonationalism, totalitarianism, religious fundamentalism, language wars, India's head-long rush towards modernity, and the caste system. For these, Saleem—"nine-fingered, horn-templed, monk's tonsured, stain-faced, bow-legged, cucumber-nosed, castrated, and [...] prematurely aged" (*MC* 447) as he is—is the exemplary sufferer.

We learn that Saleem's face replicates the political geography of the subcontinent when his fundamentalist, nationalistic school-teacher Mr. Zagallo mocks him:

> In the face of thees ugly ape you don't see the whole map of *India*? [...] These stains [...] are Pakistan! Thees birthmark on the right ear is the East Wing; and thees horrible stained left cheek, the West! Remember, stupid boys: Pakistan ees a stain on the face of India! [231–32].

In the impurities of Saleem's physiology, Zagallo perceives the impurities of Indian society. When Zagallo pulls Saleem's hair out, creating a permanent monk's tonsure, Saleem notes that he takes on even more the appearance of India's topography: "the curse of my birth, which connected me to my country, had managed to find yet one more unexpected expression of itself" (232). His body suffers from a great deal more violence: he loses a finger when it is slammed in a door; his parents force him to have an operation to clear his sinuses, a side-effect of which is that he loses his telepathic powers; and he is forcibly sterilized during the Emergency. Each of the numerous deformations and acts of violence that Saleem suffers parallel events of historical violence in India: partition, language riots in Bombay, the Indo–Pakistani war, the Bangladeshi War, the State of Emergency. Such conflicts leave the country radically fragmented and disassociated from what Rushdie perceives to be its strengths: ethnic, cultural, and linguistic heterogeneity.[14]

Saleem embodies (or at least sees himself as embodying) the Indian populace, which is portrayed in equally grotesque terms. Saleem's mother Amina's journey to the heart of Delhi to have her fortune told echoes the grotesquerie of Joyce's nighttown, another famous literary site in which a disempowered people are portrayed as grotesque[15]:

> Look, my God, those beautiful children have black teeth! Would you believe ... girl children baring their nipples! How terrible, truly! And, Allah-tobah, heaven forfend, sweeper women with—no!—how *dread-ful!*—collapsed spines, and bunches of twigs, and no caste marks, untouchables, sweet Allah! ... and cripples everywhere, mutilated by loving parents to ensure them of a lifelong income from begging ... yes, beggars in boxcars, grown men with babies' legs, in crates on wheels. [...] It's like being surrounded by some terrible monster, a creature with heads and heads and heads [81].

But she corrects herself immediately: "no, of course not a monster, these poor poor people—what then? A power of some sort, a force which does not know its own strength, which has been decayed into impotence through never having been used ... No, these are not decayed people, despite everything" (81). These are the excluded, disempowered masses who have been "contained" in the dehumanizing depictions of imperial narratives. As Amina rightly discerns, they represent an untapped power which is also, despite her correcting herself, potentially monstrous. After independence, Indian neo-nationalism replaces British imperialism as the dominant myth, and these masses return as a powerful and united yet grotesque, uncontainable force: "The monster in the streets has already begun to celebrate; the new myth courses through its veins, replacing its blood with corpuscles of saffron and green. [...] The monster in the streets has begun to roar" (115–6).

Later still, the people on the margins of Indian neo-nationalism will suffer under the reign of the Widow, who does not tolerate alternatives to the narrative of totalitarian unity. As Una Chaudhuri observes, "One thing that makes the Widow really evil is that she sets herself up as a sole god, as a monotheistic deity, and challenges, of course, the whole pantheon in doing that" (46). India, a country constituted by a multitude of stories, gods, religions, cultural traditions, and versions of the truth is denied the expression of that diversity under the Widow's/Gandhi's monolithic leadership.

But India's people, Rushdie suggests, can never be crushed into an artificial conformity. After the Indo–Pakistani war, Saleem settles in Delhi's "ghetto of magicians," peopled exclusively by "Communists [...] [i]nsurrectionists, public menaces, the scum of the earth—a community of the godless living blasphemously in the very shadow of the house of God!" (*MC* 397). Like the midnight's children, the magicians are a heterogeneous group who represent an alternative and therefore a threat to Indira Gandhi's "official" monolithic reality. The ghetto is invaded one night by a group of government representatives, all of whom are fantastically identical in appearance to Sanjay Gandhi (Indira Gandhi's politically powerful younger son) or his wife, a magic realist trope that emphasizes the Gandhi government's project of unification-by-force. To further that project, they have come to implement a program of mass sterilization—eugenics, basically, under the pretense of egalitarianism. The scene dramatizes an actual program of enforced sterilization carried out on the "Untouchable" caste during Indira Gandhi's Emergency rule (though naturally it was subsequently denied). On behalf of the government, one of the Sanjay-clones declares that "all men are created equal" (398), but in an ironic reversal of logic it is the magicians—the masters of illusion and fraud—who demonstrate that such rhetoric of social equality is fraudulent political posturing. Picture Singh, "the Most Charming Man In the World," debunks the idea by putting a cobra's head in his mouth. "You see, captain," he tells the Sanjay-clone after performing this fantastic feat, "here is the truth of the business: some persons are better, others are less. But it may be nice for you to think otherwise" (398–9). Of course all people should be *treated* as equals by their government—the magicians are communists, after all— but the notion that everyone is "created" equal is merely a convenient piece of rhetoric to enforce a fundamentalist/fascist ideal of social homogeneity, in part through eugenics. Intolerant of voices of dissent, deviations or aberrations from the prescribed norm, the Widow's representatives bulldoze the community and sterilize its populace.

Saleem, in his typically egocentric way, attributes the attack on the ghetto to the Widow's attempt to capture and neutralize him personally: "*Indira is India and India is Indira* ... but might she not have read her own father's letter to a midnight child, in which her own, sloganized centrality was denied; in which the role of mirror-of-the nation was bestowed upon me?" (427). What is at stake in the conflict Saleem imagines between himself and the Widow is who will have the power to narrate the history of India: will it be the univocal, monolithic embodiment of the state or

Saleem, who claims to have the key to the "unofficial" but "true" narrative (even if his "truth" self-consciously takes liberties)? In *Culture and Imperialism*, Edward Said argues that "The power to narrate, or to block other narratives from forming and emerging, is very important to culture and imperialism, and constitutes one of the main connections between them" (xiii). Said implies that the power to narrate is a significant tool by which rulers acquire and retain power as well as shape the past, present, and future of their people.[16] It is for this reason, *Midnight's Children* suggests, that a totalitarian government must expunge "alternative versions of the truth." And since the midnight's children "literally/metaphorically" embody those alternatives, the government captures, sterilizes, and surgically removes the magical powers from nearly all them in an attempt to ensure that the state will retain the exclusive right to narrate a univocal history of India. Rushdie's portrayal of this final, brutal act demonstrates how real-world political power is generated and sustained through acts of violence: in sterilizing and operating on Saleem and the other children, the Gandhi government symbolically eliminates the radical potential of those voices and their capacity to proliferate. It is a scene of tremendous horror and suggests that the future holds only further despair.[17]

But Saleem's narrative remains to challenge the monolithic "official" narrative of Indian history. In "Imaginary Homelands," Rushdie explains that

> the novel is one way of denying the official, politicians' version of truth. [...] The "State truth" about the war in Bangladesh, for instance, is that no atrocities were committed by the Pakistani army in what was then the East Wing. [...] And the official version of the Emergency in India was well expressed by Mrs. Gandhi in a recent BBC interview. She said that there were some people around who claimed that bad things happened during the Emergency, forced sterilizations, things like that; but, she stated, this was all false. [...] So literature can, and perhaps must, give the lie to official facts [*IH* 14].

This is one of the goals of *Midnight's Children*—to point out the fraudulence of "official facts" about India's post-independence history and provide an alternative, if fictionalized, portrait of that history. It is not an attempt at verisimilitude; on the contrary, it is purposefully littered with falsifications, exaggerations, and obvious distortions of received historical facts in order to demonstrate, as does Julian Barnes (see Chapter Two), that all versions of the truth are subjective versions.[18]

Saleem's story, however, is one that emphasizes complexity over simplicity. In defiance of the linear and causal logic of historiography and the traditional *Bildungsroman*, it takes over one hundred pages for the novel to get to the point of Saleem's birth, it is full of seemingly frivolous digressions, and it repeatedly goes back and forth to clarify, summarize, or complicate previous points and hint at future developments. But Saleem repeatedly insists that he cannot be understood without an understanding of everything else that had any real of perceived effect on his life:

> I am the sum total of everything that went before me, of all I have been seen done, of everything done-to-me. I am everyone everything whose being-in-the-world affected was affected by mine. I am anything that happens after I've gone which would not have happened if I had not come. Nor am I particularly exceptional in this matter; each "I," every one of the now-six-hundred-million-plus of us, contain a similar multitude. I repeat for the last time: to understand me, you'll have to swallow a world [*MC* 383].

Saleem and the story he tells rebel against the notion that lives can be encapsulated and fully explained in narrative. Similarly, Rushdie implies, there can be no simple understanding of India and its history. The history of India, like the history of Saleem's life, is multitudinous, full of loops, digressions, and other complications. Underlying all of this is the notion that the lives, cultures, and fates of all the individuals in India are intertwined, and that to attempt to erase the complex eclecticism of the country is to consign it to a terminal form of fragmentation such as that from which Saleem suffers. Saleem's magic realist physical decay is a literalization of a metaphor which critiques the consequences of India's unwillingness to accept its racial, religious, cultural, economic, and linguistic diversity.

Saleem makes a number of assertions (like the one above) that he embodies multitudes. Similarly, the pickle-jars Saleem supervises in his job as production supervisor at Braganza Pickles also figure as metaphorical containers of multitudes. At the very end of the novel, Saleem speculates that

> all the six hundred million eggs which gave birth to the population of India could fit inside a single, standard-sized pickle-jar. [...] Every pickle-jar [...] contains, therefore, the most exalted of possibilities: the feasibility of the chutnification of history; the grand hope of the pickling of time! I, however, have pickled chapters. [...] [I]n words and pickles, I have immortalized my memories [459].

To chutnify is to blend discrete elements into a whole that will be preserved—a telling metaphor made literal in the mixed heritage of Saleem as well as the mix of realism, fantasy, the grotesque, and other genres in the novel. Like the combination of elements which have gone into the composition of his story, Saleem himself is a kind of pickle-jar full of chutney, preserving the disparate parts of modern Indian history in his grotesque physiology and the improbable magical events of his personal history. The image of Saleem as a kind of human chutney is bizarre, but as Saleem states, "If I seem a little bizarre, remember the wild profusion of my inheritance ... perhaps, if one wishes to remain an individual in the midst of teeming multitudes, one must make oneself grotesque" (109).

Despite—or, rather, because of—his grotesqueness, Saleem represents a dynamic and life-affirming alternative to the life-depriving Widow. At the end of the novel, Saleem's narrative is complete, preserving a counter-"official" narrative, and he has reared a son who also possesses fantastic attributes—two grotesquely large ears in the image of the elephant-headed god Ganesh. And whereas the midnight's children "rushed wildly and too fast into our future," Saleem's son, "Emergency-born, will be is already more cautious, biding his time" (425). Although Saleem himself is destined to "be sucked into the annihilating whirlpool of the multitudes" (463), he has left a powerful legacy in words, chutney, and flesh.

How To Be a "goodandproper Englishman"

The conflict between ideals of cultural purity and ideals of cultural heterogeneity is also integral to Rushdie's 1988 novel *The Satanic Verses* and the ensuing international controversy. In the dramatic opening scene of *The Satanic Verses*, the two principle characters, Saladin Chamcha and Gibreel Farishta, fall from an airplane which has been blown up in midair by terrorists. They fall and banter. They sing. They flap their arms frantically and magically decelerate their descent. And then they land, softly and safely, reborn. Rushdie speaks directly to the reader with a self-conscious comment on the generic liberties he is taking: "Let's face it," he says, "it was impossible for them to have heard one another, much less conversed and also competed thus in song. Accelerating towards the planet, atmosphere roaring around them, how could they? But let's face this, too: they did" (*SV* 6). How, then, are we to reconcile the impossibility and the reality? Similar to the literalization of metaphor so prominent in *Midnight's Children*, Rushdie is offering a magic realist literalization of the migrant experience. As they fall through the clouds, a succession of "Hybrid cloud-creatures [press] in upon them, gigantic flowers with human breasts dangling from fleshy stalks, winged cats, centaurs," and

Saladin is "seized by the notion that he, too, had acquired the quality of cloudiness, becoming metamorphic, hybrid" (6–7). This is Rushdie's fundamental idea of what it is to be a migrant: out of place with one's surroundings, but also hybrid, metamorphic, adaptable.[19] And so, adapting to their new environment, Saladin and Gibreel begin to fly.

Early in the novel, Rushdie asks: "How does newness come into the world? [...] Of what fusions, translations, conjoinings is it made?" (8). Though the answers to these questions are pursued throughout the novel, one kind of answer is already posed by the question: newness is the product of "fusions, translations, conjoinings." Rushdie dramatizes this in the shifting identities of Saladin and Gibreel, two characters caught between nationalities, cultures, religions, and languages. Saladin, for example, is increasingly troubled by internal and external conflicts between his native (Indian) and adoptive (English) cultures. One of several interesting ways in which this is depicted has to do with his shifting between Anglo- and Anglo-Indian language genres. Before the airplane carrying him and Gibreel is hijacked by terrorists, Saladin wakes to find a stewardess asking him if he wants something to drink:

> Saladin [...] found his speech unaccountably metamorphosed into the Bombay lilt he had so diligently (and so long ago!) unmade. "Achha, means what?" he mumbled. "Alcoholic beverage or what?" And, when the stewardess reassured him, whatever you wish, sir, all beverages are gratis, he heard, once again, his traitor voice: "So, okay, bibi, give one whiskysoda only." [...] How had the past bubbled up, in transmogrified vowels and vocab? What next? Would he take to putting coconut-oil in his hair? Would he take to squeezing his nostrils between thumb and forefinger, blowing noisily and drawing forth a glutinous silver arc of muck? [...] Damn you, India, Saladin Chamcha cursed silently. [...] I escaped your clutches long ago, you won't get your hooks into me again [34–35].

As is evident from this, Saladin has a strongly negative view of his own people—a kind of Naipaul-esque self-hatred. His language use reflects his cultural ambivalence. He perceives the Anglo-Indian English as a corruption of the purity of his "British" English and therefore his identity as a British citizen. He has tried desperately to unmake himself as an Indian and re-make himself as a "goodandproper Englishman" (43), and, until the time at which the book picks up the chronicle of his life, he had succeeded. But his heritage is more complex than that, and *The Satanic Verses* is in part the story of his past catching up with him.

The shifting between language genres that Saladin experiences dramatizes the mix of language genres that makes Rushdie's writing so distinctive. David Bleich discusses the permeability of language—how different genres of language like Yiddish and German or Black English and "standard" White English interact and influence each other, creating new genres, new languages (40–41). From this, Bleich derives a "principle of mixed genres of language": "there are no pure kinds, genres, species, or languages because culture is always changing" (38). The premise of Rushdie's idiom, which is composed of a mix of "British" English, film slang, Indianized English, Caribbean English, youth slang, and many others, is the same: languages are not pure, incorruptible entities, but changing with history as societies and cultures interact. Rushdie's mixed idiom is perhaps the most distinctive feature of his work, and it reflects the experience of cultural mixing which is happening all the time, especially for immigrants, migrants, or exiles like himself. Similarly, the conflict of language which Saladin experiences reflects the deracination of immigrant experience in general.

Bleich suggests that in society there is an "ideal of purity" about language which masks a fantasy ideal of cultural homogeneity. As we've seen with *Midnight's Children*, this desire for cultural purity is of special concern to Rushdie. He suggests that for post-colonial societies and individuals to try to get back to some uncorrupted, pre-colonial national/ethnic/religious identity is to buy into a dangerous fallacy. What would it mean to be truly "pure"? In one of Gibreel's dreams, Rushdie paints a portrait of such an individual—a fundamentalist Imam (satirically modeled on the Ayatollah Khomeini) who lives in exile from his homeland but surrounds himself with guards so that he never interacts with his host environment and becomes "impure." His curtains

> are kept shut all day, because otherwise the evil thing might creep into the apartment: foreignness, Abroad, the alien nation. [...] When he leaves this loathed exile to return in triumph to that other city beneath the postcard-mountain, it will be a point of pride to be able to say that he remained in complete ignorance of the Sodom in which he had been obliged to wait; ignorant, and therefore unsullied, unaltered, pure [*SV* 206–207].

Such "purity" means being ignorant and utterly cut off from history and the contemporary world outside one's own small sphere.[20] Thus, when the Imam returns home to lead the Islamic revolution, it is to stop the progress of time itself, to throw Islamic society back into a "timeless time" of the past (214–215), for history is the intoxicant, the creation and possession of the Devil, of the great Shaitan, the greatest of the lies—progress, science, rights—against which the Imam has set his face. History is a deviation from the Path, knowledge is a delusion, because the sum of knowledge was complete on the day Al-Lah finished his revelation to Mahound [210].[21]

In contrast to this horrifying figure, Saladin and Gibreel represent Rushdie's notion of the hybrid post-colonial individual. They are in no way "pure"; they both change and adapt to new environments, new cultural surroundings. But it is also important to note that Rushdie is not recommending unqualified assimilation with a host nation. Saladin, for example, has convinced himself that he has left behind his Indian self and become a "pure" Englishman. A master of vocal disguise, Saladin has adopted the accent, mannerisms, and, most importantly, the attitudes of the British bourgeois, as well as a stage name (Saladin Chamcha is the shortened version of Salahuddin Chamchawalla) in an attempt to mask his origins. For his Anglophilic mimicry of the British, he is the object of much of the novel's biting satire. A compelling way of interpreting his subsequent sufferings is as a kind of retribution for this betrayal of his origins.

One aspect of Saladin's character is particularly ironic and instructive: even as a child in India, he exhibits the signs of a colonized mind. The young Salahuddin roots for the English cricket team to "defeat the local upstarts, for the proper order of things to be maintained" (37). He is already in the process of "mutating" into Saladin Chamcha: he dreams of "flying out of his bedroom window to discover that there, below him, was—not Bombay—but Proper London itself, Bigben Nelsoncolumn Lordstavern Bloodytower Queen" (38) and becoming a "goodandproper Englishman" (43). His one ambition is to assimilate, to erase the marks of his difference, and so, when sent to school in England, he begins "to act, to find masks that these fellows would recognize, paleface masks, clown-masks, until he fooled them into thinking he was *okay*, he was *people-like-us*" (43). But what he later learns is that he can never fully be that, because the English will not accept him as one of them and because the repressed part of himself must eventually re-emerge.

That re-emergence begins on his trip to India, prior to the airplane explosion. There, he first notices his voice beginning to "betray" him (49). And then he re-encounters Zeeny Vakil, an old lover who makes it her project to "reclaim" him (52). She ridicules Saladin for his Anglophilic mimicry: "For Pete's sake," Zeeny tells him, "*Chamcha*. I mean, fuck it. You name yourself Mister Toady and you expect us not to laugh" (54).[22] Zeeny sees through the colonialism that Saladin has played into and confronts him with it. Responding to the career he has made as a voice-over actor, she says:

> They pay you to imitate them, as long as they don't have to look at you. Your voice becomes famous but they hide your face. Got any ideas why? [...] Such a fool, you, the big star who has to travel to wogland with some two-bit company, playing the babu part on top of it, just to get into a play. They kick you around and still you stay, you love them, bloody slave mentality [60–61].

In contrast to Saladin and Gibreel, both of whom are portrayed in the novel as culturally and spiritually lost, Zeeny is a figure of strength, possessed of a self-certainty that comes from a pride in her mixed heritage:

> She was an art critic whose book on the confining myth of authenticity, that folkloristic straitjacket which she sought to replace by an ethic of historically validated eclecticism, for was not the entire national culture based on the principle of borrowing whatever clothes seemed to fit, Aryan, Mughal, British, take-the-best-and-leave-the-rest?—had created a predictable stink. [...] "Why should there be a good, right way of being a wog? That's Hindu fundamentalism. Actually, we're all bad Indians. Some worse than others" [52].

Valuing cultural "eclecticism" as she does here is of course an ideal that Rushdie espouses throughout his fiction and essays.[23] Zeeny's opposition to the notion of essential identities is also important for understanding Saladin's dilemma, for he has implicitly accepted the essentialist ideologies of his own people's inferiority and of "goodandproper" English superiority. He has, in other words, accepted a set of insidious myths or lies about national identities, even to the extent of adopting English xenophobia: in response to the Falklands War, he tells his English wife that the Argentinean reclamation of the islands is akin to "Intruders in the home. It won't do" (175). After his fall from the plane, however, his whole experience in the novel is to learn what it is to *really* be an intruder in the British home.

The mythic notions of national identities manifest themselves in dramatic ways upon his return to England after surviving the airplane explosion. Having washed up on the coast, he and Gibreel are given shelter by Rosa Diamond, an old widow. The police are tipped off about a suspicious looking person, possibly an illegal immigrant, who had been seen on the beach. When the police arrive at Rosa Diamond's, they find Saladin, who has begun to magically grow devilish horns from his temples. The

police seize him while ignoring Gibreel who, in an antithetical transformation, is now emanating divine light from a halo. In the back of the police
van, Saladin notes that he is fully transformed into a grotesque image of
the Devil, complete with cloven hooves, a tail, horns, hairy legs, halitosis,
and a monstrously erect penis (157). The policemen verbally abuse him,
beat him severely, and force him to eat his own excrement. "'This isn't
England,' [Saladin] thought, not for the first or last time. How could it
be, after all; where in all that moderate and common-sensical land was
there room for such a police van in whose interior such events as these
might plausibly transpire?" (158). Deny it as he might, however, this *is*
England.

This was one of the episodes that provoked a notorious criticism of
the novel from British Foreign Minister Geoffrey Howe: "The British government, the British people, don't have any affection for the book. The
book is extremely critical, rude about us. It compares Britain with Hitler's
Germany" (qtd. in Barnes, *LL* 269).[24] Rushdie's defenders were quick to
point out that the author was giving a valid portrait of the immigrant's
experience in a racist society and, indeed, Rushdie was attempting to
debunk numerous myths of Britain's "greatness," to expose what is essentially a kind of national hypocrisy about race and nationalism. Howe's
statement reinforces exactly the social problem that Rushdie is criticizing:
it implicitly separates British society into different classes of people—the
"real" British and the immigrants who, though they may have a British
passport, though they may have grown up and been educated in the most
traditional of English institutions as Rushdie was, are not really British.
Ironically, Rushdie's depiction of Saladin's metamorphosis is aimed precisely at bringing to the surface the racial tensions which Howe glossed
over in his fawning attempt to appease Muslim protestors by suggesting
that the novel insults "British" as well as Muslim sensibilities.

Rushdie self-consciously calls attention to the seeming anomaly of
the policemen's response to Saladin's fantastic appearance:

> What puzzled Chamcha was that a circumstance which struck him as
> utterly bewildering and unprecedented—that is, his metamorphosis into
> this supernatural imp—was being treated by the others as if it were the
> most banal and familiar matter they could imagine [*SV* 158].

It is a common convention of magic realist literature that characters fail
to exhibit any kind of disbelief when confronted with the fantastic. In this
case, Rushdie has employed this convention for a critical purpose: to suggest that discriminatory and prejudicial attitudes about race are so embed-
ded in the British national consciousness that they aren't even recognized

as problems. There is nothing extraordinary, Rushdie suggests, about the way they see him and *that* is the tragedy.

Saladin Chamcha's transformation is strongly reminiscent of Kafka's portrait of Gregor in *The Metamorphosis*. Just as Gregor's transformation into a giant insect is a literalization of an intolerable situation of racial degradation, Saladin's transformation into an archetypical Devil figure is a literalization of culturally pervasive racist metaphors. Saladin becomes what a significant proportion of British society perceives him to be—a repulsive monster.[25] The scenario echoes Rushdie's interpretation of how Kipling's Wali Dad is treated by Europeans: "a native remains a native beneath his European jackets and ties. Blood will out" (*IH* 79). The veils of assimilation with which Saladin has concealed his identity as a foreigner (an "Other")—his British voice, mannerisms, and stage name—are torn from him, forcing him to experience, in a concentrated way, all of the degradations suffered by outsiders in a country that wants to believe in its homogeneity. Saladin tries desperately to reassert his Britishness with a haughty and authoritative idiom: "my good fellows, you had best understand your mistake before it's too late" (*SV* 159). But his new body betrays him and he soils his pants. He comments to himself: "Such degradations might be all very well for riff-raff from villages in Sylhet or the bicycle-repair shops of Gujranwala, but he was cut from a different cloth!" (159). Even as he is confronted with the evidence of his difference, of his despicability in their eyes, he clings to his identification with his oppressors. But to the policemen—those representatives of British law—he is the same as any other immigrant. "Look at yourself," they tell him. "You're a fucking Packy billy. Sally-who?—What kind of name is that for an Englishman?" (163).

As bad as his subsequent sufferings are, Saladin's transformation is an *educative* process which forces/enables him to reconnect with other non–British natives and Indians, for they are the only ones who will accept him as he is without the layers of artifice. His first step to making this reconnection is in a sanitorium which the police dump him in. He finds himself in a ward full of foreigners who, like himself, have magically transformed into hybrid, animalized creatures. A man in the form of a manticore who befriends him tells Saladin that "There's a woman over that way [...] who is now mostly water-buffalo. There are businessmen from Nigeria who have grown sturdy tails. There is a group of holidaymakers from Senegal who were doing no more than changing planes when they were turned into slippery snakes" (168). When Saladin asks how this happens, the manticore replies: "They describe us. [...] That's all. They have the power of description, and we succumb to the pictures they construct"

(168). Again, language proves instrumental in these transformations. Like Saladin, the sanitorium inmates have mutated to literalize Orientalist metaphors which have depicted non–Westerners as bestial. As with other magical elements in *The Satanic Verses*, these mythical beings highlight the dehumanization of racial minorities in Britain.

Escaping with these other mutated individuals is Saladin's first major act of solidarity with others like himself. When he attempts to return home, his wife is horrified by his appearance, a rejection that forces him further away from his life as an Englishman. His friend, Jumpy Joshi, takes him to the Sufyan family who offer him shelter in the attic of the Shaandaar cafe and Bed and Breakfast they own and operate. Here, the conflict of his identity continues. Sufyan, the father, at once welcomes Saladin despite his appearance, sensing that such mutations have been somehow forced upon him: "Where else would you go to heal your disfigurements and recover your normal health? Where else but here, with us, among your own people, your own kind?" (253). But when Saladin is left to himself, he struggles against this notion of affinity: "I'm not your kind. [...] You're not my people. I've spent half my life trying to get away from you" (253). To Sufyan's teenage daughters, Mishal and Anahita, who are actually instantly enamored with him for the rebellious, anti-establishment connotations of his appearance, he tries

> to explain that he thought of himself, nowadays, as, well, British ... "What about us?" Anahita wanted to know. "What to do you think we are?"—And Mishal confided: "Bangladesh in't nothing to me. Just some place Dad and Mum keep banging on about."—And Anahita, conclusively: "Bungleditch." [...] But they weren't British, he wanted to tell them: not *really*, not in any way he could recognize. And yet his old certainties were slipping away by the moment, along with his old life [258–259].

Mishal and Anahitas' self-identification as British complicates Saladin's hitherto polar conception of identity, for Mishal and Anahita do not fit either of his ideas about what it is to be an Indian immigrant or an English native. Like Saladin himself, they are a mixture of East and West, old and new. Many different combinations can be made from these elements. Mishal and Anahita are one such combination and Saladin is another, although they share one particular thing in common: they are all hybrid or "impure" individuals. The very important implication here is that in addition to there being no right or wrong way to be an Indian, there is no right or wrong way to be British. The pervasive belief that underlies British racism is that there is such a thing as a pure British identity that is being corroded by immigrants.[26] Thus, the "myth of authenticity" works both ways.

Saladin's transformation blurs the line between fantastic and realist narrative genres. In a sense, his experience as a mutated being desublimates and forces him to confront all of the inegalitarian aspects—which he has until now been able to repress and ignore—of what it is to be a racial minority. Those things that appear most fantastic to him are actually most "real" to the experience of immigrants, migrants, and racial minorities, which helps to explain why no one except himself finds the actual fact of his transformation particularly shocking. For the racist policemen, he is exactly what they expect him to be; for Jumpy Joshi and the Sufyans, his appearance merely confirms British society's extreme racism, and confirms the fact that there are no norms in society: "the transformation of Saladin Chamcha," thinks Jumpy, "had precisely to do with the idea that normality was no longer composed (if it ever had been) of banal, 'normal' elements" (280). It is the heightened awareness—evident in so much postmodern art—that reality is more complex than it seems that has made magic realism such a popular genre: its conventions speak directly to that contemporary loss of the sense of reality as mundane.

In Rushdie's portrait of contemporary life, especially that of postcolonial immigrants, the intertwining of fantasy and reality seems to have become a relatively common occurrence. Mishal tells Saladin of a man who obsessively rearranges his sitting-room furniture like a single-decker bus and compels his family to pretend that they're on their way to Bangladesh; Anahita explains: "you're not the only casualty, round here the freaks are two a penny, you only have to look" (283). Rushdie's repeated emphasis on the blurred distinction between reality and fantasy or dream dramatizes the deracinating sense caused by migrancy: the feeling of being in two places—one materially or physically "real," the other emotionally, mentally "real"—at the same time.

Bizarrely and ironically, Saladin becomes popular as a counter-cultural figure. The image of Saladin as a devil "rising up in the Street like Apocalypse and burning the town like toast" (285) begins to penetrate the dreams of contemporary Londoners, threatening white complacency and stirring non-white rebelliousness:

> While non-tint neo–Georgians dreamed of a sulphurous enemy crushing their perfectly restored residences beneath his smoking heel, nocturnal browns-and-blacks found themselves cheering, in their sleep, this what-else-after-all-but-black-man, maybe a little twisted up by fate class race history, all that, but getting off his behind, bad and mad, to kick a little ass [286].

There is an exuberance and comedy to this strange turn of fortune that typifies Rushdie when he is simultaneously at his most playful and most critical. *The Satanic Verses* thrives on such reversals of expectation: a devil becomes a hero, an angel a madman, a Muhammad a Mahound, etc. Vendors mass-produce Saladin's devil-image on buttons, sweatshirts, and posters: "he was a defiance and a warning. Sympathy for the Devil: a new lease of life for an old tune" (286). Mishal elaborates: "Chamcha [...] you're a hero. I mean, people can really identify with you. It's an image white society has rejected for so long that we can really take it, you know, occupy it, inhabit it, reclaim it and make it our own" (286–287). Explaining this strange turn of events, Timothy Brennan writes that "Opposition to British hegemony within the black community takes the form of accepting the devil's role assigned to them by Britain, not passively but as a means of resistance" (156). Saladin, as might be expected, is horrified by all of this, but he is overcome with bitterness and hatred focused on Gibreel for having betrayed him at Rosa Diamond's, and he begins to "be what he had become: loud, stenchy, hideous, outsize, grotesque, inhuman, powerful" (*SV* 289). Ironically, when he gives expression to his repressed rage, and in the process destroys a dance-club which Mishal has taken him to, he is restored to his human form, as if becoming fully conscious of his status as a part of the community of marginalized, disempowered, and abused persons reconciles him to those long-repressed aspects of his cultural background.

After his metamorphosis back into his human self, Saladin begins to move away from the old image of himself as a purely "goodandproper Englishman." He sees a program on television about hybridizing trees and finds in it a new metaphor for his life: "There it palpably was, a chimera with roots, firmly planted in and growing vigorously out of a piece of English earth. [...] If such a tree were possible, then so was he; he too, could cohere, send down roots, survive" (406). He comes to reject the "portrait of himself and Gibreel as *monstrous*" (408). Is this a new beginning for him?

Faith and Doubt

Gibreel undergoes a similar though antithetical transformation to Saladin's. Whereas Saladin's experience in the novel deals with issues of race, Gibreel's focuses on issues of religion. While Saladin starts the novel as a man who has lost his sense of racial and national identity, Gibreel starts the novel as a man who has lost his faith. Suspecting that God does not exist because there is no divine intervention while he suffers from an illness, Gibreel decides to gorge himself on pork. When there is no ostensible act of retribution for this transgression, his loss of faith is confirmed.[27] But in fact he does suffer a very serious form of retribution. Renowned for playing divine figures in the popular Indian film genre of the "theological," he is forced in a series of tormenting dreams to play the role of his namesake, the archangel Gabriel/Gibreel. As the angel, he interacts with Muhammad (here called Mahound) in the desert at the time of the founding of Islam; the exiled Imam who returns to his homeland to effect an Islamic revolution; and a young seeress named Ayesha who leads a present-day pilgrimage of Indian villagers to Mecca.

Gibreel becomes a chronicler of the struggle between the faith and doubt of various characters in his dreams who demonstrate a range of positions from fanatical belief to unwavering skepticism. It is the content of the dream involving Muhammad and the founding of Islam that most inflamed many Muslims' religious sensitivities. In these parts of the novel, Rushdie is doing something very similar to what Jeanette Winterson and Julian Barnes do in re-writing the Old Testament story of Noah and the ark (see Chapters Two and Three): casting doubt on religious texts by treating them not as sacred and authoritative but as akin to fictional literature.[28] Therein lies the problem, for orthodox Muslims consider the Koran to be the direct and inviolable "Word of God," whereas the Bible is not generally treated as such.[29]

Some of the sense of affront the novel caused is simply the product of misunderstanding—of having heard about or read bits of the novel out of context. For example, the fact that the Muhammad figure is called "Mahound"—the derogatory name applied to him by medieval Christians—is explained in the novel: "To turn insults into strengths, whigs, tories, Blacks all chose to wear with pride the names they were given in scorn; likewise, our mountain-climbing, prophet-motivated solitary is to be the medieval baby-frightener, the Devil's synonym: Mahound" (93).[30] These are the kinds of reversals Rushdie makes throughout the novel (for example, when he has Zeeny use the term "wog" to describe herself, or, more dramatically, when he turns the Devil into an icon of liberation for formerly colonized people). This isn't to say that the novel is positive press for Muhammad; it presents a morally complex picture of a prophet as a human being with faults and attempts to desacralize him as a figure invested with divinity by many Muslims.

In any case, the central focus of Rushdie's criticism is the text of the Koran rather than the person of Muhammad or his wives. The issue of the "Satanic verses" arises when Abu Simbel, the crafty leader of the magical desert city Jahilia (Mecca), recognizes that Mahound and his one God represent the future: "Why do I fear Mahound? For that: one one one, his terrifying singularity. Whereas I am always divided, always two or three or fifteen" (102). He tempts Mahound to accept just three (Lat, Uzza, and Manat) of the city's three hundred and sixty idol gods as "worthy of worship" (105). The prophet consults Gibreel and returns with a set of verses which allow this modification of the incipient theology. But in response to news that Simbel may betray his pledge of loyalty to Allah, Mahound consults Gibreel again and returns with a disavowal of the previous verses as the product of Satan.[31] Gibreel, however, informs us that both the first revelation and its repudiation came from him, and in each case the words were somehow forced from him by Mahound. The way in which all of this is dramatized is complex, but a sense emerges and begins to grow that Mahound's recitations (the verses that would make up the Koran) were not the direct "Words of God"; instead, they were conveniently fabricated to suit whatever purpose he had at any given time. The disavowed "Satanic verses," for example, helped him to convert the Jahilians to his new religion. Both the mytho-historical tale of the "Satanic verses" and Rushdie's dramatic recreation of it conflates imaginative with "revealed" genres of literature, calling into question the putative "purity" and revelatory sanctity of the Koran.

Mahound's scribe, Salman the Persian, confides to the poet and satirist Baal many years later that he thinks the prophet is a fake. Fleeing persecution in Jahilia after the incident of "the Satanic verses," the prophet and his followers go into the desert where Mahound, Salman recounts,

> became obsessed by law. […] Gibreel appeared to the Prophet and found himself spouting rules, rules, rules, until the faithful could scarcely bear the prospect of any more revelation […] rules about every damn thing, if a man farts let him turn his face to the wind, a rule about which hand to use for the purpose of cleaning one's behind. It was as if no aspect of human existence was to be left unregulated, free. The revelation […] told the faithful how much to eat, how deeply they should sleep, and which sexual positions had received divine sanction [363–364].

Talal Asad points out that most of the strictures Rushdie mocks have no basis in the Koran itself. According to Asad, most Islamic rules come from the documented accounts (called *hadith*) of Muhammad and his followers' lives, and different Muslim sects follow different *hadith* (293). So Rushdie is conflating different religious and legal traditions for literary convenience, but his irreverent mockery is, like that of his contemporaries Barnes, Winterson, and Carter, aimed at a general criticism of religion and its ideological underpinnings. Rushdie suggests that religious texts are in large part early law books which dictate restrictions on human behavior that do not—cannot except through deliberate re-writing—change with changing social values. Although religious law does get re-interpreted to accommodate social change, Rushdie's concern is with radical fundamentalists who treat it in an absolutist fashion.

One of the most troublesome areas in this regard is religious positions on women, a subject I treat in depth with regards to Jeanette Winterson and Angela Carter in Chapters Three and Four. The tradition of purdah, which Rushdie has repeatedly spoken against, has its origins in the Koran.[32] Marina Warner suggests that the contemporary resurgence of purdah in and outside of Britain "represents a retrenchment against the yielding of boundaries, against slippage of distinctions, against assimilation"; thus, women become "keepers of the religion's [...] integrity" (*RF* 192).[33] Even worse, the Koran validates the idea of men's superiority over women and their right to abuse them:

> Men have authority over women because God has made the one superior to the other, and because they spend their wealth to maintain them. Good women are obedient. They guard their unseen parts because God has guarded them. As for those from whom you fear disobedience, admonish them and send them to beds apart and beat them [Dawood, *Koran* 64].

In *The Satanic Verses*, Rushdie suggests that such strictures were a matter of Mahound's personal sexism: Salman tells Baal that when the women of Yathrib (the desert oasis Mahound has fled to) begin to express their autonomy, "bang, out comes the rule book, the angel starts pouring out rules about what women mustn't do, he starts forcing them back into the docile attitudes the Prophet prefers, docile or maternal, walking three steps behind or sitting at home being wise and waxing their chins" (*SV* 367). Part of Rushdie's challenge to the sacredness of the Koran, then, is a protest against its restrictive and abusive ideologies regarding women— ideologies which are being re-invigorated because the separation of women is crucial to the fundamentalist ideal of cultural purity.[34]

Salman further reveals to Baal that Mahound started to lay down the law and then consult Gibreel to have it "confirmed." In the hope of disproving his suspicions, Salman takes to interjecting his own modifications into the recitation to see if Mahound will notice. Even more directly than the Satanic verses incident, this act changes the genre of the text by interjecting artifice into putatively pure Divine revelation: "there I was, actually writing the Book, or re-writing anyway, polluting the word of God with my own profane language" (367). When Mahound fails to notice this "pollution," Salman is forced to conclude that the recitation—the Koran—is fabricated rather than God-given.[35] From an Islamic point of view this is blasphemous, but from a secular point of view it is both a playful and serious desacralization of a religious text. This desacralizing does not defeat religious points of view; it poses alternatives, suggesting that the demand for purity of faith put forth in the Koran is a limiting one. All faith, Rushdie suggests, is subject to doubt, even *requires* doubt.[36]

Eventually Mahound does notice what Salman has done and confronts him: "Your blasphemy, Salman, can't be forgiven. Did you think I wouldn't work it out? To set your words against the Words of God" (374). It is exactly this that Rushdie has attempted in *The Satanic Verses*, and while there is a great deal of material in these parts of the novel that is straight-forwardly irreverent (even "blasphemous" according to some sensibilities), entirely apart from the arguments about freedom of expression which dominated the Rushdie controversy, it should require no apology. At one point, for example, Rushdie indirectly refers to Ibrahim (Abraham) as a "bastard" for leaving his son in the desert because it is God's will. He comments: "From the beginning men used God to justify the unjustifiable" (95). It is a common enough criticism of religious institutions, and part of the tradition of literature as social criticism. The book offers all the "justification" or "defense" it needs; within its pages is the resounding manifesto for the social function of art which I have taken as the epigraph to this study: "A poet's work," says the satirical poet Baal, is to "name the unnamable, to point at frauds, to take sides, start arguments, shape the world and stop it from going to sleep" (97). Though fundamentalists, totalitarian leaders, and some conservatives may not find this notion comforting, this has been in many societies a presumed role for literature, and it is particularly foregrounded in Rushdie's fiction and that of the other authors I discuss in this study.

Appropriately, then, it is Baal who comes to represent a "profane" alternative to Mahound's new regime upon his return to Jahilia. Once a thriving center of licentiousness where "all the talk was of fucking and money, money and sex" (380), Jahilia becomes a puritanistic city where no alcohol is allowed and wives are locked up. "The Curtain," the most popular brothel in town, is allowed to remain open during a period of transition, and Baal, disguised as a eunuch, takes refuge there and comes up with the idea of having each of the twelve prostitutes assume the identity of one of Mahound's twelve wives. For the men of Jahilia, this becomes a kind of invitation to transgress, to covertly rebel against the harsh set of strictures imposed by Mahound's recitations. Baal remarks to himself:

"There were more ways than one of refusing to Submit" (381). Soon the prostitutes lose their old sense of themselves and they decide to take Baal as their husband, making him "a secret, profane mirror of Mahound" (384).[37] Again, this part of the book can be read as deeply offensive or playfully critical, depending on one's personal orientation. When Baal and his wives are at last "found out," the crowd that gathers to hear him laughs uncontrollably at the humor of his irreverent story. Despite Baal's attempt to tell the story "using the simplest language" (391), it is outrageously funny for its profane rebuke of Mahound's newly instituted puritanism—a yoke under which all those gathered to listen suffer.[38]

The word "Islam" (which means "submission") conveys the religion's central ideal. Those who do not "submit" threaten its ideology. In *The Satanic Verses*, Rushdie suggests that it is necessary always to have voices of challenge. Just before his execution, Baal says: "Whores and writers, Mahound. We are the people you can't forgive," and Mahound replies: "Writers and whores. I see no difference here" (392). Mahound equates writers with whores because they are both profane to him: whores for obvious reasons, and writers because the mere act of writing words challenges the authority of the "Words of God" as written/revealed in the Koran. At the very founding of Islam, Rushdie asserts in an interview, there was a "conflict between the sacred text and the profane text, between revealed literature and imagined literature" (*RF* 23), a conflict manifested by the fact that when Muhammad returned to Mecca he executed only five or six people, four of whom were writers or satirical actresses.[39] In *The Satanic Verses* Rushdie replays this historical act, having Mahound execute Baal for representing a profane alternative to Islamic ideals. Sadly, it is the same intolerance of imaginative literature (because of its challenge to revealed literature) that contributed to the Ayatollah Khomeini's death sentence on Rushdie.

Pilgrimage

A parallel story of the conflict between faith and doubt in *The Satanic Verses* is that of the messianic Ayesha leading a group of Indian villagers on a foot pilgrimage to Mecca. The two parts of the novel that narrate this tale combine conventions from religious myth, quest narratives, and magic realism into an allegory about faith and doubt. Reminiscent of Gabriel Garcia Marquez's magic realist tropes, Ayesha is constantly surrounded by butterflies which provide her sole source of nourishment, and, when necessary, her only form of clothing.[40] Like Mahound, Ayesha is visited by Gibreel in her dreams and she gains magical, prophetic powers. She diagnoses cancer in Mishal Akhtar, the wife of a wealthy landowner, Mirza Saeed. Mirza, a modern, secular sceptic, attacks Ayesha for attempting to come between him and his wife. When doctors confirm Ayesha's diagnosis, however, Mishal believes her claim that the cancer is a test of faith from God and that she (Mishal) will be saved if she undertakes the pilgrimage to Mecca. Ayesha also convinces the rest of the village except for Mirza Saeed that they must walk to Mecca. To Mirza's dismay, they even believe her claim that the waters of the Arabian sea will be parted for their passage.[41]

The pilgrimage physically and ideologically divides Mirza from his wife and the rest of his village. Mishal accuses him of having identified, like Saladin Chamcha, too closely with the English: "Saeed, a thing is happening here, and you with your imported European atheism don't know what it is. Or maybe you would if you looked beneath your English suitings and tried to locate your heart" (238). Mirza Saeed accompanies the pilgrims in an attempt to persuade them away from their folly, but he does so in another European import which emphasizes his separateness— his Mercedes which, as he begins to acquire "converts" of his own, comes to be known as the "station wagon of scepticism" (481). As their journey continues, several of the very old and the very young villagers die, but Mishal never relents despite Mirza's pleas to get her the best treatments in Europe, Canada, and America: "Trust in Western technology. They can do marvels. You always liked gadgets, too" (485). Mirza, it becomes evident, is not a man without faith, but a man with faith in Western technology—the product of the Enlightenment which brought about widespread doubt of religion in Europe.[42] Ayesha, on the other hand, forsakes all such developments. Her fanatical faith aligns her with the exiled Imam of Gibreel's previous dream. But Rushdie, it becomes clear as this story progresses, and as is clear from the rest of his work, is not willing to entirely discount either of these poles: just as the real and the fantastic are intertwined in his fiction, so are faith and doubt, East and West, past and present, ancient knowledge and modern knowledge. Rushdie is looking for a synthesis of these polarities; he warns against privileging any one kind of knowledge too much.

After a sudden flood disbands the pilgrims, the butterflies seek them out, heal their wounds, and bring them back together. Mirza still maintains his disbelief in spite of this miraculous event, but his wife confronts him: "What does your science say about this?" (495). There is more to this world, Rushdie suggests, than that which science can explain. But there are also real dangers inherent in religion, as is evident when a local Imam pronounces a foundling child the product of "devilment" and, subsequent to Ayesha's cryptic comment that "Everything will be asked of us" (397), a crowd stones the baby to death. Although this causes a temporary rebellion among her followers, Ayesha returns with renewed promises of salvation. She interprets the rebellion as a test of faith: Mirza's offer to fly some of the remaining pilgrims to Mecca "had contained an old question: *What kind of idea are you? And she, in turn, had offered him an old answer. I was tempted, but am renewed; am uncompromising; absolute, pure*" (500). The novel suggests that such fundamentalism is extremely dangerous: the infirm pilgrims die, a baby is stoned, and, finally, the pilgrims themselves drown in the Arabian Sea.

Or do they? The believers walk willingly into the sea while Mirza and his "converts" look on with disbelief for they see nothing. At the last minute, the unfaithful run into the water to try to save the others, and all of them except Mirza report that they saw the waters part and the pilgrims walking across the sea floor. Police investigators inform them that the drowned bodies have floated to shore, but those left behind persist in believing that they had witnessed a miracle from which they were excluded. The implication is that those who lacked faith missed out on something of immense importance. If anything, this part of the novel offsets some of the more aggressively anti-religious sentiments of other parts of the novel, for it is the doubters who are "left behind" in the literal and symbolic/spiritual sense. When Mirza returns home, for example, he slowly rots in solitude amid a village which has "crumbled into dust" from drought (506). In contrast, the faithful pilgrims shared a solidarity and common purpose which gave them strength and communal identity.

Did the villagers perish in the waves or did they walk across the sea floor to Mecca? It's pointless to try to choose which version of events was "real," for they were each "real" to the individuals experiencing them. Rushdie's mix of realism and fantasy allegorizes how people perceive the world in rationalistic *and* fantastic ways. The ambiguity of the end to this story suggests that Rushdie isn't discounting the reality of peoples' faith in religious miracles. Many readers who responded negatively to the novel, however, ignored the ambiguity at the end of the Ayesha pilgrimage and other parts of the book, reading it simply as an attack on religion. Syed Ali Ashraf, for example, asserts that "Ayesha and her followers are destroyed by their false beliefs" (*RF* 20).[43] But Rushdie actually gives a lot more validity to the possibility of miraculous or mystical experiences than someone like Angela Carter would. In his essay "In Good Faith," Rushdie writes that "The mystical, revelatory experience is quite clearly a genuine one" (*IH* 408). Similarly, in an interview he affirmed that in India and Pakistan "Religion is the air everyone breathes. If you're trying to write about the

Despite his newly recharged faith, and even in his most messianic moments, Gibreel is, like Salman the Persian, invaded by "Satanic" doubt:

> how unconfident of Itself this deity was, Who didn't want Its finest creations to know right from wrong; and Who reigned by terror, insisting upon the unqualified submission of even Its closest associates, packing off all dissidents to Its blazing Siberias, the gulag-infernos of Hell [332].

Gibreel soon banishes his doubts, however. Like Saladin, he grows angry and becomes an avenging figure who then levitates menacingly over London: "He would show them—yes!—his *power*.—These powerless English!—Did they not think their history would return to haunt them? [...] He would make this land anew" (353). Gibreel sees himself as the embodiment of England's colonial history returning for vengeance. But how to accomplish this? Comically, he decides that the trouble with the English is their weather and resolves to transform London into a tropical city, reasoning that it will bring "increased moral definition" to a people who suffer from seeing everything in their unchangingly cold, damp, and grey country as "much-the-same, nothing-to-choose, give-or-take" (354). In tropicalizing England, he intends essentially to colonize the former colonizers, something that in the minds of xenophobic white Britons is already occurring through immigration. Frantz Fanon's words spring to Gibreel's mind: "The native is an oppressed person whose permanent dream is to become the persecutor" (353). The alternative, Gibreel begins to believe, is embodied in his adversary, Saladin/Satan: "the nature of the adversary: self-hating, constructing a false ego, auto-destructive. Fanon again: 'In this way the individual'—the Fanonian *native*—'accepts the settler and his lot, and by a kind of interior re-stabilization acquires a stony calm'" (353). Again Rushdie presents a conflict between two extremes: the native can *either* submit to and identify with the oppressor *or* become the oppressor. But neither of these alternatives is really acceptable, and as Gibreel and Saladin move towards a confrontation, alternative possibilities arise.

Reconciliation

Because of Gibreel's treason at Rosa Diamond's, because of Saladin's jealousy of Gibreel's commercial success (Saladin has been dropped from his contracts), and because Saladin has lost his English trophy wife and Gibreel has attracted the love of the stately and blonde Alleluia (Allie) Cone, Saladin decides to avenge himself against Gibreel. The latter suffers from attacks of irrational jealousy, and Saladin exacerbates this condition by making phone calls in his thousand and one stage voices to recite "Satanic verses" of intimate knowledge about Allie.

Saladin's revenge forces Gibreel into another messianic break and the two play out a postmodern, fantastical tale of the battle between good and evil. They come to represent opposed but interdependent ways of being: each is "the other's shadow" (426). Rushdie suggests that Saladin becomes an avatar of "evil" because of his desire to re-invent himself in the image of his oppressors, whereas Gibreel becomes an avatar of "good" because "at bottom" he wishes to remain "an untranslated man" (427). But a moment later he dismisses these ideas because they depend on the false notion that there is a such a thing as a pure essence to individual identity: "Such distinctions, resting as they must on an idea of the self as being (ideally) homogeneous, non-hybrid, 'pure',—an utterly fantastic notion!—cannot, must not suffice" (427). Rushdie further suggests that the notion of good and evil as represented by polar entities—God and the Devil—is too simple a formulation. It is a primary convention of religious literature to pit good against evil in order to teach simplistic moral lessons, but at various moments in *The Satanic Verses*, Gibreel and Saladin each seem to be good *and* evil. In portraying Saladin and Gibreel as pseudo-Divine figures who both do ostensibly good and evil things, Rushdie changes the genre of religious literature to critique and complicate its conventionally facile morality. Religious texts are dangerous, Rushdie suggests, in part because the moral paradigms they proffer lack the nuances that are inevitable in any real-life ethical conflict.

In one of the novel's most powerful scenes, Rushdie dramatizes a more complex concept of morality. London is destabilized by a slew of racial violence in the wake of the wrongful arrest and mysterious death of Dr. Uhuru Simba, a prominent minority rights activist. During that violence, the Shaandaar café is set on fire and Saladin, despite his recent evil streak, enters the burning building to try to save the Sufyans, demonstrating that good and evil can reside simultaneously in a person. It is Gibreel's realization of this, upon seeing Saladin collapsed on the floor of the café, that changes his own intentions:

> Is it possible that evil is never total, that its victory, no matter how overwhelming, is never absolute?
> Consider this fallen man. He sought without remorse to shatter the mind of a fellow human being; and exploited, to do so, an entirely blameless woman, at least partly owing to his own impossible and voyeuristic desire for her. Yet this same man has risked death, with scarcely any hesitation, in a foolhardy rescue attempt [467].

The morality of individuals, Rushdie suggests, is more complex than the polar simplicities of good and evil to be found in religious texts and many of their interpretations. Nevertheless, in depicting Gibreel and Saladin as avatars of good and evil, Rushdie does remain somewhat caught in a binary mode of thinking. Carter and Winterson, as discussed later in this study, are more sophisticated in their critique of polar systems, especially of gender and sexuality binaries.

To mark the special significance of Gibreel saving Saladin, Rushdie presents it as a miracle akin to the parting of the Arabian sea: Gibreel exhales a breath which "slices through the smoke and fire like a knife," parting the fire "like the red sea it has become [...] so that on a night when the city is at war, a night heavy with enmity and rage, there is this small redeeming victory for love" (468). It is a beautiful moment, probably the most decisively optimistic note of any of the books I discuss in this study. Amid all of the controversy over this novel, it is all too easy to forget its profound humanity, a humanity emphasized when Gibreel saves Saladin and in the last chapter which portrays Saladin's reconciliation with his father and with his Indian heritage. These reconciliations don't erase the fact of a very violent and divided contemporary world, but they are something. As Saladin flies home to his father's death-bed, he reads in the newspaper of various atrocious acts of sexist and religious violence in India. Beside him is Whisky Sisodia, the stuttering film producer, who pessimistically tells him that "religious fafaith, which encodes the highest ass ass aspirations of human race, is now, in our cocountry, the servant of lowest instincts, and gogo God is the creature of evil" (518). Again, Rushdie presents a two-edged, strongly irreverent view of religion, but it is also a valid assessment of the harm caused by religious sectarianism throughout history.

Offsetting that violence, however, is the belief in forgiveness and reconciliation between warring parties. Forgiveness is at the root of this novel: Mahound forgives the Jahilians (except for Baal) who persecuted him and his followers; Gibreel and Saladin forgive each other for their respective betrayals; Saladin and his father forgive each other for turning their backs on one another; and Zeeny forgives Saladin for having abandoned his heritage. Sara Suleri remarks that the "somewhat surprising stress of the tropes of forgiveness and reconciliation with which the narrative ends [...] emphasizes its religious impetus, exuding a nostalgia for the unitary—the Islamic—that it had earlier sought to banish" (193). While I don't agree that there is a nostalgia for the "unitary" aspects of Islam, I do think Suleri brings up a very important point: *The Satanic Verses* is, as she says, a "deeply Islamic book" (191) in that its concluding scenarios of tolerance, acceptance, and reconciliation demonstrate what Rushdie perceives to be the "true" spirit of Islam. This is not to suggest that all affronts should be forgiven, but that the ability to reconcile, to be lenient in the face of actions which have offended, is a defining feature of our humanity. For religious fundamentalists, however, forgiveness is only granted if a person repudiates the past and embraces their particular philosophy. And for the most stringent extremists, such as the Ayatollah Khomeini and his followers, there can be no forgiveness for offenders such as Rushdie. Despite the Iranian government's declaration in 1998 that they will no longer seek to fulfill the *fatwa* against Rushdie, it can never really be repealed because it is a permanent clerical judgment.

For all of its irreverent play with religion, *The Satanic Verses* is an extremely humane novel with complex human characters who make choices that are sometimes "good" and sometimes "evil"; and in addition to its scathing criticism about racial and religious prejudice and violence, this novel affirms the human capacity to change into something better. Saladin changes into something better by reconciling himself with his past, his country, his given name, and his family:

> To fall in love with one's father after the long angry decades was a serene and beautiful feeling; a renewing, life-giving thing. [...] Saladin felt hourly closer to many old, rejected selves, many alternative Saladins—or rather Salahuddins—which had split off from himself as he made his various life choices [523].

Confronted with his father's courage and the kindness of others during his father's last days of life, Salahuddin is struck by the indomitability of the human spirit: "We are still capable of exaltation, [Salahuddin] thought in celebratory mood; in spite of everything, we can still transcend" (527).

The ending of the novel is not a cliché of happiness, however. Life is more complex than that. Although Salahuddin regains himself, Gibreel sinks further into madness and despair; he kills Allie, Whisky Sisodia, and then himself. Salahuddin

> had believed [...] that the events of the Brickhall fire [...] had in some way cleansed them both, had driven those devils out into the consuming flames; that, in fact, love had shown that it could exert a humanizing power as great as that of hatred; that virtue could transform men as well as vice. But nothing was forever; no cure, it appeared, was complete [540].

Nevertheless, it is Salahuddin's renewal that takes precedence: "If the old refused to die, the new could not be born. [...] It seemed that in spite of all his wrong-doing, weakness, guilt—in spite of his humanity—he was getting another chance" (547). In contrast to Timothy Brennan's contention that Rushdie has an "inability to protest and affirm at the same time" (165), then, I would suggest that Rushdie very carefully balances these two impulses. If anything, Rushdie seems to favor gestures and conventions which affirm the human capacity to mend wounds and renew life.

Ambiguities of Magic Realism

In *The Satanic Verses*, we are often unsure about whether a specific "magical" incident has actually occurred, or whether it is merely the product of an individual or collective delusion. The most prominent of these ambiguous scenes is probably the end of the Ayesha-led pilgrimage to Mecca. The natural compulsion while reading such scenes is to want to "figure it out," but Rushdie's repeated ambiguity with regards to such events forces us to read the literal as metaphorical. This is something that Rushdie does differently than many other magic realists. Whereas most magic realists write fantastic events into their narratives as if they are no different than any other event, Rushdie usually integrates a challenge to such events, as he does in the opening scene which self-consciously denies and affirms the feasibility of Saladin and Gibreel bantering in the sky as they fall from the plane. Similarly, for every claim of a miraculous event in the novel, there is an opposing voice of scepticism: though the survivors of the Ayesha pilgrimage claim that the villagers walked across the sea-floor, the police state that their bodies washed up on shore. This self-consciousness towards the conventions of magic realism is one of the things that makes Rushdie distinctive as a postmodern writer *and* a magic realist.

These kinds of juxtapositions of the possible and the impossible continue throughout the novel. After his decision to "tropicalize" London, for example, Gibreel wakes up collapsed on Alleluia Cone's doorstep, leading us to believe that he's merely had another delusional break, but a moment later the book reveals that a tropical heatwave which could last for months has moved into England. Like the end of the Ayesha pilgrimage story, the ambiguity here makes it difficult to interpret. Similarly, the magical aspect of Gibreel saving Saladin is challenged. In response to Mishal Sufyan's suggestion that perhaps Gibreel *did* part the flames with his breath, her boyfriend, Hanif, insists: "What has happened here in Brickhall tonight is a socio-political phenomenon. Let's not fall into the trap of some damn mysticism. We're talking about history: an event in the history of Britain. About the process of change" (*SV* 469). Are such events "real" miracles or delusions and coincidences easily dismissed by the secular mind? The only reasonable response is that there is more to reality than the purely secular mind can explain. Miracles may be a sham, but they also play an important part in the way many people understand the world around them. This is a book about contending interpretations of reality and it suggests that we cannot discount a particular way of perceiving the world because it accepts the fantastic as real. Faith makes the fantastic a real factor in many people's lives.

The potential danger of ambiguous representations of the fantastic, such as those Rushdie presents, is given explicit attention towards the end of the novel in a brief exchange between Swatilekha and Bhupen, two political activist friends of Zeeny. Swatilekha, criticizing the use of religious imagery in Bhupen's poems, tells him:

> "These days [...] our positions must be stated with crystal clarity. All metaphors are capable of misinterpretation." She offered her theory. Society was orchestrated by what she called *grand narratives*: history, economics, ethics. In India, the development of a corrupt and closed state apparatus had "excluded the masses of the people from the ethical project." As a result, they sought ethical satisfaction in the oldest of the grand narratives, that is, religious faith. "But these narratives are being manipulated by the theocracy and various political elements in an entirely retrogressive way." Bhupen said: "We can't deny the ubiquity of faith. If we write in such a way as to pre-judge such belief as in some way deluded or false, then are we not guilty of elitism, of imposing our world-view on the masses?" [537]

Swatilekha espouses Jean-François Lyotard's theory that "grand narratives" have organized human social life, and she adds that this has generally kept the large majority of people ignorant and disempowered. It is clear from the rest of the novel that Rushdie agrees with Swatilekha that religion has been manipulated by the few to control society and disseminate conservative ideals such as those of racial and ethnic purity. But the novel also affirms that religion cannot be simply dismissed as some kind of universal delusion. Although it certainly does present some anti-religious, especially anti–Islamic, situations, *The Satanic Verses* is less of an anti-religious novel than a novel *about* religion.[45] It is about the dialectic between faith and doubt, which Rushdie perceives as inextricable. To have faith without doubt, he suggests, is dangerous, as he himself experienced.

These issues are very complex, and *The Satanic Verses* does not seek to resolve them all because really there are no answers. The mixed genre of magic realism allows Rushdie to present a series of situations that can be read as secular or religious, "real" or "supernatural," literal or metaphorical. Swatilekha is certainly correct that "All metaphors are capable of misinterpretation," as the controversy over the novel made all too clear. But what is the alternative? Rushdie's use of magic realism in *The Satanic Verses* affirms that, for many, metaphors, symbols, and the supernatural are as material a part of human reality as anything strictly tangible. Like Swatilekha, we may want "crystal clarity," but reality is more complex than that. One of Rushdie's earliest critics, Syed Ali Ashraf, based his objections on a denial of this complexity, stating that Rushdie

> wanted to be realistic and fantastic at the same time. Where he failed miserably is in portraying people's feelings when they see the transformation of Saladin and Gibreel as if these are normal things. In a normal situation, these abnormal things do not happen. In a fairy tale they do. His attempt to mix normalcy and fairy tale myths created by him do not carry conviction. Had we been transported into the imaginary world completely, as C. S. Lewis does in children's tales or as is done in fairy tales, it would have been convincing [RF 20].

Ashraf would impose extraordinary limits on the literary imagination, suggesting as he does that, outside of "children's tales" or "fairy tales," literature should not mix fantasy and realism. This denies the fact that literature has mixed realist and fantasy genres from its beginning and also suggests that "fantasy" literature has no relevance to the "real" world.[46] If "serious," "adult" literature were to strictly limit itself to literal representations, as Ashraf suggests, it would be extremely impoverished. Rushdie's purpose is not to be "convincing" in the realist sense Ashraf seems to expect. *The Satanic Verses* urges us to think about various ways of perceiving the world and demonstrates that the "fantastic" has an important place in many of those perceptions. That other characters do not respond to Saladin and Gibreels' transformations as if they are impossible is conventional of magic realist texts. And in *The Satanic Verses* it is essential to the ideas that Rushdie is writing about: Saladin's metamorphosis makes "visible" what is generally invisible to the populace of Britain—that immigrants are seen as monstrous; and Gibreel's transformation incarnates many believers' expectation that a figure of salvation will arrive. Finally, contrary to Ashraf's suggestion, there is nothing "normal" about the situations Saladin and Gibreel find themselves in—simply being an immigrant, Rushdie suggests, is to be a social aberration—which is partly why Rushdie uses fantasy in portraying their experience. Rushdie's persistent ambiguity towards the makeup and perceptions of reality seems to me to be one of the facets of the novel that, had it not been ignored or misunderstood, could have helped mitigate the insult protestors believed Rushdie intended.

Questioning the Unquestionable

Among the massive amounts of documentation concerning the "Rushdie affair,"[47] a few issues stand out which highlight the difficulties that impeded a peaceful resolution for so long. The controversy has been dominated by debates over freedom of expression (a concept which means very different things in different parts of the world), but genre considerations provide another useful perspective. For example, Syed Ali Ashraf's protest (above) against the novel's mix of fantasy and realism highlights an important element of the early debate surrounding the novel: Was it to be read as fantasy or as historical revisionism trying to pass itself off as fact? Part of this problem has to do with a cultural difference in how large parts of the Muslim and non–Muslim communities have perceived the relationship between "factual" and "fictional" genres of writing. A frequent assumption was that Rushdie was attempting to revise Muslim history, prompting some critics to suggest that the insult of the novel was akin to the insult of revisionary histories of the holocaust.[48] Syed Ali Ashraf, for example, assumes that Rushdie has taken the myth of the Satanic verses and treated it as true: "He has intentionally and deliberately distorted the history of the Blessed Prophet and his Companions" (*RF* 19). Similarly, an article in the London *Sunday Times* reported that "The grand Sheikh of Cairo's Al-Azhar, the 1,000-year-old seat of Islamic theology, said [...] the book [...] contained 'lies and figments of the imagination' about Islam, which were 'passed off as facts'" (*RF* 27). Rushdie's opponents, it seems, received the novel as blasphemous propaganda and were noticeably unwilling to accept what he has called the "fictionality of fiction" (*IH* 393).[49]

Defending his novel, Rushdie draws attention to issues of genre:

> I genuinely believed that my overt use of fabulation would make it clear to any reader that I was not attempting to falsify history, but to allow a fiction to take off from history. [...] Fiction uses facts as a starting-place and then spirals away to explore its real concerns, which are only tangentially historical. Not to see this, to treat fiction as if it were fact, is to make a serious mistake of categories. The case of *The Satanic Verses* may be one of the biggest category mistakes in literary history [*IH* 408–409].

While it is perhaps overstating things to suggest that the true concerns of fiction are only "tangentially" historical (a position I doubt Rushdie would really stand behind), Rushdie is correct to point out that some basic distinction between fiction and fact be maintained. To do otherwise, as Julian Barnes suggests in his *A History of the World in 10½ Chapters* (see Chapter Two), would be to submit to the dangerously radical philosophy that all versions of history are equally valid.

Rushdie introduces the conflict between fact and fiction in the novel when Gibreel's dreams become the raw material for a new series of "theological" genre movies. Billy Battuta, one of the film's producers, describes the first of them, a film that will "recount the story of the encounter between a prophet and an archangel": "'It is a film [...] about how newness enters the world.'—But would it not be seen as blasphemous, a crime against...—'Certainly not. [...] Fiction is fiction; facts are facts'" (*SV* 272). While there is some truth to this—it is important not to mistake fiction for fact—it is also important not to accept "fact" without scepticism. Battuta's remarks seem ironic given that the whole spirit of *The Satanic Verses* (and of Rushdie's other works) belies the over-simplistic division between fact and fiction or reality and fantasy. Gibreel, for example, cannot work out for himself what is real and what is the product of his own delusional mind. Even as readers with all of the clues that Rushdie gives us, it isn't really possible for us to work out exactly what is to be read as literal truth and what as metaphorical truth. As I've discussed, Rushdie's use of magic realism collapses these categories, which is one of the reasons why arguments over the book's alleged blasphemy are so vexed: on the one hand, its defenders have wanted to read it as a novel which fictionally dramatizes the conflict between faith and doubt; on the other hand, those attacking it see it as a challenge to the literalness of Islamic history and revered historical-theological figures. It is both of these things, but it does not seek to suggest that its own vision of Islamic history supplant the "official" history, just as Rushdie doesn't intend for us to *literally* believe Saleem's version of Indian history. Rather, it is suggesting that no historical or religious text should be automatically accepted as purely "factual." The point here, similar to that suggested by Julian Barnes (see Chapter Two), is that fact and fiction are inextricable in all genres of representation whether they are recognized as religious, historical, literary, or other.

Even when it was understood that *The Satanic Verses* wasn't trying to substitute its narrative for the Koran's, it met with a pervasive prejudice against fantasy in writing. Peter Mullen, a Christian reverend sympathetic to the Muslims outraged by the novel, implies that only the strictest realism can be counted as "good writing": "The further the art work departs from the real world, the more conjectural and abstract it becomes, the worse it is. [...] Good writing, like the Old Testament, eschews contrivance and gives us the world as it is" (Cohn-Sherbok 31). While Mullen's assumption that the Old Testament harbors no "contrivance" is ludicrous, the same assumption about the Koran is nearly universal among believing Muslims. One of the troubling facets of religious orthodoxy is that it insists, as Mullen does, that the world can be described in the most literal terms. *The Satanic Verses*, along with other postmodern, fantastic, or magic realist works, suggests otherwise. As Bhikhu Parekh observes, magic realism has become popular specifically because for many it is the most sensible genre for depicting "a reality that continually overtakes the imagination and refuses to conform to conventional canons of rationality or even intelligibility" (Cohn-Sherbok 73).

In the sense that magic realism is often a response to that which is inexplicable in everyday reality, then, the genre provides a similar social function to that of religious texts. By doing so, and by suggesting that miraculous events can happen without divine will, it implies a challenge to religious texts. The distinguishing conventions of magic realism— supernatural or miraculous events, apparitions, wish-fulfilling fantasies— can be seen in different kinds of literary texts and in religious texts as well, suggesting, as do the other authors I discuss in this study, that religious and literary texts have generic similarities. Religious texts, like classic fantasy stories, are characterized by miraculous events: the flood, the parting of the Red Sea, guiding pillars of fire and smoke, manna from Heaven, the immaculate conception, resurrection, etc. Much of the controversy surrounding *The Satanic Verses*, then, has to do with the fact that Rushdie depicts the Koran as a human contrivance. For Rushdie, its sanctity as scripture is culturally attributed and the divine origin of the revelations is dubious. Despite the fact that it is a text with great cultural and historical significance, Rushdie plays with the narrative of the Koran as if it were a *literary* or *fictional* intertext such as *A Thousand and One Nights* (a text which he alludes to throughout his work). A major difference between religious and literary genres of writing is that religious texts, especially the Koran, legislate individual and social behavior, often with the threat of divine retribution for disobedience. By treating religious texts as also literary, Rushdie desacralizes them and suggests that societies and individuals have taken them too literally.

In February of 1994, the fifth anniversary of the Ayatollah Khomeini's *fatwa* against Salman Rushdie, the French television network *Arté* devoted an entire evening of programming to discussing the *fatwa* and *The Satanic Verses* with Rushdie. During the interview, Rushdie spoke strongly in favor of the notion that religious texts must be treated as other kinds of texts — that they not have the kind of privileged status that forbids questioning.

"There should be no separate rules for religious texts," he said. "They should have to face the competition of other texts on their own." With this statement, Rushdie pinpointed the basis of the problems which were a response to the publication of his novel. Scripture is generally granted a privileged status in societies. For fundamentalists, religious texts are unassailable, unquestionable, absolute. The Koran, as already noted, has an inviolable status beyond that of the Torah or the Bible, for it is believed by faithful Muslims to be the only sacred text that contains the direct "Word of God."[50] Nevertheless, such texts are always being mediated by those who have been privileged as their interpreters. When those interpreters are fundamentalists, it is a dangerous situation as that interpreter wields nearly unlimited power with his (and it is almost invariably a man) followers. As Rushdie comments in one of his essay-istic asides in his novel *Shame*:

> So-called Islamic "fundamentalism" does not spring, in Pakistan, from the people. It is imposed on them from above. Autocratic regimes find it useful to espouse the rhetoric of faith, because people respect that language, are reluctant to oppose it. This is how religions shore up dictators [278].

The situation was identical in Iran during the Ayatollah Khomeini's regime, making the situation particularly dangerous not only for Rushdie, his translators, publishers, and other associates, but also for the people who died and suffered as a result of the Iran–Iraq war.

Although Rushdie's play with the Koran in the Mahound parts of the novel expresses a harsh scepticism about Islam, the novel is not aimed at invalidating Islamic faith. Instead, Rushdie wants to desacralize the Koran— at least in the sense of it as a God-given, unquestionable text—and open it and Islam as a whole to questioning, a concept that is heretical to fundamentalists. The idea of questioning scripture, as Carlos Fuentes notes in an article defending Rushdie, is inimical to the whole idea of sacred texts: "a sacred text is, by definition, a completed and exclusive text. You can add nothing to it. It does not converse with anyone" (*RF* 241). Strictly speaking, this is not true of all sacred texts or of everyone's approach to such texts: sacred texts are always being questioned, interpreted, and mediated. But it is true that for fundamentalists sacred texts are absolute, inflexible, and unchallengeable. Further, since the Koran more or less encompasses Islam, Rushdie's challenge to the text is perceived by believing Muslims as a challenge to their faith. Fuentes notes that "For the Ayatollahs reality is dogmatically defined once and for all in a sacred text" (241). The idea of questioning such texts is inherently blasphemous to

Muslims and that is what has made this conflict virtually impossible to resolve on a religious level. Syed Shahabuddin, an Indian MP who was one of the earliest figures to denounce *The Satanic Verses*, asserts that the novel "serves to define what has gone wrong with the Western civilization—it has lost all sense of distinction between the sacred and the profane" (*RF* 38). But it is not the *distinction* between the sacred and the profane that poses a problem as much as the categories themselves: declaring certain kinds of writing sacred and others profane discourages meaningful interaction with both kinds—the sacred is beyond questioning while the profane isn't worthy of serious attention. *The Satanic Verses* dissolves these categories to encourage questioning of and dialogue with religious texts.[51]

One of the reasons this kind of an attempt to question sacred texts meets with fundamentalist protest is that such questioning is often seen as a weakening of faith and therefore a weakening of the religious community's sense of unity and solidarity. Thus, the "Rushdie affair" has fostered some interesting comments about the nature of identity—a subject treated by the novel. Shabbir Akhtar, a member of Bradford's Council of Mosques and one of the earliest voices of protest against the novel, asserted: "Given that the Koran is the book which defines the authentically Muslim outlook, there is no choice in the matter. Anyone who fails to be offended by Rushdie's book *ipso facto* ceases to be a Muslim" (*RF* 228). Obviously, such a statement proposes a rather limited concept of what it is to be a Muslim. In one of his essays, Rushdie takes this notion to task and explains his own motives:

> Those who oppose the novel most vociferously today are of the opinion that intermingling with a different culture will inevitably weaken and ruin their own. I am of the opposite opinion. *The Satanic Verses* celebrates hybridity, impurity, intermingling, the transformation that comes of new and unexpected combinations of human beings, cultures, ideas, politics, movies, songs. It rejoices in mongrelization and fears the absolutism of the Pure. *Mélange*, hotchpotch, a bit of this and a bit of that is *how newness enters the world*. [...] It is a love-song to our mongrel selves [*IH* 394].

Rushdie's mixing of genres, languages, and literary traditions reflects his goal of defying values of cultural, religious, or racial purity such as those espoused by Akhtar and Khomeini. His repeated supposition is that we are hybrid individuals—the product of cultures, societies, languages, races, and religions intermixing—in a hybrid world culture: as Zeeny irreverently says in *The Satanic Verses*, "Why should there be a good, right way of being a wog?" (52). Rushdie's works teach that only for fundamentalists is there a single, "right" way of being an Indian, Pakistani, American, Muslim, Hindu, Christian, Jew, etc. For Rushdie, it is actually impossible to be culturally "authentic": neither Saladin Chamcha/Salahuddin Chamchawalla nor Saleem Sinai can erase the fact that they are the "mixed" products of a postcolonial world; they have inherited the languages and traditions of multiple nations, cultures, and religions. The only way to remain "pure" is quite ridiculous: to withdraw entirely from history and the world around oneself, as does the exiled Imam in Gibreel's dream.

The emphasis on mixing is reflected in the form of Rushdie's fictions which draw on literary traditions, religious ideas, cultural values, and languages from East and West. With all of this material co-existing within his fictions, Rushdie creates a dialogue between East and West, as announced by the title of his 1993 collection of stories: *East, West.* Carlos Fuentes writes that "Rushdie's work perfectly fits the Bakhtinian contention that ours is an age of competitive languages. [...] [I]n dialogue, no one is absolutely right, neither speaker holds an absolute truth or, indeed, has an absolute hold over history" (*RF* 241). Rushdie does not offer absolute truths, but puts different ideas into dialogue with one another. Speaking more generally, Fuentes expands on Bakhtin's concept of heteroglossia to say that "Fiction is a harbinger of a multipolar and multicultural world, where no single philosophy, no single belief, no single solution, can shunt aside the extreme wealth of mankind's cultural heritage" (243). In another article defending Rushdie's work, Edward Said concurs that

> there is no pure, unsullied, unmixed essence to which some of us can return, whether that essence is pure Islam, pure Christianity, pure Judaism or Easternism, Americanism, Westernism. Rushdie's work is not just *about* the mixture, it *is* that mixture itself. To stir Islamic narratives into a stream of heterogeneous narratives about actors, tricksters, prophets, devils, whores, heroes, heroines is therefore inevitable [*RF* 166].

It is not surprising, therefore, that those most antagonistic to Rushdie's work want to reassert ideals of cultural purity.

Although Islam has a long history of being open to cultural mixing and tolerant of other religions, Charles Paul Freund observes that, like other religions, it has had periods when a strong impulse has been to "seek self-protection from cultural and spiritual contamination" (*RF* 214). It is understandable that with the profound contemporary lack of understanding between Islamic and Western communities, especially in Britain where Muslims are the focus of severe racism, that Muslims would be inclined to see *The Satanic Verses* as an attack on their identity as Muslims. One of the things that is so frustrating, even infuriating, about the Rushdie affair, however, is that *The Satanic Verses* is unequivocally on the side of those who attacked it[52]; as Farrukh Dhondy noted early on in the affair, "it defends them [British Muslims] against the ravages of a racist society" (*RF* 184). It is worth emphasizing that the harshest portraits in the novel are of British racists and the fundamentalist Imam, not the numerous Muslim immigrants. But most Muslims in Britain and elsewhere were only exposed to the religiously irreverent parts of the book taken out of context and so were never aware that they were attacking a book that championed their own concerns.

The conflict was then used by Khomeini to further his own agenda. Khomeini exploited *The Satanic Verses* controversy in a way similar to Margaret Thatcher's exploitation of the Falklands situation (see next chapter). Whereas Thatcher sought to re-invigorate British nationalist sentiment, Khomeini sought to unite Muslims in a struggle against a common enemy.[53] Amir Taheri suggests that, after a series of setbacks, Khomeini was "looking for an issue likely to stir the imagination of the poor and illiterate masses" (*RF* 91). Khomeini's speeches confirm this view, as he claimed that the novel was "a calculated move aimed at rooting out religion and religiousness, and above all, Islam and its clergy" and part of a conspiracy on behalf of the "world devourers"—the Americans in league with Israel—"to annihilate Islam, and Muslims" (*RF* 75).[54] In conjunction with the *fatwa*, such statements can be seen as part of a network of "discourses" calling for an "imagined political community" (Anderson)—a nation of Islam that transcends the borders separating the world's communities of Muslims. Aziz Al-Azmeh argues that Khomeini's brand of Islam fosters the desire for a "restoration of a putative utopia"—a mythic time when Islam was a monolith—and that Rushdie had become "a token by means of which the authors and purveyors of this particular brand of recent Islam [could] project their demonology, and foist upon the various Muslim communities in [Britain] a uniformity that has no justification in their histories or traditions" (*RF* 213).

A reasonable way of looking at Khomeini's *fatwa*, then, is as a reaction against the diversification of Islam. Shabbir Akhtar's sentiments demonstrate the serious dangers of this insular approach: "Any faith which compromises its internal temper of militant wrath is destined for the dustbin of history, for it can no longer preserve its faithful heritage in the face of the corrosive influences" (*RF* 229). This pronouncement—the violent, uncompromising defiance of "corrupting" influences from other cultures—highlights the masculinist basis of fundamentalism. When discussing fundamentalism, it is important to keep in mind that it is almost exclusively a male phenomenon and a direct outgrowth of male social dominance. The gender power imbalance—in fundamentalism and in society as a whole—is a subject that neither Rushdie nor Julian Barnes critique in an extended way, but one which Jeanette Winterson and Angela Carter, as will be discussed, identify and aggressively critique as the factor upon which nearly all forms of social oppression are based.

Needless to say, the "militant wrath" of fundamentalists such as Khomeini and Akhtar does not leave the door open for cross-cultural understanding and tolerance. But literature, Carlos Fuentes asserts, stands against the retrenching impulses of intolerant, monolithic societies: "The novel is born from the very fact that we do not understand one another any longer, because unitary, orthodox language has broken down. [...] Impose a unitary language: you kill the novel, but you also kill the society" (RF 243).[55] In opposition to the forces of unity that would kill the diversity and richness of human society, The Satanic Verses is a powerful call for dialogue, tolerance, and understanding.

CHAPTER TWO

Julian Barnes

Julian Barnes shares Rushdie's concerns about the veracity and authority of historical representations as well as his skepticism about religion. Rushdie's novels address these subjects on an epic scale: they span vast geographical areas and large expanses of time, and they deal with the birth and growth of nations and religions as well as the experience of whole communities of peoples. In contrast, Barnes's work might be generally characterized as more "local." He writes about characters who are trying to grapple with the "knowability" of history, but their experiences are more grounded in the mundane realities of contemporary life. Even his *A History of the World in 10½ Chapters*—with its title misleadingly announcing a sprawling, epic project—is about relatively insignificant characters involved in mostly small events.

Many of Barnes's characters are academics or pseudo-academic intellectuals. They do not *live* history as does Rushdie's Saleem Sinai. Instead, they *research* history, seeking their answers by following the time-honored traditions of academic scholarship, an aspect of Barnes's work that locates him firmly within a male tradition of writing. Though Barnes interjects self-conscious commentary on the difficulties of obtaining accurate historical knowledge, he never really addresses the issue that traditional methods of historical study stem from a masculine academic tradition—something that Winterson and especially Carter explicitly critique (see Chapters Three and Four). Nevertheless, because all of Barnes's characters fail to uncover any definitive answers to their quests for historical knowledge, his work does suggest that the search for certainty is itself a flawed concept and that knowledge gleaned from academic modes of inquiry is inevitably limited.

History: Fact or Fiction?

In the last thirty years or so, there has been a tremendous amount of creative energy expended in the writing of "historical fictions." On the one hand, the literary fascination with history has led to epic novels by the likes of James Michener or Edward Rutherford, authors who exoticize past historical settings as the backdrop for page-turning romantic/adventure sagas. On the other hand, and with what is generally regarded as having more literary merit, it has led to the current prominence of a type of fiction Linda Hutcheon has called "historiographic metafiction": novels which combine an attention to verifiable historical events, personages, or milieu with a self-reflexive awareness of their status as artifacts and the literary narrative conventions they employ (Hutcheon, *Poetics* 5, 105–123).[1] John Fowles's *The French Lieutenant's Woman*, which is set in Victorian times and comments on the mores of that era via the self-conscious interjections of its twentieth-century author persona, is the signature work of this genre. Now, with works by authors such as A. S. Byatt, Don DeLillo, Michael Ondaatje, Graham Swift, Penelope Lively, Julian Barnes, and Salman Rushdie, "historiographic metafiction" has become one of the most frequently pursued literary genres, particularly among British writers.

This increased popularity of critical historical fictions is an outgrowth of the wider postmodern questioning of Enlightenment philosophies and traditional disciplinary authority. A great deal of the scholarly work of the last few decades has been to correct for the gaps in Western history (e.g. of the experience of women, people of color, the poor) and the myths disseminated in school textbooks (e.g. of the goodness and wisdom of Western projects such as colonialism). Further, historians and other scholars have intensified their analysis and questioning of the structural elements of historical kinds of writing and now suggest that historiography, contrary to nineteenth-century realist models which urged the pursuit of "scientific" objectivity, employs literary narrative conventions.

This re-orientation in thinking about history and the writing of history has been brought to prominence recently by "New Historicism," a scholarly movement which aims to see historiography as a craft rather than a science.[2] According to Hayden White, a key fault of nineteenth-century historians is that they

> continued to believe that different interpretations of the same set of
> events were functions of ideological distortions or of inadequate factual
> data. They continued to believe that if one only eschewed ideology and

remained true to the facts, history would produce a knowledge as certain as anything offered by the physical sciences and as objective as a mathematical exercise ["Fictions" 27].

History in its realist manifestation, White asserts, construed itself as a science, meaning that it was held to be an objective form of representation as opposed to the subjective imaginings of literature. As I discuss in the next chapter, the fallacy underlying this view is that science, although it strives for objectivity, is not necessarily an objective form of inquiry. The same can be said of history as a discipline. White demonstrates that historiography, the genre of writing which records the findings of historians, is not a neutral form of organizing knowledge. Objectivity has long been held to be the highest of ideals in most forms of disciplinary inquiry, but scholars like White, along with novelists such as those treated in this study, suggest that this ideal of academic certainty is a myth.[3] Historians, like scientists, do not record objective data; they select and organize their data to construct a narrative. This process is a subjective one and so inevitably conveys an ideologically-influenced view of history. Linda Hutcheon asserts that postmodern fiction draws attention to this process in order to reveal the ideological assumptions of historical narratives: "The process of making stories out of chronicles, of constructing plots out of sequences, is what postmodern fiction underlines. This [...] focuses attention on the act of imposing order on that past, of encoding strategies of meaning-making through representation" (*Politics* 66–67). Like White, Hutcheon suggests that histories are a form of fiction.

Enlightenment philosophy, however, urged historians to view fiction as the antithesis of fact. The realist historical tradition did not recognize that regardless of whether one is dealing with imaginary or "real" events, organizing events into a narrative requires the use of literary conventions:

> no given set of casually recorded historical events in themselves constitute a story; the most that they offer to the historian are story elements. The events are made into a story by the suppression or subordination of certain of them and the highlighting of others, by characterization, motific representation, variation of tone and point of view, alternative descriptive strategies, and the like—in short, all of the techniques that we would normally expect to find in the emplotment of a novel or a play [White, "Historical Text" 47].[4]

White goes on to describe the role of the individual's point of view in how history is perceived as either tragic, farcical, comic, romantic, or ironic. Like the constituent elements of a work of literature, historical events are in themselves what he calls "value-neutral" (47). It is how the historian arranges them into a story that gives them emotional and ideological impact.

Both historians and novelists, White writes, attempt to

> provide a verbal image of "reality." The novelist may present his notion of this reality indirectly, that is to say, by figurative techniques, rather than directly, which is to say, by registering a series of propositions which are supposed to correspond point by point to some extra-textual domain of occurrence or happening, as the historian claims to do. But the image of reality which the novelist thus constructs is meant to correspond in its general outline to some domain of human experience which is no less real than that referred to by the historian ["Fictions" 22].

A corollary of this observation is that neither literary nor historical genres accomplish the task of representing reality "better" than the other—that is, no one genre has a more authoritative claim to representing human experience than another. Thus, one of the key recurring assumptions of New Historicism is "that no discourse, imaginative or archival, gives access to unchanging truths nor expresses inalterable human nature" (Veeser xi). Traditional historiography does not necessarily tell us "more" (or even more "accurately") about the experience of a particular era or personage than does an imaginative or fictional representation of that era or personage. Each may focus our attention on different facets of that experience, but neither can claim, by virtue of its methods of representation, to provide a more comprehensive portrait.

I don't mean to propose the kind of radical poststructuralist notion that history is indistinguishable from fiction. Rather, history is recorded in a variety of narrative genres of which the historical chronicle is just one. There is no "objective" view of history to be obtained by strictly following the axioms of traditional realist historical research. As Hayden White points out, New Historicists have "discovered [...] that there is no such thing as a specifically historical approach to the study of history, but a variety of such approaches, at least as many as there are positions on the current ideological spectrum" (Veeser 302). Understanding that historiography uses literary conventions helps build awareness of the limitations of such narratives and show that "fictional" texts are useful contributions to historical knowledge. Postmodern historical fictions such as Barnes's don't necessarily critique historiography or the traditional methods of historical research as much as they imagine, explore, and narrate alternative understandings of history, often in an effort to compensate for the gaps or areas of neglect in existing narratives.

How Do We Seize the Past?

This is the question that Julian Barnes is preoccupied with in his novels, especially in his *Flaubert's Parrot* and *A History of the World in 10½ Chapters*. The pervasive questioning of traditional epistemologies in this "postmodern" era has led to a general uncertainty about how to understand history and the world around us. According to Jean-François Lyotard, the grand systems of thought or "metanarratives" (e.g. Christianity, Marxism, Reason) which, for many people, used to explain things are no longer sufficient (xxiv). It is debatable as to whether they ever were really sufficient, but Lyotard is correct in that they are certainly less influential now than in previous historical eras. A. S. Byatt goes so far as to suggest that this explains why there has been such a boom in historical writing among contemporary British writers: it "is part of a project of reassessing the past, our own ancestry, without the old framing certainties of Christianity or Marxism" (444–45). The existential confusion and general uncertainty of individuals deprived of such "framing certainties" is one of the more notable features of postmodern literature, and is especially foregrounded in Barnes's work. Barnes looks to history for answers and usually only finds more questions.

Barnes draws on an extremely diverse spectrum of writing styles to show how history is recorded in a variety of genres which all make use of literary conventions. Many critics and reviewers have noted that *Flaubert's Parrot* and *A History of the World* consist of a mix of what are usually considered "historiographic" and "literary" genres.[5] James Scott, in particular, identifies *Flaubert's Parrot* as a "trans-generic prose text" (58), and notes that Barnes deconstructs "prose genre taxonomies [...] so that [...] the conventional signification patterns (biography presents fact; fiction presents fancy) no longer function" (65). This observation captures the general spirit of Barnes's work, but a more detailed examination is needed of the specific genres that Barnes employs in his fiction and the self-consciousness or "metafictional" ways in which he confronts the limitations, frustrations, and occasional rewards of their various conventions of representation.

Whereas *A History of the World* (discussed later in this chapter) addresses the problems of historical representation in a globalized sense, *Flaubert's Parrot* focuses on the problems of narrating the history of an individual's life, that is, the genre of biography. *Flaubert's Parrot* records the exploits and musings of Geoffrey Braithwaite, a retired British medical doctor turned amateur Flaubert biographer. Early in his quest for information about Flaubert, Braithwaite reflects upon history's deviousness:

> How do we seize the past? Can we ever do so? When I was a medical stu-
> dent some pranksters at an end-of-term dance released into the hall a
> piglet which had been smeared with grease. It squirmed between legs,
> evaded capture, squealed a lot. People fell over trying to grasp it, and
> were made to look ridiculous in the process. The past often seems to
> behave like that piglet [14].

Barnes is both fascinated and frustrated by the impossibility of getting
history "right," a conundrum which leads him to represent and reflect upon
historical events and figures through a variety of "alternative" historiographic genres. Implicit throughout his work is the idea that traditional
forms of historiography offer a limited means of understanding history.
Barnes doesn't presume to have the answer to this problem, but his work
does suggest that it is futile to try to eschew individualist perspectives and
ideologies in historical narration. Thus, Braithwaite, a self-professed "hes-
itating narrator" (89) who is typical of the narrators Barnes employs, tends
to be self-doubting, limited, and deeply subjective rather than authoritative, omniscient, and objective.[6]

Braithwaite's search for clues to constructing an authoritative biography of Flaubert leads him to confront the limitations of biography as a
discipline and a genre:

> The trawling net fills, then the biographer hauls it in, sorts, throws back,
> stores, fillets and sells. Yet consider what he doesn't catch: there is always
> far more of that. The biography stands, fat and worthy-burgherish on the
> shelf, boastful and sedate: a shilling life will give you all the facts, a ten
> pound one all the hypotheses as well. But think of everything that got
> away, that fled with the last deathbed exhalation of the biographee [38].

The specter of "everything that got away" drives Braithwaite to some rather
absurd forms of research. At one point, his effort to ascertain how accurate our perception can be of a Flaubertian metaphor comparing the sun
to a "large disc of redcurrant jam" leads him to write to a grocer's company to find out if a pot of 1853 Rouennais jam would be the same color
as a modern one (92). When assured that the color would be "almost
exactly the same," he feels vindicated: "So at least that's all right: now we
can go ahead and confidently imagine the sunset" (92). But how many
such "problems" of referentiality can be so resolved? Braithwaite's fret-
fulness reflects an extreme realist attitude towards representation which
Barnes is both satirizing and sympathizing with.

Throughout his search for information about Flaubert, Braithwaite
is preoccupied by this concern over the reliability or referentiality of language

and historical "evidence." One of his strategies for understanding the "true" Flaubert, for example, is to seek the "true" stuffed parrot that inspired Loulou in *Un coeur simple*; he thinks that if he finds the real parrot then he will have discovered Flaubert's "true voice." Having found one seemingly authentic parrot, he feels that he "had almost known the writer" (16). When he discovers the existence of another "authentic" parrot, he begins to discover the error and hubris of his search for a unitary emblem of Flaubert: "The writer's voice—what makes you think it can be located that easily?" (22). Braithwaite devotes much of his search to determining which of the two parrots is the genuine one, but at the end of the novel he discovers three more candidates—all that remains of a collection which once held *fifty*—at Rouen's Museum of Natural History. "Perhaps it was one of them" (190), Braithwaite muses. And perhaps it wasn't. Perhaps it was one of the lost ones or perhaps they were all frauds. This quest for the authentic parrot—and its failure—serves as a metaphor for the difficulties with reconstructing the past. Any authoritative account of the past is bound to be a fraud in some respects. Braithwaite is "obsessed"[7] with the idea that finding the "real" parrot will somehow give him a definitive insight into Flaubert's life and works, but over the course of his research he comes to realize that the "truth" about Flaubert is as elusive as the authentic parrot.

In addition to serving as a metaphor for the difficulties with historical research and providing a kind of skeletal plot, Braithwaite's search for Flaubert's parrot links the novel to the detective genre (to which Barnes has contributed four novels under the pseudonym of Dan Kavanagh[8]). One very common convention of detective novels, often including those written by women, is a deeply ingrained sexism. Honesty is associated with the detective's masculinity while "corruption of all kinds is often figured [...] as feminine" (Cranny-Francis 100), and the diction of the heroically independent and highly masculinized detective reflects misogynist attitudes (an archetypical figure is Dashiel Hammett's Sam Spade). Contemporary women writers of detective fiction such as Sarah Paretsky and Sue Grafton have been revising these conventions, and Barnes too has offered an innovation to the traditional model with the bisexual Nick Duffy, the protagonist of his four detective novels. *Flaubert's Parrot* is even more innovative with detective fiction conventions, albeit less obviously: Braithwaite, a backward-looking widower and ineffectual cuckold, is something of a comical antithesis to the traditional hard-boiled hypermasculine detective. Further, Barnes denies us the pleasure of the climactic resolution of the questions and mysteries which drive the plot of the traditional detective novel. Sam Spade at least has the reward of finding the Maltese Falcon, even if it is a fake, but Braithwaite, and Barnes's readers, will never know which parrot is "real" and which are fake. Similarly, many questions about Flaubert's "true" self must go unanswered. Consistent with postmodern fictions (or fictions about postmodernity) in general, *Flaubert's Parrot* unsettles us by leaving its questions unresolved: we can never "seize" the past; we can only try to do so and be "made to look ridiculous in the process."

Braithwaite's encounter with the multiple parrots in the museum at the end of his search confirms that there are as many views of an individual's history as there are constructions of them, biographical or otherwise, that we create. Such constructions appear in different genres of writing— traditionally "fictional" ones and traditionally "factual" ones. *Flaubert's Parrot* encourages us to question the limitations of any textual record of the past and thus to question the distinction between "fictional" and "factual" genres. One chapter, for example, is organized as a chronology of events in Flaubert's life. Generally, we expect chronologies to be the most value-neutral and veridical genre of historical record, but even lists of dates and events can posit dramatically different views of history. Braithwaite gives us three different chronologies of Flaubert's life: one which emphasizes Flaubert's successes; another which chronicles all of the death, failure, and despair in his life; and a final one which presents an autobiographical view by citing Flaubert's personal writings (*FP* 23–37).[9]

Despite his detail-obsessed, realist approach to reconstructing Flaubert, Braithwaite continues to provide us with unconventional, often wildly contradictory, views of his subject. Several chapters offer varying portraits of Flaubert by concentrating on his observations about and interactions with, for example, the railroad, or animals, or irony. A more radically unconventional chapter conveys a view of Flaubert in the generic form of a university exam which highlights the elusiveness of a unitary view of Flaubert's life. Another is in the form of a "Dictionary of Accepted Ideas" about Flaubert's life which imitates the writer's own *Dictionnaire des idées reçues*. This multi-genre, multi-perspective view of Flaubert does not necessarily mean that we must abandon historical inquiry to relativism: not all versions of the past are equal, but the past evades any easy attempts at encapsulation. As Alison Lee remarks, "that such multiple ways of seeing exist provides an acknowledgement that there is no single truth any more than there is a single parrot" (*Realism* 39).

Lee draws attention to the mediating role of language in how we acquire historical knowledge by observing that we can only know Flaubert through the written word—novels, letters, journal entries, etc. Belying his ostensible naiveté, Braithwaite conveys his awareness of this poststructural epistemological orientation when he remarks: "We no longer believe that language and reality 'match up' so congruently—indeed, we probably think that words give birth to things as much as things give birth to words" (*FP* 88). Since language is pluralistic (i.e. capable of offering multiple views of history) and Braithwaite can only reconstruct Flaubert through language, he can only write an indeterminate biography of Flaubert (Lee, *Realism* 39–40). But it is more than just a question of language mediating reality; it is a question of the genres in which language is recorded, for forms themselves can impose or at least encourage limitations on representation. Thus, in trying to give an account of himself, Braithwaite runs into the same kind of problem as he does with Flaubert: What form is appropriate to the task?

> You know those personal advertisements in magazines like the *New Statesman*? I thought I might do it like that.
>
>> 60+ widowed doctor, children grown up, active, cheerful if inclined to melancholy, kindly, non-smoker, amateur Flaubert scholar, likes reading, food, travel to familiar places, old films, has friends, but seeks ...
>
> You see the problem. [...] They aren't lying—indeed, they're all trying to be utterly sincere—but they aren't telling the truth. The column distorts the way the advertisers describe themselves. No one would think of himself as an active non-smoker inclined to melancholy if that wasn't encouraged, even demanded, by the form. [...] Style does arise from subject-matter. Try as they might, those advertisers are always beaten down by the form; they are forced—even at the one time they need to be candidly personal—into an unwished impersonality [*FP* 94–95].

This kind of critical, self-conscious attention to genre is typical of the writers I'm discussing. The conventions of the personal ad genre impose limitations on their subject, in this case transforming a person into a brief series of "marketable" characteristics. Granted, the personal ad is a particularly limiting genre of representation, but the principle that forms shape and sometimes limit our understanding of what is being represented holds true for others.

I have the impression that Braithwaite sincerely wants to render Flaubert's life to us in some complete, authoritative fashion, but his efforts to do this are doomed to failure for any such rendering is inevitably "compromised" by the necessity of literary narrative conventions in recreating historical events. This frustration leads Braithwaite to the following exasperated formulation: "We can study files for decades, but every so often we are tempted to throw up our hands and declare that history is merely another literary genre: the past is autobiographical fiction pretending to be parliamentary report" (90). If one sought a maxim for the genre of historiographic metafiction, this might be it. Braithwaite comes to this equation of history and literature when contemplating the contradiction between the numerous reports that Flaubert was a giant—"a strapping Gallic chieftain" (90)—and the documented fact that he was only six feet tall. The past may not be "fiction" in the traditional sense, but fictions proliferate around every personage, event, and artifact of the past. As a result, the narrative conventions of more ostensibly imaginative forms of writing inevitably influence our understanding of the past.

Other Genres: Fictions, Literary Criticism, Autobiography

The contradictions, gaps, and other indeterminacies in history preoccupy Braithwaite's research. As his awareness of and frustration with the inseparability of fictional and historical genres of writing increases, he ventures beyond the conventional concerns of the historian/biographer into literary criticism, autobiography, and even writing fictions of his own—all genres which Barnes uses to further challenge the traditional division between fact and fiction. To begin with the last of these, Barnes adds a layer to the metafictionality of the novel by having Braithwaite pose as a kind of postmodern author himself, writing a story which reimagines Flaubert's life from the perspective of his lover, Louise Colet. That chapter is an archetype of one of the most common subgenres of postmodern fiction—stories which offer an alternative version of the past from the perspective of a figure marginalized by history. Braithwaite assumes the persona of Colet, informs us that "The days of loyally believing false things about Gustave are over" (148), and proceeds to portray Flaubert as a stylistic tyrant who demeaned the personalized tone of her work while narcissistically exalting the "objectivity" of his own.

This conflict between "subjective" and "objective" or "scientific" modes of writing mirrors the opposition of historiographic methods which dominates Braithwaite's memoir. Braithwaite wants a verifiable, objective narrative of the past informed by documented fact but must face up to the reality that even first-hand documentary accounts can and do present conflicting versions of history. Historians and biographers may attempt to organize that information to come up with a balanced and "neutral" account, but they cannot possibly succeed for, as Hayden White argues, the act of mediating and scripting such information into a narrative inevitably influences the portrait it presents. On some level, Braithwaite understands this and abandons himself to writing narratives of Flaubert's past which consciously foreground all of the contradictions in the historical record. Even when ostensibly denying the indeterminacy of history, Barnes is being ironic, as when Louise Colet (via Braithwaite and hence Barnes) purports to correct us of our misconceptions about Flaubert: "You have heard different versions, no doubt? The truth is simple" (143). Of course, with Barnes the "truth" is never simple. Barnes is contesting the concept of "truth" in narration itself for, as Jeanette Winterson remarks in *Boating for Beginners*, "there's no such thing as a true story" (124).

The Louise Colet chapter claims to offer an authoritative account but it is also blatantly imaginative. It may be the most ostensibly fictitious account of Flaubert that Braithwaite gives us, but all the others—whether in the form of a chronology, literary criticism, mock *Dictionnaire des idées reçues*, or university exam—are similarly fictions, and each of them privileges different facets of the truth. This diversity of genres implies a crucial question: Which is most conducive for conveying the fullest, most accurate picture of the past? Much historiography pretends to be authoritative but is "compromised" by subjective factors and/or fictional conventions. *Flaubert's Parrot* teaches that a completely objective view of history is not possible, and that multiple views presented in different genres contribute to a fuller understanding of the past with no single genre, by virtue of its conventions, offering a "better" or more accurate account. *Flaubert's Parrot*, then, follows Braithwaite as he transforms from a stereotype of the realist historiographer seeking an authoritative and absolute truth to a kind of postmodern author who recognizes the indeterminacy of the past and attempts to account for it through a variety of self-conscious narrative genres which highlight contradictions rather than attempt to dispel them.

Braithwaite's struggle with what can and cannot be known about history parallels a similar preoccupation with what literature should and should not do. His interest in Flaubert leads him to dabble in literary criticism as he does in historical study. Literary criticism is meant to enhance our understanding of literature in the way that historiography tries to expand our knowledge about the past, but Braithwaite focuses on the need of some to taxonomize and canonize the texts they discuss, just as realist historians set out to give an authoritative view of historical events: "many critics would like to be dictators of literature, to regulate the past, and to set out with quiet authority the future direction of the art" (*FP* 97–98). Barnes suggests that such attempts at regulation tell us about the critic rather than the texts themselves, for the possible meanings of literary texts are at least as variegated as interpretations of historical events. The New Critical and structuralist impulse to define genres according to fixed principles is a prominent example of this attempt to "regulate" or even legislate art. But Barnes's persistently unconventional uses of genre defy this kind of obsession with controlling taxonomies.

Nevertheless, Braithwaite decides to "play" the game of literary regulation. Ostensibly he does so in an attempt to tell us more about himself, but, given his obsessive drive to regulate the world around him, it is likely that he simply can't resist the opportunity to set forth his own program for literature: "There shall be no more novels in which a group of people, isolated by circumstances, revert to the 'natural condition' of man, become essential, poor, bare, forked creatures" (98). This genre, he whimsically declares, must be banned because it is "easy" and "fun" to write. Similarly, there are to be "No novels set in abattoirs. This is, I admit, a rather small genre at the moment; but I have recently noticed increasing use of the abattoir in short stories. It must be nipped in the bud" (98). Braithwaite would impose further bans or quotas on: novels about incest, university fiction, fiction set in South America; representations of bestiality and sex in the shower; novels about distant and forgotten imperial wars; narrators identified only by an initial; novels which are "reworkings, sequels or prequels" to other novels; and the allegorical use of God (98–100). These mandates are given in an imitative Flaubertian spirit of irony, but they nevertheless do tell us something about Braithwaite. Braithwaite implies that each genre in this seemingly random assemblage has become a kind of contemporary cliché, where the conventions are too easy and the results too predictable. Perhaps because his own life is a kind of cliché (as discussed below), Braithwaite, like Flaubert, detests clichés—both social and, in this case, literary.

Another chapter in *Flaubert's Parrot* is directed against clichéd or conventional social and literary expectations. Organized as a series of responses to some of the traditional criticisms of Flaubert (that he was, for example, misanthropic, anti-democracy, anti-"progress," unpatriotic, etc.), this chapter provides some of the novel's more interesting insights into both Flaubert's artistic philosophy and Barnes's. It is worth citing at length Braithwaite's defense of Flaubert against the charge that he "teaches no positive virtues":

> Take all the obscenity trials from *Madame Bovary* to *Lady Chatterley's Lover*: there's always some element of games-playing, of compliance, in the defense. Others might call it tactical hypocrisy. (Is this book sexy? No, M'Lud, we hold that it would have an emetic, not a mimetic, effect on the reader. Does this book encourage adultery? No, M'Lud, look how

the miserable sinner who gives herself time and time again to riotous pleasure is punished in the end. Does this book attack marriage? No, M'Lud, it portrays a vile and hopeless marriage so that only by following Christian instructions will their own marriages be happy. Is this book blasphemous? No, M'Lud, the novelist's thought is chaste.) As a forensic argument, of course, it has been successful; but I sometimes feel a residual bitterness that one of these defense counsel, when speaking for a true work of literature, did not build his act on simple defiance. (Is this book sexy? M'Lud, we bloody well hope so. Does it encourage adultery and attack marriage? Spot on, M'Lud, that's *exactly* what my client is trying to do. Is this book blasphemous? For Christ's sake, M'Lud, the matter's as clear as the loincloth on the Crucifixion. Put it this way, M'Lud: my client thinks that most of the values of the society in which he lives stink, and he hopes with this book to promote fornication, masturbation, adultery, the stoning of priests and, since we've temporarily got your attention, M'Lud, the suspension of corrupt judges by their earlobes. The defense rests its case) [133].

Like many other contemporary writers, especially the ones discussed in this study, Barnes professes an outright admiration for subversive or irreverent tendencies, which helps us understand why he is so fascinated with Flaubert. In the above passage, Barnes applauds Flaubert's outright defiance of social conventions. The notion that the novel must provide conservative moral instruction is so pervasive that it has dictated the terms for discussions about literary merit for centuries. The traditional defense of novels put on trial for "encouraging" immorality has been to capitulate to dominant social values and argue that the fate of the immoral individual teaches a conventional moral. This argument, Barnes suggests, is a betrayal of artistic integrity and needs to be resisted.

A related criticism of Flaubert that Braithwaite takes up is the claim *"That he didn't believe Art had a social purpose."* Braithwaite responds:

No he didn't. This is wearying. "You provide desolation," wrote George Sand, "and I provide consolation." To which Flaubert replied, "I cannot change my eyes." [...] Listen to Auden: "Poetry makes nothing happen." Do not imagine that Art is something which is designed to give gentle uplift and self-confidence. Art is not a *brassière*. At least, not in the English sense. But do not forget that *brassière* is the French for life-jacket [136].

Barnes's evocation of Auden echoes Oscar Wilde's famous pronouncement in his preface to *The Picture of Dorian Gray* that "All art is quite useless" (17). And, as with Wilde, Braithwaite hints that Flaubert's stance that art has no social purpose is to an extent disingenuous: it is simply that the values depicted in *Madame Bovary* and other seemingly "immoral" texts run counter to dominant social morality; they are a "life-jacket" against moral hypocrisy.

With all of this attention to aesthetics, it becomes clear that *Flaubert's Parrot* is as much a book about art as it is a book about history and biography. As with the latter two, Barnes is suspicious of conventions of representation in art. Via Braithwaite, Barnes reflects on the ostensible differences between realist and postmodern strategies for conveying reality:

> the assumed divinity of the nineteenth-century novelist was only ever a technical device; and the partiality of the modern novelist is just as much a ploy. When a contemporary narrator hesitates, claims uncertainty, misunderstands, plays games and falls into error, does the reader in fact conclude that reality is being more authentically rendered? When the writer provides two different endings to his novel (why two? why not a hundred?), does the reader seriously imagine he is being "offered a choice" and that the work is reflecting life's variable outcomes? Such a "choice" is never real, because the reader is obliged to consume both endings. In life, we make a decision [...] and we go one way; had we made a different decision [...] we would have been elsewhere. The novel with two endings doesn't reproduce this reality: it merely takes us down two diverging paths. It's a form of cubism, I suppose. And that's all right, but let's not deceive ourselves about the artifice involved [89].

As with the dilemma over what genre is best suited for representing history, Braithwaite finds himself contemplating which kind of literary writing authentically renders reality: the self-assured, omniscient pose of realism or the characteristically open-ended, multiplicitous offerings of postmodernism?[10] And, as with historiographic genres, Braithwaite determines that neither realist nor postmodern modes are superior to the other on the basis of their representational conventions, although both employ tropes which have been interpreted as attempting to offer a "better" or more authoritative version. Realist and postmodern strategies of representation are equally dependent on artifice. In a novel that focuses on critiquing realist modes of representation, it may seem odd that this passage should draw attention to the artifice involved in a postmodern trope like giving multiple endings to a story, but, as this passage exemplifies, a characteristic feature of postmodern literature is, according to Linda Hutcheon, its self-critique and self-conscious "complicity" in the aesthetic practices it critiques (*Politics* 1–2).

The dilemma of how to render the experience of life authentically in art leads to Braithwaite's somewhat facetious idea of a truly realistic novel as something like the "Choose Your Own Adventure" genre:

if novelists truly wanted to simulate the delta of life's possibilities, this is what they'd do. At the back of the book would be a set of sealed envelopes in various colours. Each would be clearly marked on the outside: Traditional Happy Ending; Traditional Unhappy Ending; Traditional Half-and-Half Ending; Deus ex Machina; Modernist Arbitrary Ending; End of the World Ending; Surrealist Ending; and so on. You would be allowed only one, and would have to destroy the envelopes you didn't select. *That's* what I call offering the reader a choice of endings; but you may find me quite unreasonably literal-minded [89].

From his quest for the real parrot and his inquiry regarding the color of Rouennais jam, we know that Braithwaite is indeed "unreasonably literal-minded." In essence, he's asking for an extreme form of postmodern art: a novel which could somehow accommodate every conceivable genre of ending and therefore offer the most comprehensive representation of lived reality. It's not unlike what Barnes is attempting to do with this novel in presenting as many different views of Flaubert as one book can contain, but neither Barnes nor Braithwaite is naive about the limitations of even such a hybrid form. Clearly, Braithwaite's suggestion is as artificial an arrangement as any other and, given the self-critical remark which accompanies it, it is, I think, offered with knowing irony. It would only provide another illusion—in this case, a particularly cumbersome one— of reality. Similarly, *Flaubert's Parrot* may expose us to a great variety of views of Flaubert, but that variety does not somehow "add up" to a complete view; they must go on being in conflict with one another. As Barnes hints, via Braithwaite: "It's a form of cubism [...] but let's not deceive ourselves about the artifice involved."

These excursions into literary criticism, like Braithwaite's other attempts to reconstruct Flaubert, tell us as much about the biographer as the biographee. Braithwaite's dislike of clichés, for example, is not surprising considering the extent to which his life has become a cliché of the impotent cuckold.[11] Although one might criticize him for living entirely vicariously, for being obsessed by the search for information about another person's life, his search is also for self-understanding. His quest enables him to go on after the trauma of his wife's suicide,[12] as if by knowing Flaubert's past he will unlock the explanation of his own past. Though he attempts to suppress the trauma, it bubbles up from time to time and finally surfaces in a chapter titled "Pure Story" which gives an autobiographical account of his relationship with his wife and her death. The persistence of this trauma, its insistence on finally being told, directly defies realist conventions of historiography which attempt to cover up the historian's own experience and background. Braithwaite's biography of Flaubert, then, is just as much an autobiography because it reveals the point of view from which he is attempting to reconstruct the history of Flaubert's life. Thus, it is impossible for him to separate his discussion of Flaubert from a discussion of his life in relation to his wife, and he is just as incapable of presenting an objective or authoritative portrait of her as he is of Flaubert: "I have to hypothesize a little. I have to fictionalize. [...] We never talked about her secret life. So I have to invent my way to the truth" (165).[13] Braithwaite's language here self-consciously challenges the conventionally authoritative language and tone of biographical and historical writing. His admission echoes with Jeanette Winterson's claim that "We mostly understand ourselves through an endless series of stories told to ourselves by ourselves and others" (*AO* 59). All attempts to reconstruct the past are communicated and influenced by the conventions of literary production. Thus, Braithwaite cannot help but make use of the same literary conventions as he did when he imagined Louise Colet's "version."

Flaubert's Parrot asks us to consider what subjective factors might affect the construction of a biographical narrative and invites us to question the authoritative claims, often rooted in a language that masquerades as objective and omniscient, of biographical and historical forms of writing in general. By interweaving Braithwaite's autobiography with the search for evidence that will lead to an authoritative account of Flaubert's life, Barnes brings to the surface of the text the inevitable imbrication of the historian/biographer's own history in an historical/biographical narrative and so breaks down the distinction between history/biography and autobiography as genres. Salman Rushdie does the same in *Midnight's Children* by depicting Saleem Sinai as figuratively and literally "handcuffed to history" (*MC* 9). Similarly, Tom Crick, the history teacher of Graham Swift's *Waterland*, finds it necessary to tell fabulistic tales of his own family's history in order to convey to his students lessons and ideas about history that he can't manage to communicate by only talking about the French Revolution. None of this is to say that there aren't real formal differences between history and autobiography as genres; rather, they are inter-dependent, even when it is not explicit as it is in these novels.

Getting the Story "Straight"

Flaubert's Parrot may not seem explicitly ideologically motivated, unlike many of the other fictions I discuss in this study, but attempting to answer the question of "How do we seize the past?" is not an ideologically neutral pursuit. How we perceive and write about history, as the tenets of New Historicism make clear, has a great deal to do with individual ideology. Among other things, *Flaubert's Parrot* challenges the methods and underlying ideologies of realist historiography. Barnes teaches us to see historical discourses as stories that are as constructed and constructing as any other genre of story. Sounding very much like Hayden White, Barnes commented in an interview that "Even if it's taking facts which you've not invented yourself, what you're doing as a fiction writer is imposing a form and a motion on them" (Smith 73). Barnes's kind of historiographical metafiction can be seen as a reaction against what White considers a socially pervasive "reluctance to consider historical narratives as what they most manifestly are—verbal fictions, the contents of which are as much invented as found and the forms of which have more in common with their counterparts in literature than they have with those in the sciences" ("Historical Text" 42). In calling historical narratives "fictions," White is not suggesting that they are the opposite of "fact" or "truth." Rather, he and Barnes are pointing out that historical narratives are articulated through writing conventions that are also used for more ostensibly subjective and imaginative narratives.

White suggests that each new work of historiography adds to the number of texts that have to be considered and interpreted in order to obtain the most "accurate" or complete representation of an historical era. He says that the "relationship between the past to be analyzed and historical works produced by analysis of the documents is paradoxical; the more we know about the past, the more difficult it is to generalize about it" (43). Braithwaite gets caught up with this in his study of Flaubert: the more he learns about Flaubert, the less he can present a unifying portrait of him. Braithwaite is obsessed with the realist concern to "get the story straight," but he ends up undermining his intentions by offering multiple, contesting views of Flaubert. Each of Braithwaite's strategies of biographical/historical reconstruction is like an individual parrot, a way of representing Flaubert in the hope that a particular representation will yield the "truth." But the very existence of this multiplicity of perspectives indicates an acknowledgment that there is no single recoverable truth just as there is no single parrot (Lee 39).

Barnes is taking traditionally authoritative genres of discourse—in this case, the dictionary, literary criticism, historiography, biography, and university exam—and suggesting that they do not and can not tell the whole story, that their authority is created by tradition and their conventions rather than intrinsic objectivity. Barnes suggests that imaginative genres can tell us as much (or as little) about a subject of study as any other. And his work is as much about literature's capacity to help us make sense of human experience as it is about the failings of other branches of knowledge.

A "Multi-Media Collage"

Barnes's experiments with mixing genres are similarly radical in his novel *A History of the World in 10½ Chapters*. In fact, to call this book a "novel" as I have just done glosses over its generic complexity. Even on the level of primary formal categories, this work offers us a challenge: Is it a novel, a collection of short stories, or a "history," as the title suggests? Assuming we recognize it primarily as a fictional text, the "chapters" are not held together by a single narrative progression but by a series of themes, events, and objects which recur in different historical contexts: Noah's ark, sea voyages, apocalypse, irreverent woodworms, the separation of clean from unclean. Barnes is not the first to cross the genre boundary between short story collection and novel; other prominent examples include Sherwood Anderson's *Winesburg, Ohio* and Joyce's *Dubliners*.[14] Unlike these earlier naturalistic examples, however, Barnes's "novel" does not give an impressionistic portrait of one city at one moment in time; its comically over-ambitious project is to give such an impression of the "History of the World." It is, of course, an absurd task, and yet it is the organizing principle of this "novel."

The novel takes us on a whirlwind tour of history from Noah's Ark to the near future. Most of the stops along the way offer unorthodox perspectives on history told in varying narrative forms. As a whole, the novel presents a wide-ranging (if necessarily incomprehensive) survey of the different genres through which we have understood and recorded our experiences of the world and its history. It is a compendium of and critical commentary on theological, legal, scholarly, literary, speculative, and traditional historical genres of writing. Barnes mixes all of these genres to give a sense of history as "a multi-media collage" rather than "a series of salon pictures, conversation pieces whose participants we can easily reimagine back into life" (*H* 242). He makes full use of what Mikhail Bakhtin identifies as the novel form's organic proclivity for genre mixing[15] to demonstrate, as he put it in an interview, that "even if you're using art history or straight history or legal history or autobiography, the impulse behind it is to tell a story" (Smith 73). Barnes's "stories" present a view of the history of the world that revises our notion of history as a discipline to suggest that history is the sum of our attempts to make sense of our past through numerous narrative genres, no matter whether they are traditionally considered historical or not.

It begins at The Beginning, with a revised view of Old Testament historiography. The first chapter of *A History* rewrites the myth of Noah and the ark from the perspective of a stowaway woodworm. The woodworm narrator "disabuses" us of the idealized view of Noah as the pious, wise, and sober father of humanity and protector of the world's species. Barnes's narrator assures us that "It wasn't like those nursery versions" (3). Instead, Noah was a bigoted, tyrannical, ignorant, misguided, aggressive, and even murderous drunkard. Whatever happened to the basilisk, the griffin, the sphinx, the hippogriff? All were tossed overboard, the victims of discrimination: "They were all crossbreeds. We think it was Shem—though it could well have been Noah himself—who had this thing about the purity of the species" (16). This introduces a theme that echoes Rushdie's concerns about fundamentalism and runs throughout the novel: separating the "clean" from the "unclean," the "pure" from the "impure." The Bible, Barnes suggests, proposes such categories and so legitimates, even lays the groundwork for, social division and, consequently, prejudice and discrimination.

Similar to the chapter of *Flaubert's Parrot* in which the Louise Colet persona sets out to correct our misconceptions about Flaubert, the woodworm tells us that, although "accounts differ," he's going to give it to us straight and correct the "misleading" portrait presented in the Old Testament: "My account you can trust" (4). The woodworm strenuously argues that the common conception of Noah and his family, based on the Old Testament account of the deluge, is not true. Naturally, we're unlikely to find a woodworm's account of the deluge believable, but the point is that it is no less credulous than the Biblical version and so calls attention to the fictionality of both:

> It rained for forty days and forty nights? Well, naturally it didn't—that would have been no more than a routine English summer. No, it rained for about a year and a half, by my reckoning. And the waters were upon the earth for a hundred and fifty days? Bump that up to about four years. And so on [4].

Barnes calls our attention to some of the more fanciful elements of the Bible to highlight its dependence on fictional conventions. He desacralizes the Bible to suggest, like Rushdie, that religious texts need to be relieved of the privilege and authority which many believers invest in them.

Among its other roles, the Old Testament is the most widely accepted Western narrative of the ancient history of the world and, as Barnes implies, an overtly ideological history. In addition to creating categories for discrimination, the Old Testament is essentially an early law book for the Hebrews which presents a series of cautionary tales or parables of the harsh consequences of disobedience: God casts humanity out of Paradise, purges the Earth of life in a storm that lasts forty days and nights, unleashes plague on Egypt, and kills first-born sons. One of the Bible's ideological functions, then, is to ensure obedience, presumably to God but in reality to the various secular and religious authorities who assume the privilege of interpreting it. That people let others interpret such texts for them or are incapable of doing so for themselves is the principle danger of such texts.

In the third chapter of *A History*, "The Wars of Religion," Barnes presents a farcical view of the potential conflicts caused by varying inter-pretations of scripture. The woodworm returns, though in an off-stage capacity, as the central figure in a dispute over Biblical law and divine intention. The woodworms are put on trial in absentia for the blasphemy of having eaten away the leg of a Bishop's throne in sixteenth-century France and thus having caused the throne to break and "Hugo, Bishop of Besançon" to "fall like mighty Daedalus from the heavens of light into the darkness of imbecility" (64). Reproducing the overwrought legal discourse of the era, Barnes presents the chapter in the form of a series of trial tran-scripts. Whereas the prosecution argues that the woodworms are never mentioned in the Bible as having been onboard Noah's ark and must there-fore be representatives of "the Devil" (72), the defense maintains there is no mention in the Bible of their *not* having been on the ark. Similarly, against the prosecution's attempt "to maintain that the *bestioles* are not granted by Holy Scripture the right to inhabit cut wood," the defense argues "firstly that the Scripture does not in any patent form forbid them from so doing, [and] secondly that if God had not intended them to eat the cut wood He would not have given them the instinct to do so" (75). Thus, the Bible is used to both defend and condemn the woodworms. The entire trial is absurd, though it is, as Barnes informs us in an afternote, based on actual legal precedents. The absurdity is critical, however, for it demon-strates the extremes to which interpretations of theological and legal texts can vary. Such texts, Barnes implies, are often invoked to legitimate insti-tutional acts of control, as when the judge who decides in favor of the pros-ecution then declares that, to uphold the decision, "the *habitans* of Mamirolle are hereby instructed to pay heedful attention to the duty of charity, to yield up their tithes as commanded by the Holy Church, [and] to refrain from any frivolity in the House of the Lord" (79).

The kind of polarized dispute between interpretive camps exemplified in the trial of the woodworm is an organizing narrative convention which recurs in each of the novel's chapters. Sometimes this convention results in critical comedy, as with the woodworm's "correction" of the traditional account of the Flood, or, in the final chapter, with the narrator's experience of a grossly materialistic Heaven instead of the traditionally spiritual one. At other times, the polarization of interpretive points of view is overtly serious. Chapter Two, for example, deals with an Arab hijacking of a cruise ship. Seeking to justify or at least explain to the hostages the necessity for their execution, the Arab leader forces the self-impressed historian/anthropologist and tour guide, Franklin Hughes, to relate to them the Arabs' anti–Zionist view of history. Hughes complies and delivers a lecture on the Israeli persecution of the Arabs that suggests the lesson the Jews learned from history was that "the only way to survive was to be like the Nazis" (55). The Zionist position, of course, would hold that they are defending themselves against Arab aggression.

The dispute is over who will survive, who, in fact, has the right to survive—the Israelis or the Arabs? The result of this dispute is that everyone is caught up in a vast historical cycle of killing. The Arab leader explains that "There are no civilians any more. [...] The Zionists, at least, understand this. All their people are fighting. To kill a Zionist civilian is to kill a soldier" (51), and Hughes relays this message to the hostages. Grounding this view is a philosophy of history as a destructive force: "The world is only advanced [...] by killing people" (50–51). The violence and either/or thinking that underpins these ideas is, like Rushdie's dramatization of the conflict between good and evil, a product of androcentric social codes. While Barnes obviously abhors the idea that progress is achieved through violence, he fails to make the connection between violence and androcentrism in this chapter and only passingly critiques it in the next chapter (see below).

As a scholar, Hughes is an authority figure for the hostage passengers. They look to him to explain their plight and, in order to save his own life, he betrays his values by using his authority to attempt to pass on a very slanted view of history as true. He asks innocent people to see their imminent deaths as "justified" by historical "logic." In doing so, he perpetuates the male myth that history is constituted by acts of violence and requires violence to progress. Historiographic metafiction is often mistakenly interpreted as suggesting that all versions of history are equal, but in Hughes's collaboration Barnes presents us with an allegory of the dangers of historical relativism.

We are all, Barnes implies, at the mercy of the whims of a violent history. Some survive through ingenuity and resourcefulness, like the woodworms who smuggle themselves onto the ark in a ram's horn. Less nobly, some survive by collaborating in the destruction of others, as does Franklin

Hughes. Barnes gives another portrait of survival in Chapter Four, "The Survivor." Like most of the chapters, it is organized around a conflict between two alternative perceptions of reality or history. It tells the story of Kath Ferris who, in one "reality," has anticipated nuclear war and, like Noah operating without God's instructions, sets off to sea in a boat with two cats to find a new land and rebuild the world. In the alternative reality, which she ascribes to nightmares brought on by radiation poisoning, she is a psychiatric patient suffering from delusions after a break-up with her chauvinist boyfriend Greg. Slipping in and out of these two worlds, Kath makes some interesting observations about history. On the boat with her cats she formulates a basic feminist critique of male-scripted and sculpted history, the only time Barnes draws a clear connection between androcentrism and historical violence:

> This happened, they say, and as a consequence that happened. There was a battle here, a war there, a king was deposed, famous men—always famous men, I'm sick of famous men—made events happen. [...] I look at the history of the world, which they don't seem to realize is coming to an end, and I don't see what they see [97].

In the other reality, she is condescended to by a doctor who tells her she has a self-victimizing pattern of behavior which he calls "persistent victim syndrome" (108). Wryly, Kath observes that "The whole bloody world's a persistent victim" (109), but he doesn't really listen to her, lending credence to her critique of androcentrism. If a reader accepts the doctor's version as the "true" one, then one could conclude that Kath and her feminist position are being mocked, but by portraying the men as chauvinistic and insensitive Barnes seems to privilege Kath's version of events.

The doctor explains that she has been engaging in "fabulation": "You make up a story to cover the facts you don't know or can't accept. You keep a few true facts and spin a new story round them" (109). In other words, her "delusions" of radiation sickness and having settled on an island are the product of her attempt to imaginatively make sense of the world. She decides, however, that she has been fabulating her experiences with the doctor in an attempt to account for the horrifying symptoms of radiation sickness:

> It was all about her mind being afraid of its own death, that's what she finally decided. When her skin got bad and her hair started falling out, her mind tried to think up an alternative explanation. She even knew the technical term for it now: fabulation. Where had she picked that up from? She must have read it in a magazine somewhere [111].

Though there is no definitive way for a reader to decide which reality is "true," in either case she is fabulating—making sense of what has happened by mixing fact with fancy.

"Fabulation" is also a useful generic description of how Barnes views the writing of history and how his own stories are scripted: all forms of historical writing are on some level creative narratives which make use of verifiable historical referents. Barnes's explanation of fabulation further suggests the conciliatory function of such narratives: they aid the process of coming to terms with the forces of a destructive, even merciless history. Barnes's *History* often seems like a catalogue of human disasters (or the threat of human disasters): the flood, terrorism, nuclear war, shipwreck, earthquakes, murder, the Holocaust. As Claudia Kotte observes, it is a view of history which contrasts with Hegel's assumption that history unfolds rationally (120). It is also a view which parodies the whole notion that history can be understood and recorded in a purely rational or academic manner.

One of the ways we deal with history's destructive side, Barnes implies, is through artistic representations:

> We have to understand it, of course, this catastrophe; to understand it, we have to imagine it, so we need the imaginative arts. But we also need to justify and forgive it. [...] Why did it happen, this mad act of Nature, this crazed human moment? Well, at least it produced art. Perhaps, in the end, that's what catastrophe is *for* [*H* 125].

Art, according to Barnes, helps us interpret and understand history's horrors if not conquer them. This is the premise behind "Shipwreck," one of the more compelling chapters in the novel. "Shipwreck" is split into two sections divided by a fold-out reproduction of Theodore Géricault's 1819 painting "The Raft of the Medusa." The first part of the chapter re-tells Savigny and Corréard's account (published as *Narrative of a Voyage to Senegal*) of the shipwreck of the Medusa off the African coast in 1816, while the second is an excursion into the genre of art criticism which also serves as a metafictional commentary on Barnes's own work. While the first section records the events in a more or less documentary prose, it is already a second-hand account and is therefore necessarily speculative in its reconstruction of events. The account is colored by Barnes's attempt to find patterns in the historical events he is narrating. Thus, when the healthy survivors on the raft decide to cast the wounded into the ocean in order to preserve their provisions, Barnes comments: "The healthy were separated from the unhealthy like the clean from the unclean" (121). Later, when a butterfly appears fluttering over their heads, Barnes imagines that to some "this simple butterfly was a sign, a messenger from Heaven as white as Noah's dove" (121). So much historiography is similarly speculative.

The second section is a much more overtly speculative attempt to reconstruct and explicate the process of the painting's composition. Barnes gives a fair amount of attention to what Géricault *didn't* paint: the various mutinies, the healthy casting the wounded into the sea, the arrival of the butterfly, the moment of rescue (126–130). "A painting is a moment" (128), Barnes declares; the challenge is for that moment to at least hint at an entire story, to gesture beyond the one moment frozen in time. Géricault, Barnes notes, was at the start faithful to the details of the shipwreck, so much so that he went to the trouble of having the ship's surviving carpenter build him a scale model of the raft. Still, he made a number of glaring departures from documentary reality: "The incident never took place as depicted; the numbers are inaccurate; the cannibalism is reduced to a literary reference; the Father and Son group has the thinnest documentary justification, the barrel group none at all" (135). It is in these alterations that Barnes discerns the most telling lessons of the work. Contemplating the pyramid of bodies attempting to hail the Argus, a tiny ship on the horizon, Barnes suggests that the image has a visual advantage over the real event in which one of the survivors waved a handkerchief attached to straightened-out barrel-hoops: "reality offered him a monkey-up-a-stick image; art suggested a solider focus and an extra vertical" (131); in other words, "Truth to life, at the start, to be sure; yet once the process gets under way, truth to art is the greater allegiance" (135). One might add that "truth to art" is inevitable, for all representational genres mediate reality.

Perhaps the most glaring departure from mimetic reality is the glowing, muscular health of the bodies depicted: "Where are the wounds, the scars, the haggardness, the disease? [...] Why do they look as if they have just come from a body-building class?" (136) asks Barnes. His language becomes interrogative and takes on the tenor of an academic inquiry—a characteristic idiom in Barnes's work. It is as if the voice of Geoffrey Braithwaite is speaking to us, struggling with the complexities between contradictory bits of historical evidence. A mimetic portrait—a portrait which showed "Shrivelled flesh, suppurating wounds, Belsen cheeks"—would, Barnes decides, too easily inspire a superficial emotional response, whereas Géricault wants to take us "beyond mere pity and indignation" into a realm of "deeper, submarinous emotions [...] through currents of hope and despair, elation, panic and resignation" (136–137). A painting is a moment, but this painting gestures to a despairing past and a redeeming future, hinting at the full narrative of the wrecked Medusa and functioning as a metaphor for human history:

> The painting has slipped history's anchor. [...] There is no formal
> response to the painting's main surge, just as there is no response to
> most human feelings. [...] How hopelessly we signal; how dark the sky;
> how big the waves. We are all lost at sea, washed between hope and
> despair, hailing something that may never come to rescue us [137].

Art helps us makes sense of the hopelessness of history: "Catastrophe has
become art; but this is no reducing process. It is freeing, enlarging, explaining. Catastrophe has become art: that is, after all, what it is for" (137).

Géricault's painting attempts to capture the twin poles of hope and
despair experienced by those on the raft. To that end, balanced against the
figure frantically summoning the Argus on the horizon is an old man in
a pose of "resignation, sorrow, despair" (132). Barnes remarks that he "might
have strayed in from a different genre" and "incites us to read 'Scene of
Shipwreck' as an image of hope being mocked" (132). The painting suggests two principle paths for interpretation: those in the raft are about to
be saved; or they are within sight of salvation only to have it denied them.
It is an interpretive dilemma which again foregrounds a conflict between
two opposed senses of reality.

Barnes's discussion of the painting compares artistic and historical
methods of representation. As with Hayden White's explanation of historiography, Géricault has selected among the recorded historical facts to
faithfully reproduce some while suppressing or modifying others. Clearly,
Géricault has not attempted to offer a strictly realist portrait of the events.
The painting, like Barnes's novel, is a mix of genres: a combination of gritty
realism and heroic fantasy. Barnes implies a similar suspicion of realism
to the one he makes explicit in *Flaubert's Parrot*: realist genres (whether
aesthetic or historical) have no particular claim to representational authority; they do not necessarily tell us more or more accurately about a particular historical event than forms of representation which blatantly take
liberties with documented historical reality. In part, this is because the ideal
of an authoritative realist or mimetic representation is, as Geoffrey Braithwaite discovers, an unachievable fantasy. Géricault's painting, like Barnes's
"history," doesn't seek to hide its fabulation; though it departs from documentary realism, it offers a kind of knowledge about its subject unavail-
able within the limitations of a realist approach.

The question of how art influences our experience of life and history
which this chapter raises is one that runs through all of Barnes's novels.
In his debut, the *Bildungsroman* titled *Metroland*, this question preoccupies
the precocious and cynical young narrator, Christopher, and his like-minded
school friend, Toni. To address it, they take to observing people who are
themselves observing art in the National Gallery. They "scientifically" note

the physical responses people manifest, hoping that a twitch, squirm, or puffing of the cheeks will help them to understand art's influence on people. Many years later, they debate the utility of their experiments. Toni, who has become a stereotypical embittered radical, declares that "at least we were looking, at least we believed that art was to do with something happening, that it wasn't all a water-colour wank" (165). Chris, who has assimilated to (or, as Toni might have it, been assimilated by) the comfortable life of the bourgeois, is more doubtful: "I just don't see that it makes anything happen. Very nice for us that the Renaissance occurred and all that; but it's all really about ego and aggro, isn't it?" (167).

There's no resolution to this dilemma in *Metroland*. In *Flaubert's Parrot*, as I have already suggested, Barnes denies the validity of aesthetic philosophies which ascribe a simple social or moral function to art; simultaneously, he suggests that the arts can help us understand (if not resolve) the complexities of culture, society, and history. With *A History of the World*, Barnes does at one crucial point in the "Shipwreck" chapter propound a more assertive stance: art is "freeing, enlarging, explaining." Still, art does not have the transcendent status in Barnes's work that it has in Winterson's (see next chapter). In "Parenthesis," the meditative "half-chapter" of *A History*, he hedges his praise for the educative and freeing value of art: "Art, picking up confidence from the decline of religion, announces its transcendence of the world (and it lasts, it lasts! art beats death!), but this announcement isn't accessible to all, or where accessible isn't always inspiring or welcome" (244–245). Because art is often available only to a social elite, and because it often challenges received values, art can not be a source of salvation. Adding his protest to that of the other writers discussed in this study, Barnes asserts that religion is similarly enfeebled as a belief system: it "has become either wimpishly workaday, or terminally crazy, or merely businesslike—confusing spirituality with charitable donations" (244–245). "[R]eligion and art," he concludes, "must yield to love. It gives us our humanity, and also our mysticism" (244–245).

"Parenthesis" is the keystone to this novel. A self-conscious or metafictional essay, the chapter poses love as the antidote to history's horrors:

> Love won't change the history of the world [...] but it will do something much more important: teach us to stand up to history, to ignore its chin-out strut. I don't accept your terms, love says; sorry, you don't impress, and by the way what a silly uniform you're wearing [240].

Barnes can get a bit smarmy about the idea, as when he declares a page later that "How you cuddle in the dark governs how you see the history of the world" (241). He admits the difficulty of discussing love seriously in prose, asserting that while poets "write this stuff called love poetry," "there is no genre that answers to the name of love prose" (227–8). Strictly speaking, this isn't true. Love letters, for example, could be considered a genre of "love prose," but Barnes's frustration is with the fact that poetry is generally considered to be *the* genre of love.

Barnes's ideas about love are similar to Winterson's. However, Winterson, as discussed in the next chapter, mixes prose and poetic diction to express ideas about love, contradicting Barnes's notion that poetry is the only genre truly suited for talking about love. Barnes, on the other hand, ironically falls back on his academic idiom, a rationalist approach which seems inappropriate for the subject: love, he tells us, is "anti-mechanical, anti-materialist" (244); it is also the "starting-point for civic virtue. You can't love someone without imaginative sympathy, without beginning to see the world from another point of view" (243). It may seem a naive position, but there is a more characteristic display of self-doubt when Barnes quotes the final line of Philip Larkin's "An Arundel Tomb"—"What will survive of us is love"—and then comments: "What will survive of Larkin is not his love but his poetry: that's obvious" (228). And towards the end of the chapter Barnes expresses a clear belief in the ultimate futility of love as an answer: "It will go wrong, this love; it probably will. [...] Our current model of the universe is entropy, which at the daily level translates as: things fuck up" (246). Images of such decay, especially of decaying art, litter Barnes's work: the woodworm is in the frame of Géricault's painting of the shipwreck and the painting itself is dissolving (139); the paintings Gillian works to restore in *Talking It Over* have been degraded by "wood-smoke, grease, candle-wax, cigarette smoke and fly-shit" (119); the statues of Flaubert at Trouville, Barentin, and Rouen are in various states of disrepair—one lacks half of a mustache, another is discoloring and the "left leg is beginning to split," and another is streaking with "cupreous tears" (*FP* 189).

Underlying Barnes's appeal to the redeeming features of love, then, is a fear of history as degenerative, destructive, and inexplicable. We want to think of history as progress, as a continuum that makes sense; our most basic concept of history—as a series of sequential dates on which important events occurred—encourages this view. But "Dates don't tell the truth," Barnes asserts. "They want to make us think we're always progressing, always going forward" (*H* 241). Barnes critiques this notion:

> History isn't what happened. History is just what historians tell us. There was a pattern, a plan, a movement, expansion, the march of democracy; it is a tapestry, a flow of events, a complex narrative, connected, explicable. One good story leads to another. [...] [A]ll the time it's connections,

> progress, meaning, this led to this, this happened because of this. And
> we, the readers of history, the sufferers from history, we scan the pattern
> for hopeful conclusions, for the way ahead [242].

The idea of history as rational progression underlies Western philosophies
of history. As Claudia Kotte demonstrates, various discourses—religious
(Jewish and Christian), Marxist, Hegelian, Darwinian—have been used or
adapted to explain, predict, and help find patterns in historical events. Such
systems of thought seek to rationalize history's frequent indifference to
human suffering: catastrophe may be incomprehensible when it happens,
but not if it is thought of as part of a divine plan; or: history is moving
inevitably towards the liberation of working people and the establishment
of a communist utopia; or: history is progressing towards universal rationality; or: history proceeds according to the "survival of the fittest" principle. Barnes's novel, Kotte concludes, demonstrates the failure of such
explanatory models to account for the chaos and destructiveness of history. They are all "fabulations"—soothing attempts to understand and
combat history's indifference to humanity. And fabulation is dangerous
because it tricks us into viewing irrational, horrific events as part of the
"rational" unfolding of history. As Kath Ferris comments: "You mustn't
fool yourself. That's what Greg did, that's what most people did. We've
got to look at things how they are; we can't rely on fabulation any more.
It's the only way we'll survive" (*H* 111).

Barnes reiterates this sentiment in "Parenthesis": while we "fret and
writhe" in the present, "we fabulate. We make up a story to cover the facts
we don't know or can't accept; we keep a few true facts and spin a new
story round them. Our panic and our pain are only eased by soothing fabulation; we call it history" (242). The "real" history of the world defies
such attempts to understand it in rational terms. Barnes views or at least
fears that history is essentially arbitrary: "The history of the world? Just
voices echoing in the dark; images that burn for a few centuries and then
fade: stories, strange links, impertinent conclusions" (242). Strangely, however, Barnes insists on the pursuit of objective knowledge:

> We all know objective truth is not obtainable, that when some event
> occurs we shall have a multiplicity of subjective truths which we assess
> and then fabulate into history, into some God-eyed version of what
> "really" happened. This God-eyed version is a fake. [...] But while we
> know this, we must still believe that objective truth is obtainable; or at
> least that it is 99 per cent obtainable; or if we can't believe this we must
> believe that 43 per cent objective truth is better than 41 per cent. We
> must do so, because if we don't we're lost, we fall into beguiling relativity,

we value one liar's version as much as another liar's, we throw up our hands at the puzzle of it all, we admit that the victor has the right not just to the spoils but also to the truth [245–246].

This appeal to believe in an objective truth seems extremely odd considering the great lengths Barnes has gone to in order to demonstrate that an objective view of history is impossible and that absolute "truth" is a fabrication of history's victors. Barnes is committing to the ideal of always *improving* historical knowledge, but he knows that this can not be achieved by eschewing subjectivity. If we were somehow to rid ourselves of all subjective involvement, what would we be left with? As Barnes demonstrates in *Flaubert's Parrot*, even a list of dates and events conveys a particular point of view. Rather, Barnes suggests that we must recognize how our experiences and biases influence the way we view and narrate history. By doing so, we admit that, like Geoffrey Braithwaite, we do not—can not— have absolute, definitive, or total knowledge about a subject. And that admission is an important step towards developing a better philosophy of historical study.

With its "half chapter" and episodic structure held together by theme rather than traditional narrative logic, *A History of the World in 10½ Chapters* denies symmetry, teleology, totality, and hierarchy[16]—all the expected conventions of realist historiography. According to Andrzej Gasiorek, Barnes teaches that history is "narrative not event, the imposition of order where there is none, and the illusion of teleology where there is absence of meaning" (164). Barnes suggests that historical texts often misrepresent our profound ignorance of what really occurred in the past. Even the title of Barnes's novel, with its announcement of an asymmetrical half-chapter, parodically mocks the notion that an inclusive, "total" history can be narrated. Which is not to say that we don't or can't have any knowledge at all; it means that historical narratives are inherently partial, that each contributes something to our understanding of the past, and that this understanding is always being revised. It also means that we need to question all such narratives so that we can recognize and challenge ideologically dangerous revisionary histories.[17] In demonstrating that historical and religious forms of writing depend on fabulation, Barnes is implicitly urging us to be suspicious of the truth claims and ideological inflections of such narratives. As Gasiorek notes: "For Barnes, to surrender to fabulation is not only to embrace relativism, thus refusing to differentiate the less accurate from the more accurate, but also to submit to the metanarratives of those who are all too willing to falsify history in the interests of power" (165).

The Search for Answers

Barnes's fictional works depict many individuals facing epistemological crises. Braithwaite, for example, is driven by the need to find a way "to seize the past." Similarly, Gregory, one of the characters in Barnes's *Staring at the Sun*, consults a computer called TAT (The Absolute Truth), hoping that it can make sense of life. The pursuit of such answers is often destructive: Graham Hendrick, the protagonist of *Before She Met Me*, destroys his life by obsessively searching for the details of his wife's sex life before he knew her; and Miss Ferguson, the Christian zealot in Chapter Six of *A History of the World*, dies on Mt. Ararat while searching for the remains of Noah's ark.

The characters in these novels search for answers to deeply troublesome questions about human experience in the contemporary era. Sometimes they confront very serious questions about the purpose of life, the politics of race, gender, and nationality, or how technology is going to affect our lives. Other times, the questions seem trivial but mask more profound human concerns. Jean, the protagonist of *Staring at the Sun*, for example, is plagued by questions which are seemingly trivial: looking at an old painting in her room with a caption reading that "The mink is excessively tenacious of life," she wonders why, and continues to wonder why; told that Charles Lindberg took five sandwiches on his transatlantic flight, she wonders what happened to the three and a half that he *didn't* eat. She continues to search for the answers to these questions, asking both Tommy Prosser, a grounded World War I fighter pilot, and Michael, her future husband, as if such answers would somehow make up for a deeper lack of knowledge about the world. But these questions, trivial as they may seem, exemplify the unanswerable-ness of many of our most profound questions about ourselves and our world. When she is older, Jean realizes that her childhood impulse was correct: we make our own answers.

The narrator of "The Dream," the final chapter of *A History of the World*, learns a similar lesson. "The Dream" portrays heaven as a place where every individual gets exactly what he or she wants heaven to be. The narrator's vision of heaven is corporeal and sybaritic: he spends his time playing golf, eating, shopping, having sex, and meeting famous people. This too is a transformation in genre: Barnes does not depict Heaven, as is conventional in art, as an ethereal realm of peace, serenity, and spiritual grace, but as a place that offers activities that reflect the dominant values of a selfish, narcissistic, and materialist twentieth-century society.[18] Once the novelty of this wears off, however, the narrator decides that he also needs to be judged: "It's what we all want, isn't it? I wanted, oh, some kind of summing up, I wanted my life looked at" (293). He gets what he wants and a "nice old gent" reviews his history and concludes, simply: "You're OK." When the narrator expects a little more, the old gent says, "No, really, you're OK," a summation which leaves him feeling a "bit disappointed" (294).

Even this extremely shallow narrator conceives of heaven as a place where questions are answered, lives are validated, and the world is made sense of, but this belief is revealed to be hollow. He learns that "getting what you want all the time is very close to not getting what you want all the time" (309), and that pressing existential questions go unanswered. "So what's it all for?" he asks. "Why do we have Heaven? Why do we have these dreams of Heaven?" Margaret, his guide to the afterlife, speculates: "Perhaps because you need them. [...] Because you can't get by without the dream" (309). Our religious narratives, like our historical narratives, Barnes implies, are fabulations designed to comfort people by making sense of their suffering. In an interview, he admitted that he is making an "argument [...] against the existence of a man-created God, an approvable God or a just God. [...] There is either a God and a plan and it's all comprehensible, or it's all hazard and chaos, with occasional small pieces of progress. Which is what I think" (Saunders G9). For Barnes, dreams of heaven and a "just God" may help some endure history's violence, universal entropy, and death, but they are ultimately a kind of self-delusive wishful thinking.

A. S. Byatt suggests that the final chapter of *A History of the World* typifies a nebulous "sense of something missing" which underlies a great deal of contemporary British literature ("A New Body" 444). As in Graham Greene's *The Power and the Glory* and *The Heart of the Matter*, absence, loss, and decay pervade the work of contemporary writers such as Kazuo Ishiguro (e.g. *The Remains of the Day*), Graham Swift (e.g. *Waterland*), Martin Amis (e.g. *Time's Arrow*), Ian McEwan (e.g. *The Child in Time* and *The Innocent*), and others. Despite the absence of answers to the questions that plague us, and despite history's violence, many of the stories in *A History of the World* demonstrate that individuals are not powerless with their destinies. The book is deeply concerned with the struggle for survival, from the stubborn woodworms that save themselves by stowing away on the ark, to the narrator of "The Dream" who puts off the day of his complete dissolution until it becomes apparent that there is no other option. Although some, such as Franklin Hughes, survive through their ignoble actions, the remarks of the woodworm after its successful voyage on the ark present a more exultant and life-affirming portrait of survival against the odds:

When the seven of us climbed out of that ram's horn, we were euphoric. We had survived. We had stowed away, survived and escaped—all without entering into any fishy covenants with either God or Noah. We had done it by ourselves. We felt ennobled as a species [28].

The World According to Thatch

In addition to writing fiction, Barnes had a five year stint as the London correspondent for *The New Yorker*, during which time he wrote a number of excellent journalistic, sociological essays (collected in *Letters From London*) which reflect principally on Britain's politics and scandals from 1990 to 1994. "Mrs. Thatcher Remembers,"[19] a commentary on Margaret Thatcher's autobiography *The Downing Street Years*, is of particular interest here as it demonstrates the potential dangers of individual bias in historical narratives by pointing out some of Thatcher's more egregiously self-serving views of history. Barnes describes her account of the Falklands War as "history with little nuance or complication, whether political or moral. [...] [T]he British were defending 'our honour as a nation'; while our wider duty was to ensure that Aggression did not Succeed, and that international law be not flouted" (*LL* 224). Barnes further notes that Thatcher portrays herself as a "hands-on" leader, uninhibited about getting "down on her knees at Chequers measuring territorial water on naval charts with the Attorney General" (225). The language Thatcher uses to narrate the events of the embarrassingly unnecessary war suggests an epic tale with herself cast as the hero: Was "a common or garden dictator" to "rule over the Queen's subjects and prevail by fraud and violence? Not while I was Prime Minister" (qtd. in Barnes, *LL* 225).

It is ironic that she should refer to the Argentinean leadership as perpetrators of fraud when Thatcher herself was so adept at lying to those in her own country, as is evidenced by her insistence that the Argentineans were responsible for the war when it was *she* who provoked hostilities by ordering the British navy to open fire on the Belgrano, an Argentinean ship several miles outside the military exclusion zone and on its way back to Argentina, on the eve of a peace negotiation.[20] *The Downing Street Years* poses its subjective, autobiographical narrative as the authoritative, accurate, and objective account of history. As such, it is a practical and recent example of what writers of contemporary historical fictions like Barnes find potentially dangerous about historical narratives—they're proclivity for serving oppressive ideological interests. Many people understand that the Falklands War was provoked by an act of unwarranted and illegal military aggression for the sake of having a cause to unite Britain's populace behind the Tory government. And it may be easy for some to reject the kind of nationalism fostered during the Falklands war, but many were (and still are) entranced by the nostalgic prospect of resurrecting, through military victory, the myth of Britain's "greatness"—a myth which Thatcher evoked and tapped to her own benefit. Thatcher's autobiography gives a view of history designed to be "a justification and a continuation of her rule" (230).[21] "Her vision," Barnes notes, is "ruthlessly monocular" (227). Quite simply, Barnes accuses Thatcher of promulgating a series of fraudulent claims about her administration. Echoing Braithwaite's frustration about the contradictions he finds in various archival documents pertaining to the life of Gustave Flaubert, Barnes encapsulates his view of *The Downing Street Years* by declaring that "Every so often, you have to shake your head and remind yourself that just because a book is heavy this doesn't make it history" (230). It is for this that Barnes, in "Parenthesis," asserts the importance of pursuing objective truth despite the difficulty of obtaining it.

The recognition of Thatcher's self-congratulatory excesses are nothing particularly novel either to her detractors or even many of her admirers. Nevertheless, *The Downing Street Years* has been and will continue to be one of the most widely read (or skimmed) accounts of Britain's late twentieth-century history and so it is important that Barnes has drawn attention to how the narrative voice biases the view of its subject. Is this history, autobiography, or fiction? Barnes's point in "Mrs. Thatcher Remembers"—as in *Flaubert's Parrot, A History of the World in 10½ Chapters,* and his other fictions—is that these genres are inextricable.

The Gender Divide

Rushdie, Barnes, Winterson, and Carter address a common set of issues relating to global social changes and the interactions of cultures. One of the key issues that all of these writers converge on is that of fundamentalism, whose major forms have been instituted and led by men. The social codes of orthodox religions, especially when enacted by extremists, demand the hierarchical separation of men and women. In the Old Testament, Adam is authorized as Eve's superior, a paradigm that abets male supremacy in Western civilization. Islamic and Hindu scripture are similarly androcentric and have led to extremely inegalitarian traditions. In Islam, the tradition of *purdah* mandates that women veil their bodies and be isolated from all men except their relatives. Hinduism instituted the tradition of *suttee* (now officially outlawed but still practiced in many families) in which women immolate themselves on their husband's funeral pyres to prove their devotion. Further, female children are often neglected in Hindu families because they are seen as economic liabilities. Through such practices, religions have helped to subordinate half the population of the world. As a result, women have not until very recently, and only in a relatively small number of places, had sexual, political, or economic freedom. While many gender inequalities have been ameliorated in recent history, fundamentalists seek a return to the strict enforcement of the gender codes that keep women in servitude to men.

While Rushdie and Barnes address many social problems including fundamentalism, classism, racism, and nationalism, they do not, in any sustained way, extend their critique to the issue of gender inequality which is one basis for these other manifestations of social inequities. They see that traditional hierarchical models of social organization are failing and they encourage their dissolution because they are unjust, but Carter and Winterson specify that social traditions are failing because they are androcentric. They forcefully claim that the fundamental model for social injustices is that of gender inequity and they demand that the sources of gender injustice be dismantled. They critique religious systems, especially Christianity, because they are the most widely disseminated and "authoritative" sources of sexism and unequal gender roles.

Winterson is particularly concerned with the sexism and heterosexism of Christian scripture and fundamentalist manifestations of Christianity. Winterson was adopted and raised by Pentecostal Evangelists and her experiences with them inform her fiction, especially her first two novels. The fact that Winterson was raised in an environment of strict orthodoxies about gender roles and sexuality motivates her attempt, through her fiction, to critique traditional ideologies about gender and explore more egalitarian ideals. For Winterson, religious-based orthodoxies about gender and sexuality need to be desacralized because they are real and present dangers to her own life as a woman and a lesbian, and to the life of our society.

Even more aggressive is Carter's fierce denunciation of the myths that constitute religion as "extraordinary lies designed to make people unfree" ("Notes" 71). Whereas Rushdie and Barnes are skeptical of religion and mock the notion that religious stories have been received from divine sources, Carter is an unabashed anti-religious crusader. Rushdie's cameo portrait of God in *The Satanic Verses* comically deflates the idea of a supremely wise being, but it is also a very androcentric portrait: the humor stems in part from the God character objectifying Alleluia Cone. In *A History of the World in 10½ Chapters*, Barnes presents a parodic portrait of Noah as well as several chapters which highlight a world devoid of a divine force that could grant meaning to human life. In contrast, Winterson and Carter focus their critique on the fact that God and other divine figures are almost exclusively men with stereotypically male characteristics. Winterson's *Boating for Beginners*, for example, depicts God, Noah, and his sons as egregiously misogynist (see next chapter). Though Winterson's critique of gender and religion is important, it is not as sophisticated, far-reaching, or as creatively articulated as Carter's. Carter views religion, and Christianity in particular, as the wellspring of women's subordination. Carter does not distinguish between fundamentalists and more liberal worshippers. No matter how liberal the interpretation, Carter perceives Christianity as harmful because it institutes the notion that sexism and the gender hierarchy are "natural" and the products of divine will. As a result, Carter is ruthless in her grotesque parodies of deific figures and demands that they be desacralized.

CHAPTER THREE

Jeanette Winterson

The Limitations of Sex

Winterson's first novel, *Oranges Are Not the Only Fruit*, is a semi-autobiographical lesbian coming-of-age story and an attack on Christian fundamentalism. *Oranges* was a huge literary success in England. It won the Whitbread prize for best first novel and soon after was adapted into a BBC film for television. From a marketing standpoint, it is certainly one of the most successful and popular "lesbian fictions," having reached a diverse audience that crosses class, gender, and sexuality lines. In comparison to many of the other novels I discuss in this study, it is a rather traditional novel in that it is principally told in a realist mode and follows the travails of a protagonist from adolescence to adult maturity. Its principle "innovative" element is its substitution of a lesbian for the traditional heterosexual male protagonist of the *Bildungsroman*. Typically, the *Bildungsroman* "naturalizes gender differentiation and heterosexual marriage" (French 84) as the climax of the protagonist's quest for self-knowledge. As a postmodern feminist re-writing of the *Bildungsroman* genre, *Oranges* alters this paradigm: it calls into question the "naturalness" of traditional gender roles and of heterosexuality as the only acceptable sexual orientation.

Like Winterson, Jeanette the protagonist of *Oranges* is adopted by an Evangelist mother who views the world in terms of the facile, binary moral categories provided by the Bible: there is that which is evil (the Devil, the heathen couple next door, sex, slugs) and that which is good (God, the family dog, Jeanette's aunt, Charlotte Brontë's novels, slug pellets [*Oranges*

3]). Winterson's comic approach to the good-evil binary suggests that such simplistic distinctions can be frivolous or downright ludicrous. As Rushdie has also explored, the failure to recognize the nuances of pragmatic morality is a dangerous consequence of the use of religious texts. This is especially common among fundamentalists, who tend to view things in binary terms: either good (pure) or evil (corrupting). As Winterson's novel progresses, it becomes more clear than it is in Rushdie's work that this polar morality stems from the androcentrism of religious systems.

At first, Jeanette is unequivocally "good" by her mother's standards: her mother grooms her to be a missionary and Jeanette demonstrates a strong aptitude for preaching and Bible study. As she enters adolescence, however, she falls in love with another girl, Melanie, and when her church discovers their affair they attempt to exorcise the demon they believe is responsible for this "deviation": "They had spent the day praying over me, laying hands on me, urging me to repent my sins before the Lord. 'Renounce her, renounce her,' the pastor kept saying, 'it's only the demon'" (107). That Jeanette's "abnormality" is automatically assumed to be the result of spiritual corruption demonstrates the extent to which religion determines sexual norms in our society. Christianity demands heterosexuality. Jeanette's lesbianism is not a threat to her soul (as the Church parishioners are led to believe) but to the authority and integrity of the Church. Forcing her to repent, then, is more about preserving the androcentric, heterosexual social structure that is advocated and relied upon by the Church than "saving" Jeanette. The pastor orders her to be locked up and starved for two days, a torture which quickly yields a duplicitous repentance. That Jeanette is insincere is of less importance than the fact that it enables the Church to sustain its masculinist hegemony.

When it becomes apparent that Jeanette has no real intention of repressing her sexual desires, however, the scandal of her homosexuality sends shock waves through the church community and forces them to reevaluate their policies. After consulting the church council, the pastor returns with their judgment that the "real problem [...] was going against the teaching of St Paul, and allowing women power in the church" (133). Jeanette recounts her mother's support of this judgment:

> women had specific circumstances for their ministry [...] the Sunday School was one of them, the Sisterhood another, but the message belonged to men. [...] She ended by saying that having taken on a man's world in other ways I had flouted God's law and tried to do it sexually. [...] So there I was, my success in the pulpit being the reason for my downfall. The devil had attacked me at my weakest point: my inability to realize the limitations of my sex [133–34].

Jeanette's mother and community respond to the threat of "unnatural passions" by re-asserting the gender hierarchy: the right to preach, to lead, to make rulings, and other expressions of power are solely masculine privileges. Jeanette's sexuality represents a threat to that order and so, as Laura Doan comments, "the church must strip away Jeanette's power by rescinding *masculine* privilege" (144, my emphasis).

The word choice in the passage above is important: it is not Jeanette's *refusal* to conform to sexual convention that Winterson emphasizes but her *inability* to do so. The notion of natural sex and gender roles which conform to society's dominant heterosexual orientation is offensive to Winterson because there is no innate or biological basis for them. Young Jeanette's sexual orientation is not a choice, which supports the anti-essentialist point of view that there is no single "natural" way to be. Jeanette's lesbianism and her success as a preacher challenge the model of what is "natural" according to Christian fundamentalism and forces her Church to re-assert clearly defined gender roles for men and women.

Winterson desacralizes the Church-authorized idea of masculine hegemony by drawing attention to the hypocrisy of the Church's dogmas: in an interview, Winterson elaborates that she was attempting, in *Oranges*, to "look at the way that the Church is offered up as a sacrament of love when really it is an exercise in power" (Barr 30). The central doctrine of Christianity is supposed to encourage love and forgiveness, but Jeanette's fundamentalist community is devoid of those things. Her adoptive parents have no love for each other (sex of any kind is anathema to her mother), and the Church demonstrates itself to be cruel and unyielding in its efforts to exorcise the love she has for Melanie. Jeanette's love, simply because it is directed at someone of the "wrong" sex, is considered demonic.

For Winterson, desacralizing the tenets of the Church is a critical part of resisting injustice in today's society. It is evident throughout Winterson's works that she is responding to the hypocrisy and outright lies of policy-setting institutions like the Church and government. In an essay for *New Statesman and Society*, she writes that we must refuse to accept the lies which perpetuate outmoded values and inegalitarianism:

> Not accepting lies means refusing crappy architecture in spite of someone in authority saying it's nice (they wouldn't live there themselves of course). It means refusing to accept that nuclear power is good for us or even necessary for us. It means facing up to the fact that the nuclear family is outmoded and bad for most of its members. It means testing every cherished assumptions and seeing whether or not it's just hogwash ["All Teeth 'N' Smiles" 33].

Winterson's fiction focuses particularly on "refusing" lies related to sex and gender roles. She attacks various artificial sources of sexism which disseminate and perpetuate lies about what is "natural" behavior for men and women: religion and scripture; androcentric political, economic, and familial hegemony; romance novels; and scientific discourses about bodies. Winterson's protagonists shun the world of limitations based on sex. Young Jeanette, for example, does not allow herself to be limited by the androcentric and heterosexist ideologies of her fundamentalist family and church. Whereas in *Jane Eyre* (a key woman's *Bildungsroman* and the one book besides the Bible that Jeanette is allowed to read) the heroine capitulates to the *Bildungsroman* convention of settling into heterosexual marriage, Jeanette refuses to forsake her sexual identity and settle into a heterosexual orientation as social and literary convention dictates. Instead, she leaves her narrow-minded Northern town for London. Similarly, in *Boating for Beginners* (discussed below) a rebellious group of women determine to survive the Biblical flood without the help of Noah and his sons. And later in this chapter I will discuss a particularly innovative novel, *Written on the Body*, in which Winterson frustrates our expectations about gender by presenting us with a narrator whose gender remains ambiguous.

Surviving the Flood

In contrast to *Oranges Are Not the Only Fruit*, Winterson's second novel, *Boating for Beginners*, has been virtually ignored by critics, no doubt partly because Winterson herself has effectively "disowned" it as inferior to her other work. Winterson has acknowledged having written it very quickly, she never speaks of it in interviews, and it is not listed as one of her credits in her other books. From an aesthetic point of view, the characters have no depth, the plot is as contrived as a pantomime, and the writing lacks the emotional charge and inventive language which distinguishes Winterson's later work. Nevertheless, it is written in a spirit of irreverence similar to that of the other novels discussed in this study and it is often funny in its mockery of received Christian myths. That it is not a particularly good book according to certain traditional criteria of literary merit does not mean that it is unworthy of critical attention. Though postmodern works such as the ones discussed in this study have generally been granted the status of "Literature" by the scholarly and critical establishment, part of the purpose of all of the genre mixing in postmodern literature is to traverse the boundaries of "high" and "low" culture and challenge conventional notions of what "Literature" is. *Boating for Beginners* deals with important subject matter consonant with that of the other texts I have been discussing, but, more so than the others, it is in the form of a "lowbrow" farce. In this respect, it is not so different from texts now considered great literary classics—for example, Fielding's *Tom Jones* or Gay's *The Beggar's Opera*. I doubt that history will treat *Boating for Beginners* so kindly, but the novel merits some attention here because of its focus on desacralizing Christian doctrine and criticizing its androcentric bias.

Like Carter and many other postmodern women writers, Winterson rewrites old stories—whether in the form of fairy tales, religious scripture, romances, historical accounts, or other genres—for feminist ends. In *Boating for Beginners*, Winterson, like Barnes, rewrites the story of Noah and the Ark, in this case to insert women into one of the founding tales of Western androcentrism. The novel mixes and parodies the conventions of genres such as mass-market romance, gothic fiction, and Biblical scripture to suggest that that which much of society reveres as God-given and authoritative is as artificial and fanciful as any literary narrative.

Winterson's first desacralizing gesture is to transplant the characters and situation of the Noah story into a milieu that resembles modern Western society—a world of capitalism, technology, mass-market books, and blockbuster cinema. Taken out of their epic and historical context, the personages, events, and other narrative elements of the Old Testament appear less authoritative: we are confronted with characters instead of historical figures, plot elements instead of historical record, entertainment instead of dogma. The novel quickly takes on the characteristics of a farce which, with its stream of irreverent conventions, might be considered the generic opposite of scripture.

Winterson presents "God," for example, as the Frankenstein-like result of a freak accident involving a bolt of lightning and some decomposing cake and ice-cream. Desi, the wife of one of Noah's sons, discovers a secret chamber in Noah's mansion and a manuscript which reveals the "truth" of the creation of "God." Noah's language in this manuscript, with its references to "natural decay and corruption of the human body" and nights spent in "vaults and charnel houses" (82) is parodically reminiscent of Mary Wollstonecraft Shelley's *Frankenstein*. The gothic tenor of his diction continues but the subject material takes a pantomime-like turn towards the outrageous when a fork of lightning strikes a decaying piece of Black Forest Gâteau and ice cream and sparks a new form of bacterial life which Noah then uses to animate a series of corpses. Using this "technology," Noah creates a being of gigantic stature who possesses miraculous powers. The creature takes to living in a cloud and comes to be known as

"Yahweh the Unpronounceable." Thus, Winterson inverts the Biblical paradigm by suggesting that God/Yahweh is the creation of "Man." The gothic parody further suggests that Yahweh is a monstrous creation—one destined, like Frankenstein's Creature, to cause havoc and destruction.

Reminiscent of (though more malevolent than) Rushdie's whimsical personification of God in *The Satanic Verses*, Winterson's Yahweh immediately manifests the egotism and petulance of a spoiled child. He surrounds himself with sycophants, including Noah, and, with Noah's help, rewrites history to convince people that the entire world is his creation. Like Barnes's Noah, Winterson's Yahweh rewrites history to depict himself in a favorable light: Noah announces that he and Yahweh are writing a history of the world that would show that "the Lord had always been there, always would be there and what a good thing this was" (14). The idea which Julian Barnes demonstrates is futile—writing a comprehensive history of the world—is exactly what Yahweh attempts. Winterson's portrayal of the circumstances surrounding its composition similarly suggest that such efforts are inevitably imaginative fictions rather than veridical "truth." Yahweh's attempt to rewrite history with himself as its source serves as an allegory of the birth of fundamentalism (he names his movement "Fundamental Religion"), and it calls special attention to the narcissism and artificiality of fundamentalist movements.

Yahweh also declares that he is interposing himself in human affairs in order to lead them away from their "false gods and socialism" (13). This reference (and others like it) to Yahweh's capitalist orientation contributes to Winterson's desacralizing portrait of God and the Church. What could be less exalted than the idea of God motivated by worldly profit? She suggests that the Old Testament's true value is as a best-selling commodity rather than a spiritual guide. Yahweh and Noah's collaborative manuscript, which is issued in "installments starting with *Genesis, or How I Did It*" and continued in "*Exodus or Your Way Lies There*," finds its appropriate place in the contemporary market culture: on the best-seller list. With the subtitles "*How I Did It*" and "*Your Way Lies There*," Winterson suggests the Old Testament is on the same level as celebrity autobiographies or motivational self-help books, two popular genres which dominate the publishing industry in contemporary society.

Winterson further suggests that the Old Testament is akin to mass-market paperback fiction. As we might expect with any enormously successful fiction, it is quickly adapted into other forms—a theatrical tour and a film—to maximize its profit potential. Noah tours with the book and becomes the principal missionary for a new era of conservative values which it attempts to naturalize: "There was no need, after all, to be vegetarian, charitable and feminist. Noah promised a return to real values" (14–15). Winterson cleverly mocks conservative values by sardonically setting up progressive, humanitarian value systems—feminism, altruism, vegetarianism—as the banes of society which need to be eradicated. The traditional values of society—such as those called "family values" in America—are presented in political discourse, the media, and from the pulpit as the "real" values, implying that others are unreal or less valid than those which have been presented to us as "natural" in scripture. Throughout Winterson's fiction it is obvious that, for her, the most troublesome of these "real" values are those which perpetuate capitalism, patriarchy, and compulsory heterosexuality.

Rendering the Bible as a mixed-genre narrative—a combination of history, adventure, allegory, myth, and fantasy—is crucial to Winterson's attempt to desacralize it and search for alternative, more egalitarian ways of organizing society. Winterson draws attention to the fictive, dramatic make-up of the Bible by having Gloria Munde (whom Noah has recruited to help collect pairs of animals for the tour) reflect that the book, with its denunciation of pagan gods, its bloody war scenes, and Yahweh's world-destroying flood, "was good box office material" (50). Gloria's recognition of the cinematic potential of the *Genesis* story emphasizes its entertainment value and further complicates the generic ambiguity of the Old Testament: the story is dramatic, engineered to appeal to large audiences; Winterson suggests it is not so much holy scripture as fiction ideal for adaptation into a mass-market medium such as film.

One of the things that Winterson is getting at with *Boating for Beginners* is the sheer outrageousness of the flood myth. The idea of a Divine Being who has created humanity only to utterly destroy it when it appears unruly is both absurd and malevolent. Re-imagining the illogic that leads to the decision to wipe out humanity, Winterson emphasizes its petty vindictiveness. On a whim, Yahweh decides to model reality on the film and cause a real flood; then he and Noah can "change the book, put it out under a new cover, stick a bit on the price. No one will know because they'll all be dead" (90–91). Winterson rewrites the story of *Genesis*, then, so that God's decision to flood the Earth is inspired by a film-script and motivated by greed[1] and contempt for humanity. Framed in such a way, Winterson makes the flood seem fickle and comical.

Like other Biblical tales, myths, fairy tales, and fables—which together can be seen as constituting an umbrella "cautionary tale" genre—the flood myth has a pedagogical function: to arouse fear that will ensure social order through obedience to religious law. In one of Winterson's increasingly characteristic authorial asides, she expands upon her implication that the

Bible is manipulative fiction rather than veridical history: "The Bible writers didn't care that they were bunching together sequences some of which were historical, some preposterous, and some downright manipulative. Faithful recording was not their business; faith was" (66). Rather than seeing the Bible as a divine compendium of God's laws, Winterson views it (and invites her readers to view it) as a convenient way of making sense of the world without really confronting the complexities of the world. It is what Angela Carter would call "consolatory nonsense."[2] Winterson aims to desacralize the Bible by highlighting its role as a legitimator of social power structures. She suggests that the *Genesis* we know is, as Barnes would say, a "fabulation" of a small group of men designed to protect their own interests: Noah tells his sons in secret, "We can write what we want in our book [...] and call it the inspired word of God" (111). Winterson further suggests, as Barnes does not, that the Bible is intentionally misogynistic (or at least that misogyny is rampant in it). Reflecting on his many disappointing experiences with women, Noah decides that his re-drafting of *Genesis* will "make sure everyone knew where the blame lay. Women; they're all the same" (117). At the foundation of Jewish and Christian thought, Winterson implies, is a conspiracy to create a set of myths that concentrate and maintain power in the hands of men. For centuries they have legitimized a social structure in which women have had little or no economic, sexual, and intellectual freedoms.

History demonstrates other dangers of religious myths. The God of the Old Testament is punitive and destructive, setting an appalling example for the faithful. Other cautionary tales within the Old Testament, such as those about God killing the first-born sons of Egypt and annihilating idol worshippers, encourage extremist ways of dealing with one's enemies. Of particular concern to Winterson, with her fundamentalist upbringing, are those believers who would destroy anything to preserve their faith: "Believers are dangerous and mad and may even destroy the world in a different deluge if they deem it necessary to keep the faith" (66). Here Winterson comes off as quite angry and iconoclastic, equating faith with destructiveness. The link between faith and violence is portrayed throughout the Old and New Testaments and, more specifically, in God's actions. God's putative goodness appears to be yet another manifestation of religious hypocrisy: If God is such a benevolent force, then why is the Bible full of tales of his wrath? There are no second chances for those who disobey his laws; failure to obey leads to harsh responses such as immediate ejection from the garden of Eden, a flood which eradicates all but two of every living thing on Earth, and Moses being barred from the promised land. Winterson concedes that the Bible should be read because it's "very beautiful" but warns that the "mistake is to use it as a handbook" (66–67). The fact that it is compelling literature has made it a dangerous tool of tyrannical political agendas. The Old Testament idea that the Earth must periodically be purged of the unfaithful, the wayward, or the unclean has provided a model for atrocities such as the Crusades, the Spanish Inquisition, the Holocaust, and other political-religious conflicts.

Religious ideals contribute to the hierarchical division of society, "justifying" legal discrimination and violence against individuals and groups of people according to their gender, race, sexual orientation, or whether their beliefs match those of the majority. Winterson emphasizes the hypocrisy underlying this social problem by portraying Noah as a kind of "right-wing," charismatic, Evangelical preacher (69). Noah creates a sense of community, even "family," among the believers, but the ideology of the Noah story—with its pairings of one male and one female of each species—insists upon a heterosexual community. The Noah story even suggests a form of eugenics: the population of the world will be destroyed to clear the way for a new order of obedient creatures whose primary task, as suggested by the collection of creatures in male/female pairs, will be that of heterosexual reproduction. In order to maintain this orthodox social order, non-believers (in God, in compulsory heterosexuality) are excluded: "although they might claim to love your soul the rest of you could literally and metaphorically go to hell" (70). Though the Noah story pre-dates the advent of Christianity, it is apparent that Winterson is reading and critiquing it according to Christian notions (e.g. of the soul and hell). It is easy to hear in this the echo of some Christians' "love the sinner but hate the sin"-policy towards homosexuals. As Winterson demonstrates in *Oranges Are Not the Only Fruit*, it is difficult to reconcile the Christian message of peace and love with its intolerance of behavior that does not meet traditional norms.

For Winterson, Christianity and other religions in their orthodox manifestations have too often "legitimized" persecution. In her novel *Art and Lies*, one of the narrators reflects that

> In 1936, when the Catholic hierarchy was colluding with the Nazis, Hitler was not in favor of Concentration Camps. He advocated compulsory sterilization for the "hereditarily diseased." His advisor, Cardinal Faulhaber, disagreed: "From the Church's point of view, Herr Chancellor, the State is not forbidden to isolate these vermin from the community, out of self-defense, and within the framework of the moral law. But instead of physical mutilation, other defensive measures must be tried, and there is such a measure; interning the people with hereditary diseases." [...]

Strict Catholics. Orthodox Jews. The other day I heard an ex–Chief Rabbi arguing in support of genetic cleansing for homosexuals. It would be kinder, he said, than imprisonment [*AL* 108].

Like Barnes and Rushdie, Winterson suggests that scripture, especially the Bible, provides the basis for religious institutions to separate people into categories of "clean" and "unclean" and so "justify" orthodoxy's persecution of unbelievers. For her, religious scripture has been one of the most powerful forces for perpetuating androcentric, heterosexist, racist, and misogynistic ideologies.

That Winterson disapproves of the social uses of the Bible does not mean that she would have us ignore the text itself. Winterson re-reads the Bible on the level of literature or art, praising it for being an "anti-linear text" (*BB* 65). It is exactly this aspect of its artistry, however, that Noah intends to alter. To make the story accessible to a wider audience, Noah enlists Bunny Mix, a mass-market romance writer, to write the screenplay. Doris, one of the women Gloria meets on the film set, objects that Bunny tries to turn the story into a more conventional, linear narrative. Noah employs Bunny to alter the generic conventions of the Bible in order to make the film accessible to a lowest-common-denominator audience and so cash in on its mass-market potential.

The romance novel genre takes quite a beating in *Boating for Beginners*. Though not in the same league as scripture, it too is a source of sexist ideologies. Bunny Mix is the author of almost a thousand romance novels, "all of which had the same plot" (16), though for novelty she rotates hair colors for the heroines and occupations for the heroes. Typical of Harlequin or Mills and Boon-type romances, Bunny's novels "compensate" readers for the mundane realities of their lives by enabling them to escape into gratifying fictions about exotic locals and idealized sex (Radway 86–118).[3] For Winterson, mass consumption of such fictions facilitates women's retreat from the real world of actions and relegates them to the subordinate and passive roles expected of them by male-dominated society.

Gloria and her mother are both devout fans of Bunny Mix. When Gloria reads Bunny's novels, she falls into a "semi-hypnotic state" (*BB* 39), manifesting the kind of passivity Winterson believes such fictions engender. Gloria appears entranced when reading the blurb of one of Bunny's novels and appreciating its "sensuous prose" (39). That "sensuous prose" is a collection of dreadful melodramatic clichés which parody the tropes of romance fiction: "When slim brunette Naomi travels across the desert with her uncle's caravan she doesn't expect to find true love. A mysterious thunderstorm forces the party to take shelter in a nomadic village [...] where she meets Roy, the most fearless camel tamer of them all" (39). The novel-blurb is itself a genre, designed to capture the reader's imagination so that he or she will purchase the book. The blurb assures the reader that the expected conventions—in this case, a young woman's sexual awakening, a transgressive love, exotic and dangerous settings, and high adventure—will be met by the book.

It is perhaps a great missed opportunity for Winterson's novel that she does not give us a sampling of the *Genesis* screenplay Bunny devises, but Winterson does "reproduce" several pages of Bunny's romance narrative, further parodying the genre's excesses. Roy, the camel tamer Naomi meets, conveniently reveals himself to be a wealthy prince and proposes marriage within seconds of meeting her. When her uncle refuses to give his consent, Roy cuts off his head and melodramatically declares: "I do not beg for what I want!" (43). Naomi's response is ludicrous: "You had to do it Roy, I know that, but we must send Auntie some flowers" (43). Winterson mocks the romance novel (in its contemporary, mass-market form) by condensing its plot conventions—"a man and a woman meeting, the obstacles to their love, and their final happy ending" (Radway 199)—into the space of a few sentences. Carolyn Allen writes that the "gender codes" of romance novels are "rigidly conservative: the woman must be Feminine, the man Masculine, as the dominant culture [...] uses these terms" (70). Winterson has Roy and Naomi play these parts to an extreme, parodying the stereotypical association, perpetuated by the romance genre, of masculinity with violence and femininity with passiveness. The portrayal of Roy ridicules the idealized, brutal expression of masculinity common to romance novels, while Naomi's support of Roy murdering her uncle satirizes the warped romance ideology that women should support any action as long as it advances their prospects of marriage.

Winterson further implies that the romance genre perpetuates outmoded ideologies about feminine beauty. Winterson mocks Naomi's laborious efforts to use cosmetics to give herself the appearance of natural beauty: "After about three hours she was satisfied that she looked as if she had made the minimum effort and achieved spectacular results. She wanted to be thought natural" (*BB* 42). Unlike Angela Carter's Leilah, who self-consciously uses cosmetics in *The Passion of New Eve* to create an *artifice* of beauty (see next chapter), Naomi actually believes that creating a "natural" look requires intense cosmetic preparation. Romance novels, Winterson suggests, perpetuate the absurd notion that to be "naturally" beautiful and feminine a woman has to employ artifice.

Another convention of many romance novels that Winterson suggests is particularly insidious is the chaste avoidance of the physical realities of sex. In the excerpt Winterson provides of one of Bunny's novels, Naomi's aunt reflects back on her first sexual experience (on the eve of her marriage, of course): "after he had gently pulled back the sheets, she felt a thunderclap melting her and a thick tenderness deep inside. It was like a fairy tale" (40). This kind of idealized language obscures the physicality of sex and depicts it as a magical, transcendent experience that bears little or no relation to reality. Romance fiction, Winterson suggests, tames sex for a readership ashamed of its own sexual desires or, in Gloria's case, ignorant about her own sexuality.

At the beginning of *Boating for Beginners*, Gloria's experience of the world is more or less limited to what she has learned from her mother's religious beliefs and Bunny's ideologically regressive novels: her world was assembled "from a kit composed of spiritual certainties and romantic love" (23). Throughout the rest of the novel, Gloria learns that the real world does not conform to the expectations with which she has been instilled. She meets Marlene, a transsexual former synchronized swimmer whose unconventional gender status distresses Gloria. Gloria is unclear about how to interact with Marlene because the latter does not fit into the binary view of human nature. But for Winterson, gender and sexual orientation should have no bearing on human relations; Gloria's distress is the naïve product of a sexually orthodox culture. Disconcerted over her conversation with Marlene, Gloria approaches her friend Desi, the wife of Noah's son Ham, for guidance. Desi tells her that "There are always people who ... whatever you can think of. Whatever combination, innovation or desperation" (37). The range of human possibilities, Gloria learns, is infinite, not constrained by narrow social conventions. In Gloria's ignorance and confusion, Winterson mirrors the difficulties so much of society has when confronted with the unknown.

The world of limits which Gloria wants to believe in is exactly what Winterson's fiction attempts to transcend. Gloria's encounter with Marlene, who does not allow her gender identity to be limited by biological factors, is the beginning of her move away from the notion of certainties and limits. She becomes involved in a rebellion against the social expectations for women. While production plans for the film proceed, Noah and his sons prepare for an actual flood. They conspire to drug and even beat their wives unconscious to insure they'll come along, a plan that emphasizes their misogyny and unilateral resolve.

Desi, however, overhears Yahweh's decision to make the film's premise a reality. When she relates the news to Gloria and Marlene, a sprite-like creature called "the orange demon" appears without warning. Winterson uses this orange demon in *Oranges Are Not the Only Fruit* and *Boating for Beginners* to personify her authorial intrusions and act as a kind of "spirit-guide" who challenges the ideas of her protagonists and influences their actions. In *Oranges*, the demon appears to the adolescent Jeanette to help her negotiate the difficulties of being a lesbian in a fundamentalist Christian family and community. In *Boating for Beginners*, the demon appears to Gloria, Desi, and Marlene to charge them with the task of surviving the flood so that an alternative to this male-authored plot can exist; people must "realize that there's no such thing as a true story" (124). In what is for the most part a light-hearted comic novel, this comes across as a rather weighty injunction. As Susan Suleiman asks, "what could be more serious than the realization (if indeed it is true) that 'there is no such thing as a true story'?" (197). It is a serious consideration because it suggests that all narrative explanations of the world, whether they are generically classified as historical, scriptural, or even scientific (the discourse that carries the most veridical authority in the contemporary Western world), are questionable. In having the orange demon suggest that they "invent something else" (*BB* 124) if they need to, Winterson is commenting on her own project in *Boating for Beginners*—to provide an alternative so obviously fabulated that it calls into question the veracity of all authoritative stories, especially those of the Bible.

Winterson imagines that all of the elements of the Noah story are deliberately scripted for dramatic effect and to convey the *appearance* of truthfulness. Winterson's Noah plans to "plant" gopher wood at the peak of Mt. Ararat to add legitimacy to the story he will write. Gopher wood, as opposed to the fiber-glass and reinforced steel that his ark is actually made out of, fits more appropriately with the mythopoeic genre he trying to create. Similarly, Bunny collaborates with Noah to solve the plot problem of how they are to know when the waters have subsided; she comes up with the idea to write that they sent a dove in search of land. Bunny also proposes that the appearance of a rainbow—which they would pretend never existed before—could "round off" that segment of the story. Winterson suggests, then, that it is at least in part the poetic quality of the language and imagery that makes scriptural texts so compelling, but, for the same reasons, scriptural texts can be viewed as literary works employing literary conventions designed to garner mass appeal. *Genesis* is not *the* story of the creation of the world and its early history; it is one such story among many.

Gloria, Marlene, Desi, and Doris must survive to debunk or at least provide an "alternative" to this story. They are prototypical feminists, determined to assert their independence from male rule. In addition, their act of solidarity and defiance symbolically asserts women's right to choose to live and even reproduce without men and the heterosexual social order represented by all of those pairs of animals on Noah's ark. Thus, the end of the novel celebrates life's persistence in its many guises; Gloria resolves to find a way to survive: "[N]o flood myth would destroy them" (146). And so she, Marlene, Desi, and Doris gather themselves, canoes, rain-gear, and other survival equipment in the attic of a high-rise hotel and wait for the flood waters to arrive. Reminiscent of Angela Carter's New Eve setting off to sea in a small skiff (see Chapter Five), they await the waters that will deliver them into a new era of independence.

As with *Oranges Are Not the Only Fruit*, *Boating for Beginners* urges women to forge their own paths rather than follow those laid out for them by social convention. Winterson's work teaches that the autonomy of women has been limited by androcentric ideologies perpetuated in scripture, romances, fairy tales, gothic fiction, and other genres. By mixing religious myth, romance, and the gothic in a self-consciously fictional text, *Boating for Beginners* suggests an equivalence between popular fiction and the Bible. In a short epilogue to the novel, an archaeologist and his assistant look for remnants of Noah's ark on Mt. Ararat. Reflecting on the Biblical account of the flood, the assistant comments: "Damn good story" (158). This is exactly how Winterson would have us view the Bible: as a gripping fiction, a mass-market best-seller which has unduly been invested with too much authority and veracity.

Science as Salvation

As Winterson's career has progressed, her approach to her subject material has become somewhat less whimsical. Her more recent novels maintain some comic overtones but are generally serious and meditative in tone as they grapple with profound questions ranging from those about interpersonal relationships and human ethics to metaphysics and the material reality of the universe. As her early fiction demonstrates, Winterson finds religion inadequate as a resource for understanding the world. In her later work Winterson looks to and interrogates other belief systems. Her fiction from *Sexing the Cherry* to the present demonstrates an increasing fascination with religion's alter-ego—science.

Historically, faith in religion has been steadily metamorphosing into faith in science for some time. This change became particularly prominent during the Enlightenment and the later development of positivism by Auguste Comte in his *Cours de Philosophie Positive*. Beginning in the seventeenth-century with the work of pioneers such as Francis Bacon and Isaac Newton, and continuing into the eighteenth- and nineteenth-centuries, Reason, Rationality, and Science began to take the place of religion as the privileged belief system for understanding the world. Christianity achieved dominance in part through its promise of human salvation. Modern science, with its promise of curing human ailments and solving life's mysteries, has offered a similar hope of salvation.[4]

For Winterson, science is as limited and limiting a belief system as religion. At times she portrays them as two facets of the same belief system, which helps highlight the masculinism underlying each: as David Noble demonstrates in *A World Without Women*, Western science emerged from the male, ascetic Christian clerical tradition (see especially 163–278). Handel, one of the narrators of Winterson's *Art and Lies*, personifies this dualism. He is both a priest and a surgeon, yet he is tormented by the inadequacies of religion *and* science. He comments:

> when you tell people you know what's good for them particularly if you're a doctor, they will believe you. Having no beliefs of their own they believe. It's a truism that as faith in God has declined, belief in science, especially medical science, has increased. Yet most people know even less about science than they did about God. Science is now incomprehensible to the layman, but the layman accepts it, even though one of the arguments against God is that He doesn't make sense [*AL* 8–9].

The human need to put faith in something beyond ordinary comprehension allays fears that life and the universe are directed by random factors. Religion provides the illusion that we are immortal—that there is something rewarding beyond the meagerness and disappointments of the material world. Similarly, science, especially medical science, provides an illusion of immortality by holding out the hope that all human ailments can eventually be "fixed."[5]

Among other re-orientations in belief during the Enlightenment and positivist eras, the Christian idea of the human body as a vessel for a "soul" which encompasses individual identity and assures life beyond corporeal existence was challenged by a conception of the human body as a pure machine that harbors no essential, unduplicatable self and can be repaired no matter what ails it, even, as Mary Wollstonecraft Shelley fictionalized in *Frankenstein*, to the extent of overcoming death.[6] As is evinced by the contemporary debate over recent scientific developments such as cloning and genetic manipulation, this ideal—the perfectibility and immortality of the human body—continues to dominate medical-scientific study today, while it is strenuously opposed as "unnatural" and dehumanizing from some quarters.

The early goal of Comte's positive philosophy was to "search out the objective principles governing the external world and the human world (individual and social). Science and its methodology would [...] reveal its unity, and such knowledge would enable man to control life more effectively" (Strandley 125). This early privileging of scientific epistemology remains an influential belief system in this "postmodern" era of mass technological expansion: geneticists are racing to decode the human genome and thereby decode the "mysteries of life"; physicists are striving to formulate a Grand Unified Theory (GUT) which will unlock the mysteries of the universe by explaining the relationship between the strong and weak nuclear forces, electro-magnetic forces, and gravity. One of the defining features of postmodern art is its pervasive suspicion of such scientific projects. The modern championing of science and technology has been a particularly persistent source of anxiety for Winterson, who is as skeptical of science and its impact on human society as she is of religion.

Gender Bias in Scientific Discourse

Among other concerns, science has a history of conveying sexist ideologies. At least since the nineteenth-century, science has served as a legitimizing basis for the disparities between the social status of men and women. Scientific and medical genres typically assume a tone of anonymous authority and have often employed a diction which conveys stereotypical gender characteristics in describing the body and body processes. Feminist thinkers such as Ruth Hubbard and Emily Martin have written on this matter at length. Hubbard, for example, argues that nineteenth-century male scientists claimed that women's biology was extremely frail and so women were unfit for anything but childbearing and child rearing; this belief "justified" women's exclusion from public life and ensured the continuing male dominance of the social and political spheres (*Women's Biology* 27).[7]

Similarly, Emily Martin points to how descriptions of human reproduction have attributed the most negative feminine stereotypes to the human egg: it is passive, receptive, fragile, and dependent; while sperm, the product of the male body, is active, searching, determined, penetrative, productive. Such scientific knowledge, Martin argues, "is often able to masquerade as 'natural fact'" ("Body Boundaries" 411), a masquerade which perpetuates these stereotypes and the ongoing limiting of women's potential. Martin critiques the language used in scientific discourse by exposing its often essentializing, androcentric assumptions. She connects the language conventions of scientific forms of writing about the body to sexist power dynamics, showing the latter to be a product of the biases "naturalized" by the former.[8]

How, then, can the authority of scientific/medical depictions of the body be challenged? Analysis of the ideologically inflected genre conventions of scientific discourse such as that provided by Hubbard and Martin is one important avenue of resistance. Literature and other arts provide another. It is the relation—analyzed by Hubbard and Martin—between language, narrative, authority, and power in scientific discourse which Jeanette Winterson's *Written on the Body* in part speaks to. In this novel, Winterson directly confronts the limitations of science as a source of knowledge, as a promise of salvation, and as a "naturalizer" of gender biases. To do this, *Written on the Body* has two main strategies: first, it uses an anonymous narrator of unspecified gender; and second, it mixes several language genres to talk about the human body and therefore challenges the authoritative characteristics of much scientific discourse. As Salman Rushdie and Julian Barnes do with historical and religious discourses, Winterson demonstrates that scientific discourses are forms of story.

Reading for Gender

Written on the Body is a love story; by using a narrator of unspecified gender, however, Winterson departs from the conventions of most love stories which delineate clear sexual roles. As a result, reading this novel can be a disorienting experience: we want to know the narrator's sex so that we can better understand his/her relationships, but every attempt to discern the narrator's sex must rely on inferences based on misleading gender stereotypes.

This confusion, along with an ambivalence about Winterson's departure from narrative convention, is evident in the comments of many of the novel's reviewers. Many are reluctant at best in approving this choice, calling it a "gimmick" (Annan, Miner, Kendrick) or a "trick point of view" (Kirk). One reviewer writes that the

> his/her ambiguity is a gimmick that works until the turning point of the story, with a scatter of teasing, misleading clues. [...] But once the lovers are separated, the narrator [...] comes out: "I thought difference was rated to be the largest part of sexual attraction but there are so many things about us that are the same" [*WB* 129] [Annan 22].

This particular reviewer makes the assumption that the narrator's reference to difference and sameness necessarily refers to sexual difference and sameness when the purpose of what he calls a "gimmick" is to thwart such assumptions.

Many reviewers (e.g. Sutherland, Sheehan, Stuart) assumed that the narrator is female, associating him/her with the author or finding hints accreting towards such a reading, but at least one critic jumped to the conclusion that the narrator is male: "he [the narrator] broadcasts his current affairs without hesitation, even to near-strangers; it's difficult to imagine that such love is not heterosexual" (Kendrick 131). This interpretation does nothing but demonstrate the limitations of the reviewer's own imagination: influenced by a heterosexual society, he assumes that all homosexuals would "closet" their feelings. Another reviewer recognizes Winterson's critical purpose, but implies it's a failure: "At first the concealment of his/her sex forecasts interesting theoretical questions about essentialism, but Winterson doesn't carry these identity questions beyond the *gimmick*. Gender is just one unknown about this strangely disembodied, decontextualized character" (Miner 21). Even though most reviewers agreed the narrator was female, the only evidence they give to support this is highly contestable and exposes the often stereotypical and hetero-normative biases in their own reading practices. Aurelie Jane Sheehan, for example, asserts that the narrator's erotic pleasure in Louise's leg-stubble is virtually a dead give-away that the narrator is female (209). And John Sutherland argues that Winterson's "general avoidance of male characters" in combination with the fact that the narrator apparently sits down to urinate, is highly suggestive that the narrator is a woman (19). Sutherland wants to know more about the "mechanics of the lovers' love-making [...] whether it is orally, prosthetically or digitally penetrative; whether one partner takes an exclusively active, the other a passive role; whether it is confined to ecstatic fondling, kissing, smelling and tasting of each other's private parts" (19). Without an explicit description of the narrator's genitalia, however, knowing these details cannot tell us the narrator's sex. But the important questions that should be asked here are: What motivates the desire to know the narrator's sex, and how would knowing affect our reading of the text?

What becomes apparent in these early responses to the novel is the degree to which readers found it necessary to decide on one sex for the narrator, a sexually ambiguous reading being beyond the bounds of the socially gendered reader. As Julia Cream writes, "In our society sexual ambiguity is untenable" (33). The fact that this novel can be generically classified as a romance makes sexual ambiguity all the more disconcerting for, as Carolyn Allen writes, "the plot conventions of the romance require individual readers to sex the narrator according to their own desires" (70). But any attempt to determine the narrator's sex is dependent on essentialized and/or stereotypical readings of gender. The fact is, there is no information about the narrator's body that can lead us to determine whether the narrator is male, female, transsexual, intersexed, or XXY.[9] And that is exactly the point: it implies that such information is or *should be* irrelevant. Confirmation of the narrator's sex would merely reinforce false gender stereotypes rooted in male-authored scientific "knowledge" about sexed bodies (for example, that men are "naturally" aggressive and women are passive, that women are innately more nurturing, less stable, and less intelligent).[10]

Ute Kauer proposes that "simply by the narrator's denial to be classified according to gender, the question of the *consequences* of gender for the act of narration is forced on the reader" (Grice and Woods 41, my emphasis).[11] Winterson's aim, I believe, is to suggest that gender is or at least should be *inconsequential* to narration. Kauer presents an impressive set of evidence to support the notion that the narrator is a woman. Many would no doubt agree with Kauer and most of the novel's reviewers that the evidence points in favor of that conclusion,[12] but by doing so they are attempting to force conventionality on a novel that is not conventional. The clues we may take to be signs of one gender or the other are, as Kauer readily admits, red-herrings. Nevertheless, Kauer relies on stereotypical notions to demonstrate that the narrator's "point of view is clearly a female one" (50) and concludes largely on that basis that it is more likely that the narrator is a woman than a man. She simultaneously concedes that she perhaps "falls prey to Winterson's design in trying to trace the gender of the narrator" (50). I agree. To suggest that there is such a thing as a specifically female point of view is to essentialize. Winterson is criticizing our need to apply gender stereotypes when reading. It is in the act of reading that we project expectations—informed by dominant social ideas about gender—upon literary characters. We look to sex as an important clue for interpreting literary texts, but Winterson frustrates that tendency, demonstrating that such acts of interpretation are dependent on gender biases. Such gender biases are also often linked to a heterosexually-normative view of the world. Ideally (although the majority of book's reviewers failed to grasp this), the narrator's sexual ambiguity teaches us to become aware of how we view the world in polar, sexualized, and essentialized terms, implicitly challenging the "naturalized" status of positivist-influenced biological essentialism.[13]

Love in the Postmodern Era

The central story of *Written on the Body* concerns the narrator's love affair with a woman named Louise. Their rapturous affair inspires frequent meditations on the narrator's behalf about the nature of love and human relationships. Throughout such meditations, the narrator strives to understand and articulate his/her love in a way that is not bound up with all the old clichés. In the process, the narrator interacts with many genres about love from the lofty to the trivial:

> I used to read women's magazines when I visited the dentist. They fascinate me with their arcane world of sex tips and man-traps. I am informed [...] that the way to tell if your husband is having an affair is to check his underpants and cologne. The magazines insist that when a man finds a mistress he will want to cover his prick more regally than of old. [...] No doubt the magazines know best. [...] If Mrs. Right is having an affair it will be harder to spot, so the magazines say, and they know best. She won't buy new clothes, in fact, she's likely to dress down so that her husband will believe her when she says she's going to an evening class in mediaeval lute music [74–75].

Winterson implies a dissatisfaction with this genre as a source of knowledge—its fatuous advice columns and their inevitable gender stereotyping perpetuate sexist ideologies.

Ironically, the discourse that proves to be richest for the narrator's poetic imagination of Louise and love is, ostensibly, scientific. It is ironic in that the history of science has been dominated by a search for absolute answers, while the tradition of literary and philosophical discourses about love are distinguished principally by their inability to definitively comprehend this human experience. Here is an example of the narrator employing a metaphor based in scientific discourse to explore the vagaries of love:

> Molecular docking is a serious challenge for bio-chemists. There are many ways to fit molecules together but only a few juxtapositions that bring them close enough to bond. [...] [M]olecules and the human beings they are a part of exist in a universe of possibility. We touch one another, bond and break, drift away on force-fields we don't understand. Docking here inside Louise may heal a damaged heart, on the other hand it may be an expensively ruinous experiment [61–2].

At the same time that the narrator uses scientific discourse for new metaphors about love, Winterson's ambivalence about the role of science and technology in contemporary culture is evident. In the above passage, both molecular and human bonding are seen as equally fickle, rare, and random. This leveling, I would suggest, challenges the common conception of science as a discipline of absolute laws which will eventually assure the predictability of events in the "natural" world. In fact, relatively recent developments in our scientific understanding of the material world provided by particle physics and quantum theory show that the physical properties of matter are as mysterious and impossible to predict as matters of the heart.[14]

At another point, the narrator laments the pseudo-scientific approach to modern-day love:

> Dating agencies stress the science of their approach although having a computer does not make one a scientist. The old music of romance is played out in modern digital ways. Why leave yourself to chance when you could leave yourself to science? Shortly the pseudo-lab coat approach of dating by details will make way for a genuine experiment whose results, however unusual, will remain controllable. Or so they say. (See splitting the atom, gene therapy, in vitro fertilization, cross hormone cultures, even the humble cathode ray for similar statements) [96].

While the conflation of computer-assisted dating with such cataclysmic scientific projects as atom-splitting is over-stated, this passage demonstrates a severe (and common) distrust of technological innovation. Even the most innocuous experiments, Winterson implies, can lead to more insidious technologies.

Tied up in the perceived threat of technological progress is an anxiety about postmodern culture and its latest promise of instant gratification through virtual reality:

> If you like, you may live in a computer-created world all day and all night. You will be able to try out a Virtual life with a Virtual lover. You can go into your Virtual house and do Virtual housework, add a baby or two, even find out if you'd rather be gay. Or single. Or straight. Why hesitate when you could simulate?
>
> And sex? Certainly. Teledildonics is the word. You will be able to plug in your telepresence to the billion-bundle network of fiber optics crisscrossing the world and join your partner in Virtuality. Your real selves will be wearing body suits made up of thousands of tiny tactile detectors per square inch. Courtesy of the fiberoptic network these will receive and transmit touch. The Virtual epidermis will be as sensitive as your own outer layer of skin. [...] The scientists say I can choose but how much choice have I over their other inventions? My life is not my own, shortly I shall have to haggle over my reality [97–8].

Scientific advances threaten to render material reality and the body super-fluous, a situation Jean Baudrillard warns of when he asserts that the post-modern era is characterized by an increasing "virtualization" of what is real. A pathologist of postmodernity, Baudrillard contends that individuals no longer actively engage with objects in the environment, but increasingly become "terminal[s] of multiple networks," participating in all the activities of life—work, play, social relations, consumption, etc.—telematically or, in other words, via virtual reality ("Ecstasy" 129).[15] Eventually, Baudrillard asserts, "what's left appears only as a large useless body, deserted and condemned" (129). Employing the vocabulary of this theory of postmodernity, the narrator of *Written on the Body* suggests that "tele-dildonics" threatens to supplant bodily love. While in some theories about identity this might be seen as a reward of postmodernity,[16] one of the sub-texts for the novel's anti-positivist thrust is the threat to organicism or what's "real" posed by an increasingly telematic culture.

Against this threat to the relevance of the material body, the narrator expresses a nostalgia—consistent with Winterson's reverence for the modernists, especially Woolf—for an idealized earlier time uncomplicated by technology and postmodernization[17]: "For myself, unreconstructed as I am, I'd rather hold you in my arms and walk through the damp of a real English meadow in real English rain. I'd rather travel across the world to have you with me than lie at home dialing your telepresence" (97). The realization of this ideal, however, is denied when Louise's estranged husband, Elgin, informs the narrator that Louise is afflicted with leukemia.

Winterson portrays Elgin, a prominent cancer researcher, playing computer games that enable him to simulate surgery and gene-splicing free from any "real" consequences (29, 104), an activity that highlights Winterson's negative view of the technological treatment of the body as a mere machine which reckless, Victor Frankenstein-like scientists deconstruct and reconstruct heedless of the humanity they circumscribe. Elgin asserts that only he—via his exclusive access to medical technology—can offer the possibility of curing Louise's leukemia. He has the "hardware" she needs, but he will only help if the narrator agrees to leave and never see Louise again. Elgin's access to the masculine world of medical technology enables him to stake his claim to Louise and position himself as the only authorized spokesperson for her. That the promise of Louise's bodily salvation persuades the narrator to cede his/her claim to Louise (his/her assumption being that a diseased person automatically belongs to science) is a measure of the predominance of faith in medical science.

Body Language

In one of her essays in *Art Objects*, Winterson claims that "if fiction is to have any future in the technological dream/nightmare of the twenty-first century, it needs, more than ever, to remember itself as imaginative, innovative, Other. To do this the writer must reclaim lineage and language" (178). In *Written on the Body*, Winterson's primary strategy for reclaiming language and the experimental spirit of Modernism which she reveres is to compose a prose poem that responds to the discourses of science. The middle section of the novel in which this occurs stands out as an example of what Winterson later explained was her ongoing project of changing and combining genres[18]:

> it is desirable now to break down the assumed barriers between poetry and prose, to let the writer use poetry when she needs intensity and prose when she does not. [...] What I am seeking to do in my work is to make a form that answers to twenty-first century needs. A form that is not "a poem" as we usually understand the term, and not "a novel" as the term is defined by its own genesis [*AO* 191].

Self-consciously, Winterson sets out to sculpt literature into new forms to respond to the alienating, depersonalized threat of scientific postmodernity.

The narrator abandons the scientific/technological world for a cottage in North England so decayed and devoid of the trappings of modernity (e.g. telephones, television, central heating) that it is on the verge of being reclaimed by its muddy, organic surroundings (107). There, in an attempt to re-capture some essence of Louise, the narrator begins to study medical textbooks. By entering into a dialogue with these texts, the narrator tries to imaginatively reclaim Louise and her diseased body from the exclusive authority of medical discourse. In the language of medical science and anatomy, the narrator uncovers a "love-poem":

> I became obsessed with anatomy. If I could not put Louise out of my mind I would drown myself in her. Within the clinical language, through the dispassionate view of the sucking, sweating, greedy, defecating self, I found a love-poem to Louise. I would go on knowing her, more intimately than the skin, hair and voice that I craved. I would have her plasma, her spleen, her synovial fluid. I would recognize her even when her body had long since fallen away [111].

The textbooks' anatomical descriptions of the body dissect, name, classify, and so seek to contain the body under a single rubric. Medical science explicates the body in terms of its components and mechanical processes, and Winterson depicts its inevitable failure to treat the individual holistically: school biology textbooks, for example, define the "characteristics of living things" merely as a set of body processes: "Excretion, growth, irritability, locomotion, nutrition, reproduction and respiration" (108).

From a seemingly sterile set of anatomy-textbook paradigms, the narrator extemporizes a prose poem, hybridizing artistic, imaginative language with the previously "pure" scientific discourse. Here, for example, is a description of the cells of the body in anatomical terms: "THE MULTI-PLICATION OF CELLS BY MITOSIS OCCURS THROUGHOUT THE LIFE OF THE INDIVID-UAL. IT OCCURS AT A MORE RAPID RATE UNTIL GROWTH IS COMPLETE. THEREAFTER NEW CELLS ARE FORMED TO REPLACE THOSE WHICH HAVE DIED. NERVE CELLS ARE A NOTABLE EXCEPTION. WHEN THEY DIE THEY ARE NOT REPLACED" (115). This clinical language assumes an implicit authority over its subject matter (emphasized by Winterson rendering it completely in capitals) while obscuring any sense of a speaker—an observer or individual generating the language. The most characteristic convention of genres such as the lab report, the scientific journal article, and the science textbook is the avoidance of personal expression.[19] Scientific writing is supposed to link the reader directly to "universal truths" about nature, but it offers a limited form of knowledge that is particularly challenged when confronting the complexities of human behavior and feeling.[20]

Winterson offers a number of alternative ways of perceiving objects usually studied by science. Here, for example, is the narrator's response to the above passage on the cells of the body:

> In the secret places of her thymus gland Louise is making too much of herself. Her faithful biology depends on regulation but the white T-cells have turned bandit. [...] It used to be their job to keep the body safe from enemies on the outside. They were her immunity, her certainty against infection. Now they are the enemies on the inside. The security forces have rebelled. Louise is the victim of a coup. [...] The faithful body has made a mistake. This is no time to stamp the passports and look at the sky. Coming up behind are hundreds of them. [...] Here they come, hurtling through the bloodstream trying to pick a fight. There's no-one to fight but you Louise. You're the foreign body now [115–6].

Not only does the narrator's diction make use of medical terminology, but, with its references to "passports," "security forces," and a "coup," it describes the body in politicized terms: Louise's body is a battlefield, at war with itself, and also the object of the war between the narrator and Elgin. The link between politics and disease has a long and involved history, as Susan Sontag demonstrates in *Illness as Metaphor* (72–88). Sontag argues that disease metaphors have often crassly been employed to describe political and historical events.[21] Winterson inverts this model, using political metaphors to describe Louise's diseased body. The passage above mixes political and medical language genres to poetically dramatize the struggle going on in Louise. It is a poetic strategy in which the narrator challenges the authority of medical discourses by refusing to abandon the representation of the body to a male-defined, depersonalized, exclusive vocabulary. The mix of genres used by Winterson's narrator encourages us to become conscious of how representations of bodies are informed by a variety of ideologies conveyed through the language genres used to describe them.

Despite his/her use of medical diction, the narrator retains a fundamentally negative attitude towards the usefulness and adequacy of scientific discourses which view the body as a conglomerate of parts and processes. By rewriting anatomical-text excerpts on the skin, skeleton, senses, cells, tissues, systems, and cavities of the body, the narrator attempts to put them in a framework that is not alienating.[22] In response to the textbook's anatomization of the face, for example, the narrator writes:

> Of the visions that come to me waking and sleeping the most insistent is your face. Your face, mirror-smooth and mirror-clear. Your face under the moon, silvered with cool reflection, your face in its mystery, revealing me. [...] Frontal bone, palatine bones, nasal bones, lachrymal bones, cheek bones, maxilla, vomer, inferior concha, mandible.
>
> Those are my shields, those are my blankets, those words don't remind me of your face [132].

This passage clearly articulates the tensions between artistic and scientific discourses: the narrator associates Louise's face with fertile poetic images (e.g. the moon; mirrors that reveal the narrator to his/herself) while declaring the anatomical taxonomy of the face sterile and unevocative. Taxonomies, by definition, seek to define boundaries for sets of information. In doing so, they delimit, constrain, and construct the objects of the taxonomy. Taxonomies are not, in other words, a neutral form of organizing knowledge. As Ruth Hubbard writes, "scientists do not simply go out and look at nature or hold up a mirror to it. They define and isolate the pieces of nature they choose to look at and, in so doing, change them by removing them from their natural context. They thus construct the nature they describe in science" (4).[23] When the body is anatomized for the purpose of scientific definitions, the anatomy tells a particular story of the body: one that privileges form over substance, parts over wholes, processes over gestalt, and mechanism over person. In leveling scientific and literary discourses, Winterson urges us to see scientific genres of writing not as "natural" but as a set of stories, as constructed and constructing as any other genre of story. Elizabeth Grosz comes to a similar conclusion:

> The body has thus far remained colonized through the discursive practices of the natural sciences, particularly the discourses of biology and medicine. [...] The way in which bodies, men's and women's bodies, are understood by the natural sciences is, however, no more accurate than the ways the social sciences and humanities understand them [x].

Grosz's comments support the notion that the authority of scientific "stories" over others is unwarranted and often damaging to the ideals of social equality. When pertaining to attributes associated with gender, for example, such stories can lend themselves to the naturalization of gender-based forms of oppression.[24] The basis of this oppression is challenged in the genre mixing Winterson uses here and, as I have already discussed, by the narrator's sexual ambiguity.

In an attempt to understand what Louise might be going through or might soon go through, the narrator takes to visiting terminal wards in hospitals to learn people's stories. There, one of the doctors admits the limits of scientific knowledge and the relative primitivism of medical technology: "How little we know. It's the late twentieth century and what are the tools of our trade? Knives, saws, needles and chemicals. I've no time for alternative medicine but I can see why it's attractive" (*WB* 150). Contrary to the modern view of science as the ultimate authoritative source of knowledge, this doctor construes the "miracle of modern medicine" as a charade. It is something akin to a priest admitting that Christian doctrine is fraudulent. Even Elgin, at one point, admits the limits of scientific knowledge: "Cancer is an unpredictable condition. It is the body turning upon itself. We don't understand that yet. We know what happens but not why it happens or how to stop it" (105). As with the biology textbook's definition of life, one of the key shortcomings of Western science according to Winterson is its reluctance to view the body holistically:

> It is usually metastasis which kills the patient and the biology of metastasis is what doctors don't understand. They are not conditioned to understand it. In doctor-think the body is a series of bits to be isolated and treated as necessary, that the body in its very disease may act as a whole is an upsetting concept. Holistic medicine is for faith healers and crackpots, isn't it? Never mind. Wheel round the drugs trolley, bomb the battlefield, try radiation right on the tumor. No good? Get out the levers, saws, knives and needles [175].

The narrator's poetic imagination of Louise's body is clearly a counternarrative to the scientific body of parts and processes. As such, it represents at least a partial movement away from the objectification of bodies that the narrator participates in with his/her earlier lovers: for example, with Inge—the "anarcha-feminist" (21) who wages a campaign against patriarchal oppression by blowing up urinals—whose breasts the narrator fetishizes (24). With Inge, the narrator reveals a preference for body surfaces and, hence, superficialities. It is a mark of his/her growth that in dealing with Louise, s/he is committed to a holistic view of the body, but it is still an objectifying view. Louise's status as an independent person is increasingly jeopardized as the narrator constructs her in a plethora of metaphoric terms: at turns a "landing strip" (117), a "mausoleum" whose secrets need to be mapped (119), a "musical instrument" (129), a "fallen angel" (131), a "dragonfly" (131), "the winged horse Pegasus" (131), "a perfumier of sandalwood and hops" (136), a gun "cocked and ready to fire" (136), an "olive tree whose roots grow by the sea" (137), the "fiery furnace" of the sunset (138), a "coat of many colours wrestled into the dirt" (138). As the metaphors proliferate, Louise becomes almost grotesque.[25] Further, the narrator never really thinks of Louise as an autonomous individual. Despite, or because of, all the transcendent images she inspires, she is an object for worship, and the narrator describes her in such a multitude of metaphors that Louise seems almost imprisoned in them. To an extent, the narrator exhibits the same kind of possessiveness as Elgin who, Louise asserts, "wanted something showy but not vulgar [...] wanted to go up to the world and say, 'Look what I've got'" (34).

In addition to the possessive nature of the narrator's diction, the narrator's precipitous, unilateral decision to leave Louise to Elgin denies Louise the right to make her own decisions. In the end, we know little about Louise except that she has red hair and is Australian. Nearly everything else is the narrator's subjective construction of her as an erotic object. For Elgin, also, she is an object, albeit more ornamental. Patricia Duncker writes, "She is beauty, the object of desire, the lover's fantasy projection, and not much more" (Grice and Woods 85). Louise's role in the book, then, is principally as an object to be fought over. The power struggle between the narrator and Elgin is played out in their attempts to claim Louise: each armed with their preferred narrative, they battle over who will decide Louise's destiny, whose discourse is more authoritative. Neither the narrator nor Elgin give Louise the chance to communicate her own version of her story. And yet Louise exercises her agency in the most decisive way in this book: when the narrator leaves, Louise absconds also, refusing to play into Elgin's ploy despite the fact that the narrator does.

Eventually, the narrator realizes that s/he has been complicit in the same kind of controlling tactics that Elgin has used:

> I had failed Louise and it was too late.
>   What right had I to decide how she should live? What right had I to decide how she should die? [*WB* 157].

> Why didn't I trust you? Am I any better than Elgin? Now you've made fools of us both and sprung away [172].

The narrator recognizes that s/he has participated in the fictionalization of Louise—made of her an aesthetic object and so deprived her of her personhood and agency: "It's as if Louise never existed, like a character in a book. Did I invent her?" (189). Gail, a friend s/he makes in the north of England during his/her self-imposed exile from Louise, replies: "No, but you tried to. [...] She wasn't yours for the making" (189). At another point, Gail censures the narrator for his/her fictionalizing impulses: "The trouble with you [...] is that you want to live in a novel" (160). Apart from indicating the narrator's proclivity for melodramatic ideas about love, this comment highlights the dangers of submerging oneself too deeply in these scripts—of acting out literary narratives as models for real behavior. Gail understands what the narrator, blinded by passion, cannot: "This isn't War and Peace honey, it's Yorkshire" (160), Gail quips.

Reading this, one feels as if Winterson is remonstrating with herself for her artistic flights of fancy. Her fiction demonstrates an ongoing tension between the desire to believe in the boundless potential of art to pose alternatives to vulgar postmodern reality, and art's very real limitations. In her fiction and her essays, she frequently espouses a traditional Romantic (i.e. anti–Enlightenment) ideal of art as salvation: in *Art Objects*, she writes that "the tragic paradigm of human life is lack, loss, finality, a primitive doomsaying that has not been repealed by technology or medical science. The arts stand in the way of this doomsaying. Art objects" (19). Just as religion has failed in its promise of salvation, science and technology— the positivist replacements for religion—have failed. In their place, Winterson, similar to the modernists she reveres, sacralizes art.

In *A History of the World in 10½ Chapters*, Julian Barnes suggests that art helps us to make sense of catastrophe. Winterson's view on the function of art is comparatively messianic—art not only "objects" but *saves*. Throughout her essays in *Art Objects*, her fiction, and her statements in interviews, Winterson elevates art to the status of a religion. As Lyn Pykett writes, "Poetry (or literary art) has [...] become the religion of Winterson's secular 'future,' and she has retained a sense of the immanence of the word from her Evangelical childhood" (Grice and Woods 57).[26] Winterson demonstrates that she needs to fill the vacuum she has created through her desacralization of more socially dominant belief systems. The tradition of art as resistance which Winterson draws upon has a long history, but to suggest that art can effect the kind of change necessary to revolutionize the problems of postmodern society—to propose it as a source of salvation—is to overstate its potential. Art provides extremely important venues for expressing skepticism about dominant social values, but the mistake is to believe, as Winterson seems to, that art can be a comprehensive cure-all. Such a belief is as misguided as the worship of religion and science. What Winterson *does* achieve through art is a portrait of the body that challenges the authority invested in science and the essentializing trends of scientific language.

    Written on the Body exemplifies Emily Martin's assertion that "there are many coexisting and contending knowledges of the body" (419). It is important to note that such knowledges are often "contending" with one other: representations of the body are frequently involved in power claims for science, religion, reproductive freedom, political agency, and artistic integrity. It is desirable, then, to present alternatives to representations of the body that are complicit in oppressive power dynamics (e.g. between the sexes) or that easily lend themselves to the institution of such power dynamics. In part towards this end, Jane Flax has called for a union of feminist theory which seeks to "destroy all gender-based relations of domination" ("Innocence" 459) and postmodern discourses which seek to deconstruct Enlightenment-derived beliefs (447). *Written on the Body* successfully unites feminist and postmodern projects. The narrator's ambiguous sex defies essentialist ideas and readings of gender, and the mix of language genres reclaims the body from scientific discourses, participating in the postmodern critique of what Flax calls the Enlightenment's "dreams of innocence" (446–447): contrary to the Enlightenment/positivist "dream," science is not the paradigm for all true knowledge; nor is it neutral or universally socially beneficial; and scientific language is not a transparent conveyor of fact but constructing and ideologically informed.[27]

    Nor, as Jean-François Lyotard points out in *The Postmodern Condition*, does scientific knowledge represent the totality of knowledge: "it has always existed in addition to, and in competition and conflict with, another kind of knowledge" which Lyotard calls "narrative" (7). In *Art Objects*, Winterson affirms that "We mostly understand ourselves through an endless series of stories told to ourselves by ourselves and others" (59). Such stories arrive in different genres: literary, scientific, political, mythic, romantic, culinary, cliché, women's magazine, and screenplay, to name some of the more obvious ones in *Written on the Body*. Just as there is no single approach to depicting bodies in narrative, the mixing of poetic, spiritual, political, medical, and other language genres—the narrator's "love-poem" to Louise—exemplifies how all narratives exist in hybrid forms; that is, there is no "pure" approach to story-telling. A corollary to this is Winterson's assertion in *Boating for Beginners* that "there is no such thing as a true story." This is particularly important with regard to the stories scientists tell because the convention of excising subjectivity in their language imputes an illusory purity and therefore an unwarranted authority over "Truth" to their narratives. Like Rushdie and Barnes, Winterson suggests that traditionally authoritative genres of story—in this case, those of science—do not and cannot tell the whole story. The authority of scientific genres is an illusion encouraged by tradition and language conventions rather than any intrinsic objectivity of style and method.

The conflict between narrative and scientific forms of knowledge to which Lyotard refers is primarily one of authority. The question posed by this conflict, then, is: Who will tell what/whose stories? Will we let science remain the most authoritative discourse for understanding ourselves and the natural world? The threat is not just a prominent one for women. We are all threatened by authoritarian narratives, whether they be the scientific "legitimation" of sexual and racial power disparities, the nationalistic "justification" of oppressive politics towards minorities, the religious-fundamentalist threat to non-believers and non-heterosexuals, or any other narratives that support oppressive ideologies.

Winterson's *Written on the Body* is a tale of non-compliance with one such narrative. Elgin and the narrator use scientific and hybrid literary discourses, respectively, to stake their claims to Louise. In the process, Louise's body becomes a kind of palimpsest, written on again and again with different language genres through which Elgin and the narrator try to capture her and, in a sense, deprive her of her autonomy. At the end, questions linger: Whose body is this and whose story does it tell? Though there are problems with the narrator's artistic objectification of Louise, the emphasis is on the limits and dangers of scientific knowledge. Louise, as I have suggested, defies attempts to control and contain her. At the very end of the novel, Louise appears to the narrator. Although it is ambiguous as to whether she is real or spectral, her return suggests reconciliation[28]: the narrator is forgiven for having attempted to choose her path for her. Although she may have forgiven the narrator, although she has escaped the possessive maneuverings of Elgin, and although her body ostensibly remains her own, her story remains untold. The novel ends optimistically, however, with a declaration that the ending, paradoxically, is "where the story starts" (190). This denial of closure, a common convention of post-modern works, departs from the tradition of realist novels, a tradition that imposes limits on its subjects by wrapping up all the "loose-ends." A gesture of affirmation and hope, the open-endedness of this finale suggests that this is where Louise's own story begins.

The Artistry of Science

Winterson's concern with science and technology has remained prominent in two of her more recent novels, *Art and Lies* and *Gut Symmetries*. Like Jean Baudrillard and Fredric Jameson, Winterson worries that our headlong rush into the postmodern/technological age leaves our humanity behind. What will become of love and other human feelings in a world tending toward the "virtualization" of feeling? Western society privileges the benefits of technology, but Winterson continues to ask us to consider what is lost to it. In *Art and Lies*, Handel wonders about the consequences of our worship of technology. What, he asks, will come of

> assuming that another pill, another drug, another car, another pocket-sized home-movie station, a DNA transfer, or the complete freedom of choice that five hundred TV channels must bring, will make everything all right? Will soothe the nagging pain in the heart that the latest laser scan refuses to diagnose? The doctor's surgery is full of men and women who do not know why they are unhappy.
> "Take this," says the Doctor, "you'll soon feel better." They do feel better, because little by little, they cease to feel at all [8].

Under the guise of "progress," contemporary society projects material possessions and technological advances as the cure for human discontent; technology has become an object of human society's impulse to worship. But the passage above and others like it in Winterson's fiction echo Baudrillard's warning that technology will erode our humanity. And progress, Winterson suggests, is a misleading concept:

> Progress: An advance to something better or higher in development. Are human beings better or higher in development that they were. [...] I will admit that we have better scientists, if by better, we agree that they are more sophisticated, more specialized, that they have discovered more than their dead colleagues. But if we ask, are they more ethical, more socially aware, more disciplined, more relevant to the happiness of the whole, then our scientists have failed the age they claim to have created. The masses are fobbed off with gadgets, while the real science takes place

behind closed doors, the preserves of the pharmaceuticals and the military. Genetic control will be the weapon of the future. [...] The white coat will replace the khaki fatigues as the gun gives way to the syringe [107].

It is not that science is innately dehumanizing or absolutist; it is the destructive uses to which scientific knowledge has been put and the widespread willingness of people to invest science with deific expectations that Winterson contests. With science having taken over many of the traditional functions of religion, Winterson attempts to desacralize it by critiquing the myth of the universal good of scientific progress.

Winterson's skepticism toward the worship of science and technological developments is strong, but she is not wholly dismissive of science or scientific inquiry. Though *Written on the Body* is extremely critical of science, elsewhere Winterson invokes scientific language and ideas to marvel at the way they have influenced our understanding of the material world. The passage below, which epigraphically precedes the text of *Sexing the Cherry*, exhibits a fascination with the near-magical insights that science has made possible:

Matter, that thing the most solid and the well-known, which you are holding in your hands and which makes up your body, is now known to be mostly empty space. Empty space and points of light. What does this say about the reality of the world? [8].

Framed this way, knowledge about the atomic structure of matter appears, ironically, more mystical than scientific. This equivalence of science and mysticism is further developed in *Gut Symmetries*, a novel which sees numerology, the Tarot, astrology, and ancient, medieval, modern, and postmodern science as equally valid (or invalid) systems of thought for understanding the universe.

In *Gut Symmetries*, Winterson suggests that science often offers theories that seem to be the work of poetic imagination. The physicist Jove (one of three narrators) studies Superstring theory. Alice, Jove's mistress and fellow physicist, explains:

According to the theory, any particle, sufficiently magnified, will be seen not as a solid fixed point but as a tiny vibrating string. Matter will be composed of these vibrations. The universe itself would be symphonic. [...] If the Superstring theory is correct there is no table. There is no basic building block, no firm stable first principle on which to pile the rest. The cups and saucers are in the air, the cloth levitating under them,

> the table itself is notional, we would feel uncomfortable eating our dinner without it, in fact it is a vibration as unsolid as ourselves [100, 161].

Modern science, from atomic and quantum theory to astrophysics and Superstring theory, tells us things which defy empiricism: that everything we think of as solid isn't, that appearances deceive, that solid objects are "notional" or "provisional": "Can we talk about reality anymore when reality means 'that which actually exists. Not counterfeit or assumed.' What does actually exist?" (211). To Alice, whose perspective Winterson seems to privilege, science looks more and more like a modern form of mysticism, even offering hopes of a kind of afterlife, the traditional consolation of religion:

> According to quantum theory there are not only second chances, but multiple chances. Space is not simply connected. History is not unalterable. [...] If we knew how to manipulate space-time as space-time manipulates itself the illusion of our single linear lives would collapse. And if our lives here are not the total our death here will not be final [162].

From the sub-atomic to the macro-cosmic universes, modern science—contrary to its desire for Grand Unifying Theories (GUTs) or "Gut Symmetries"—has uncovered chaos and unpredictability. Science searches for absolutes but its most recent developments reveal that nothing is absolute.

This paradox perhaps explains why the reflections of Winterson's characters on science have become more ambivalent in her recent work. Science breeds destructive technologies, but it is also the product of aesthetic aspirations: "Inside the horror of Nagasaki and Hiroshima lies the beauty of Einstein's $E = MC^2$" (105). Einstein's revelation was used for destructive purposes, but the revelation itself has a kind of poetic beauty for Alice. Similarly, in Einstein's theories about time Alice discerns a poetic mind at work:

> Einstein understood time as a river, moving forward, forceful, directed, but also bowed, curved, sometimes subterranean, not ending but pouring itself into a greater sea. A river cannot flow against its current, but it can flow in circles; its eddies and whirlpools regularly break up its strong press forward [106].

But it takes a poetic sensibility to appreciate these insights in this way. Comparing her perceptions of science to Jove's, Alice observes that "What to him were manipulatable facts were for me imaginative fictions" (211). Whereas Alice delights in the mysteries and magicality of modern science,

Jove, as Helena Grice and Tim Woods suggest, "is certain of a rationalis-
able and determinate universe, and cannot abide the mystical and metaphysical, regarding it as a typically effeminate form of thought" (121).[29]
Grice and Woods highlight that Winterson once again portrays science as
a male-dominated endeavor in which the ideas of value are thought of as
the product of "strong," "objective," and "masculine" thinking. Criticizing his wife Stella, a poet, Jove disavows non-literal understandings of the
world:

> Unhealthy individuals understand their dreams and fantasies as some-
> thing solid. An alternative world. They do not know how to subordinate
> their disruptive elements to a regulated order. My wife believes that she
> has a kind of interior universe as valid and as necessary as her day-to-day
> existence in reality. This failure to make a hierarchy, this failure to recog-
> nize the primacy of fact, justified her increasingly subjective responses.
> She refused to make clear distinctions between inner and outer. [...] At
> first I mistook this pathology for the ordinary feminine. [...] There is
> nothing mystical about the universe. There are things we cannot explain
> yet. That is all [*GS* 194–195].

In contrast to men, women's way of thinking, Jove suggests, is "weak,"
fanciful, "subjective," and undisciplined. It is this dichotomy of modes of
thinking that Winterson is criticizing. Jove's idea that there are exclusive
and specific male and female ways of thinking about the universe is an
androcentric over-simplification of reality. Jove's assumption that science
will inevitably yield answers to all the mysteries of the universe and that
such "progress" is unquestionably desirable allies him with positivist thought
and its masculinist biases. But Winterson portrays Jove and his faith in
science as exceedingly limited. In contrast to Alice and his wife Stella, Jove
is unimaginative and completely unlikable: he is a manipulator, a sexist,
an anti–Semite, and even a cannibal (to survive being lost at sea, he eats
part of his wife Stella's leg and hip).

Jove's condescending, androcentric, and misogynistic comments
might seem to suggest, as Grice and Woods have argued, that Winterson
herself "lapses into some rather tired gendered stereotypes" (121). Winterson often seems to be equating men with science and fact and women with
creative fertility and flights of fancy. But she is not falling prey to those
stereotypes. She is demonstrating one of the ways in which society has been
shaped according to gender: science has been, until very recently, an exclusively male discipline (see Noble). Even with women now working in the
sciences, all of the methodologies and goals of scientific study have been
pre-determined by centuries of male direction. A more open-minded

approach to life's mysteries than Jove's requires an artistic sensibility. As a poet, Stella "espouses a view of the world which is mystical and eschews the rigidity of disciplinary thought. [...] She is far more interested in a fluid concept of interrelationships between things [...] more attuned to the vibrations of the cosmos than Jove" (Grice and Woods 120). And Alice, a woman scientist who also recognizes the tentativeness of scientific knowledge and celebrates the aesthetic spirit of scientific inquiry, represents the possibility of science and society moving beyond their historical androcentrism.

Like Alice, Winterson perceives science as a set of "imaginative fictions" or stories. And stories, as she writes in *Oranges Are Not the Only Fruit*, are "a way of explaining the universe while leaving the universe unexplained. [...] Everyone who tells a story tells it differently, just to remind us that everybody sees it differently" (93). There are no final explanations, no absolute answers, but there is art. Whereas scientific knowledge is founded on the positivist ideal that the present is always better than the past, on the unquestionable good of an ever-increasing technical knowledge base, on purity, objectivity, and the elimination of ambiguity, literature and other art forms (according to Winterson) value past, present, and future equally, parade their subjectivity, thrive on ambiguity, and present alternatives to narratives of purity:

> each new generation considers itself more enlightened than its predecessor; a view that science both encourages and depends upon. Literature (all art) takes a different view; human nature, emotional reality is not seen as a progress from darkness to light but as a communication, with ourselves and across time, so that work entirely out of date by scientific standards is as fresh and meaningful to us as it ever was. Whereas science outdates the past art keeps it present. Whereas the language of science tries to eliminate error, chiefly by the use of agreed symbols carrying an agreed value, the language of literature seems to be able to contain error by being greater than it [*AO* 166].

The fundamental bases of scientific and literary/artistic thought, Winterson argues here, are opposed. Calling our attention to the founding image of the "Enlightenment"—of reason, rationality, and science leading us out of the darkness and into the "light"—Winterson asks us to reconsider its assumption: the past might not be as dark as we sometimes think, and the future may not be so bright.

CHAPTER FOUR

Angela Carter

The "Demythologising Business"

Of all of the writers discussed and mentioned in this study, none have been more daring, more inventive, and more incisively critical of social injustices than Angela Carter. From her first novels in the mid to late 1960s, which boldly confronted the pervasiveness of androcentrism, traditional ideas about gender roles, and the roots of female masochism, Carter distinguished herself as a stylistic and thematic innovator. Though some male writers such as Anthony Burgess and John Fowles had already begun taking British literature into the "experimental," self-conscious realms of postmodernism, Carter was one of the first and most spectacular *women* writers in Britain to do so.[1] In retrospect, it is clear that as she matured she was at the cutting edge of a new movement of writing which, while retaining the discontentedness of the "angry young men" crowd typified by Kingsley Amis, led the British novel out of its regressive and male-dominated social realist trend. It is for this reason that I have saved my discussion of her work for last. When one compares the ideas and stylistic methods of Carter to successors such as Rushdie, Barnes, Winterson, and many others, it is evident that she was tremendously influential in shaping contemporary British literature.

Carter's death in 1992 was followed by numerous encomiums of her life and work. Though most praised her for her visionary contributions to world literature, not all the reviews were entirely favorable. John Bayley's appraisal of her work for the *New York Review of Books* bears particular attention. Bayley implied that Carter's works would not endure the test of time because they were too embroiled in articulating the politically correct fashions of the present. Hermione Lee's excellent tribute to Carter defended her against this attack,[2] but Bayley's depreciation of Carter indicates a wider disdain for postmodern literature: "if there is a common factor in the elusive category of the postmodernist novel it is political correctness: whatever spirited arabesques and feats of descriptive imagination Carter may perform she always comes to rest in the right ideological position" (9). Because of his underlying conservative belief that postmodern art is always in service of the most simplistically conceived notions of political correctness, Bayley under-values the work of an important contemporary writer. But Carter's antagonistic position towards antiporn feminists as well as poststructural feminists rebuts the view that she is simplistically allied with high-profile political trends. Postmodern writing *does* rethink conventional ideological positions, but fictions such as Carter's are inquiries into and critiques of social values rather than literal prescriptions for how things should be.

Carter remains difficult to appraise as a writer. As Salman Rushdie said in his obituary of her, Carter was "a defiler of sacred cows. [...] She demolished the temples and the commissariats of the righteous" (qtd. in Sage, *Flesh* 313). *Nothing Sacred* was the title of her first collection of essays and reviews, and it serves well as an encapsulated description of the guiding principle in her own fiction. As I noted in the introduction to this study, Carter's work is self-consciously connected to the fleeting liberatory spirit of the sixties, an era in which, to reiterate Carter's assessment, "all that was holy was in the process of being profaned" ("Notes" 70). Carter herself articulates this "profanity" through a variety of registers. She skips gaily and deviously among science fiction, dystopian fiction, pornography, the gothic, magic realism, fairy tale, burlesque, tragedy, and myth. In doing so, she demonstrates the pliability of literary genres for conveying historically changing ideas about society and culture, especially, in her case, about those related to the roles women play and are expected to play in male-dominated society.

It is important not to underestimate Angela Carter's influence on contemporary women's writing. Lyn Pykett observes that Jeanette Winterson, for example, is not sufficiently cognizant of the debt she owes to Carter:

> Surely it is Carter's new way with words, her tightrope-walking risktaking, her boldness, her energetic ransacking and remaking of all manner of literary traditions, her demythologising and remythologising, that provide the models for many of the brilliant devices [...] which have been

such important elements in Winterson's success [Grice and Woods 59–60].

Carter was not only an important precursor for Winterson, but was arguably the most influential figure in British women's writing since World War II. Many of the "postmodern" strategies of contemporary women's writing (e.g. rewriting androcentric, socially conservative genres and male-authored texts from a feminist viewpoint; self-consciously analyzing how gender structures social relations; using fantasy to imagine worlds where androcentrism and traditional gender roles have come undone) were brought to a new prominence by Carter during the height of the feminist movement, marking a break with the conservative social realist traditions of the immediately postwar period.

Carter's ongoing project was to investigate and debunk "the social fictions that regulate our lives" ("Notes" 70). She viewed religion, psychoanalysis, capitalism, patriarchy, and even certain kinds of feminism as responsible for perpetuating damaging myths: "I'm in the demythologising business. [...] I'm interested in myths [...] because they *are* extraordinary lies designed to make people unfree" ("Notes" 71). This self-assessment announces that Carter's task is essentially the same as that considered by Rushdie to be the true *métier* of all writers: to "point at frauds." The myths that occupy Carter's attention throughout her fiction and essays are the ones related to gender, especially femininity. She mocks, debunks, and revises myths that have contributed to androcentric sexual norms and gender roles. As previous chapters have focused on the social critiques and genre innovations of Rushdie, Barnes, and Winterson, this chapter focuses on how Carter uses and revises the conventions of genres like the fairy tale, pornography, speculative-fiction, and the gothic to critique myths which perpetuate out-moded values about gender.

Postmodern Fairy Tales and Pornography

Because written literary traditions historically have been shaped and institutionalized by men, women writers have had to respond to literary forms that carry an androcentric bias—forms that have traditionally, often subtly, helped subordinate women to men. Anne Cranny-Francis argues, for example, that the convention that resolves nineteenth century realist tales with marriage "tells the reader that individual success and happiness means heterosexual romance and marriage [...] [and therefore] is involved in the construction of the compulsory heterosexuality which typifies patriarchal discourse" (93). Through constant repetition, such conventions came to be seen as "natural" and so the androcentric values they conveyed were reinforced as "natural" also: "The realists simply naturalised the conventions so that they seemed obvious or inevitable to readers, and so became effectively invisible. When the conventions became invisible, so did their social and ideological function" (93). While texts that defy such generic conventions can be found in every literary era,[3] trends such as the one Cranny-Francis identifies in realist writing do produce a set of dominant social values, attitudes, and beliefs.

Given the traditional social functions attributed to specific narrative genres, feminist writers have reinvented and revised generic conventions and forms to offer alternative values. As Angela Carter puts it in "The Language of Sisterhood," "It is, after all, very rarely possible for new ideas to find adequate expression in old forms" (228). While new forms have generally been fashioned of elements from old forms, Carter emphasizes that the purpose of such revision is to find ways of speaking to new realities in society. Portraying new social values about gender, then, requires new representational conventions.

A popular strategy of postmodern writers has been to rewrite stories from scripture, mythology, folk literature, and classic literature to parody, invert, or otherwise alter their traditional conventions and so draw attention to their ideological messages. This trend in rewriting suggests that writers have been undertaking the task of reading genres in relation to their historical scenes of appearance as suggested by Ralph Cohen when he links generic transformations and retellings of individual tales with the dominant values of their contemporary society ("Postmodern Genres" 19; "History and Genre" 214). Angela Carter's rewriting of classic fairy tales in *The Bloody Chamber and Other Stories* is an example of revising generic form for feminist purposes. Because fairy tales have played an important role in teaching androcentric values to children, they have been frequently revised by women writers. With *The Bloody Chamber*, Carter was one of the first of a number of contemporary women writers—including Tanith Lee, Anne Sexton, Sheri Tepper, A. S. Byatt, and Margaret Atwood[4]—who have put fairy tales to unconventional uses. In addressing the issue of fairy tales and their social influence, Carter and others have suggested an alternative starting point for social critique—in the home and child-rearing, rather than just in public policy. Changing society to promote gender equality is a difficult task, but, since gender roles are learned in early childhood, identifying and changing some of the sources of learned behavior (such as fairy tales) is an important step towards that goal.

Historically, folk and fairy tales have served numerous functions besides acculturating children. The pre-literary oral folk tale functioned principally as a peasant form of entertainment,[5] while the European literary fairy tale emerged in the late seventeenth century as an appropriation of the oral folk tale by French aristocratic women like Madame D'Aulnoy, Mademoiselle Le Prince de Beaumont, Mademoiselle L'Héritier, and Mademoiselle de La Force. Published versions of the tales they told in French salons allegorically conveyed a critique of Louis XIV's politics and expressed utopian impulses in an era of French decline (Zipes, "Introduction"). The "use-values" (Beebee) to which fairy tales have been put, then, have varied at different historical moments. Carter herself suggests yet another historical use of fairy tales when, drawing on Jack Zipes's influential studies of folk and fairy tales in her introduction to *The Virago Book of Fairy Tales*, she asserts that the Grimm brothers

> sought to establish the cultural unity of the German people via its common traditions and language. [...] Their work in collecting fairy tales was part of the nineteenth-century struggle for German unification. [...] [They] envisaged popular culture as an untapped source of imaginative energy for the bourgeoisie [xvi].[6]

Fairy tales, Carter implies here, are socially important because they provide a set of common cultural scripts—a collective mythology which naturalizes certain types of behavior. But this is not to say that the fairy tale genre is *intrinsically* conservative or conformist. If that were the case, feminist revisions of the genre would be impossible. It was the error of structuralist critics like Vladimir Propp, Jack Zipes argues in *Fairy Tales and the Art of Subversion*, to equate literary form on its own (i.e. heedless of other considerations) with a work's meaning (5).[7] Genres are tied to different ideological trends at different points in history. Carter's selection of fairy tales for the Virago collection, for example, is in part meant to demonstrate an alternative tradition of folk literature—one which exhibits "the richness and diversity with which femininity, in practice, is represented in 'unofficial' culture: its strategies, its plots, its hard work" (xiv).

Nevertheless, in certain historical and cultural eras there *is* a tradition of fairy tales being appropriated for the purposes of defining "proper" and "improper" conduct. Although literary fairy tales "are constantly rearranged and transformed to suit changes in tastes and values," Zipes adds that they readily "assume mythic proportions when they are frozen in an ideological constellation that makes it seem that there are universal absolutes that are divine and should not be changed" (*Fairy Tale as Myth* 19). This is perhaps most evident in the versions of the tales given by Charles Perrault in his 1697 collection of *Histoires ou contes du temps perdu* and in the morals he appended to them.[8] Perrault's collection rewrote the peasant folk tales to create a kind of "conduct book" on French *civilité* (Zipes, "Introduction" 19).[9] Perrault's tales became popular because they so effectively conveyed lessons of civility for aristocratic and bourgeois children, especially girls—lessons that taught the sinfulness and dangerous consequences of giving in to curiosity and sexual impulses while instilling values like humility, piety, passivity, and self-discipline. The reception of fairy tales as sexually instructive was given further currency in the twentieth-century with a variety of psychoanalytical readings by Freud, Carl Jung, Erich Fromm, Otto Rank, and Bruno Bettelheim.[10] It is this tradition (from the eighteenth-century through the present) of bourgeois fairy tales and the history of their interpretation as lessons about "proper" behavior, especially regarding sexuality, that Carter confronts in *The Bloody Chamber*.

The Bloody Chamber returns the fairy tale genre to the more physiologically explicit and individualistic themes commonly expressed in its pre-literary folk origins, while also transforming the tales so that they speak to contemporary feminist concerns. The stories in *The Bloody Chamber* revise the pedagogical subtexts of several classic fairy tales, especially Perrault's versions of "Bluebeard," "Little Red Riding Hood," "Beauty and the Beast," and "Snow White." Instead of passively accepting punishment for their transgressive behavior, Carter's female protagonists remain resolute and actively defy their male-determined fates. For example, in "The Bloody Chamber," a retelling of the Bluebeard tale, Bluebeard's bride does not repent her actions or passively go to meet her fate. She uses her sexuality to distract him from forcing her to retrieve the blood-stained key to his private chamber. Although this stratagem fails, she demonstrates a resourcefulness regarding the utility of her sexuality—something that Carter portrays as an admirable trait throughout her work. Finally, she is saved when, instead of her brothers coming to rescue her as in the Perrault version, her indomitable mother arrives on horseback and shoots the tyrannical husband. Similarly, in "Werewolf," one of Carter's revisions of "Little Red Riding Hood," Red Riding Hood defeats the wolf in physical combat, uncovers that the wolf is really her grandmother (an inversion of the traditional tale), and prospers when she takes over her grandmother's property. In "The Company of Wolves," another variation of the Red Riding Hood tale, she becomes the wolf's sexual partner, thus defying one of the tale's traditional interpretations—as a warning against female sexual agency or promiscuity. This version challenges the androcentric notion that women should not feel or express sexual desire by presenting the heroine as full of desire and actively in search of the fulfillment of that desire.

The traditional conventions of these tales are crucial to having defined the classical fairy tale as an androcentric, bourgeois, moralistic, and acculturating genre. Carter's changes to the expected conventions of the tales—mother riding to the rescue; the grandmother masquerading as a wolf rather than vice versa; the archetypically innocent girl entering into a sexual partnership with the wolf—alter the fairy tale genre by encouraging us into a more critical stance as readers. Instead of reading fairy tales and their morals passively, Carter's stories practically demand us to confront and compare the ideas being conveyed in both the traditional versions and the revisions. In changing the form and content of these tales, Carter makes a broader "conceptual change" (Cohen, "Afterword" 276) in the fairy tale genre and presents ideological messages that dispute those of the traditional tales: a husband does not have the right to make binding laws on his wife; and trust, passivity, altruism, and sexual naiveté are not essentially feminine virtues. Carter's stories function as a kind of social criticism through literature, implicitly commenting on the history of fairy tales and the uses to which they have been put. Reading Carter's fairy tales raises questions about the history and conventions of the genre, especially of their portrayal of the ideal woman as passive, powerless, and subservient. In other words, Carter enables readers of received genres like the fairy tale to re-read them from a more critical stance, and this new process of reading sets in motion further challenges to the traditional identity of the old genres.

In conjunction with this strategy of revising the formal features of specific narratives, another prominent method of revising form for feminist writing has been to combine conventions of two or more genres which are traditionally considered discrete into a mixed genre narrative. Carter took for granted that writing necessitates recycling and that fairy tales in particular are formed "out of all sorts of bits of other stories long ago and far away, and [have] been tinkered with, had bits added [...] lost other bits, got mixed up with other stories" all in an "endless recycling process" (*Virago Book* x–xi).[11] She was also conscious of the fact that her own writing followed this model. In one interview, she stated that her work "indulged in a sort of intellectual *bricolage* [...] revisiting and reutilizing our cultural heritage, as though it were a big junk shop, a gigantic scrapyard" (Bono 43).

In addition to her work with revising the traditional conventions of the fairy tale, then, Carter mixes conventions from a variety of genres. In *The Sadeian Woman*, her 1978 study of Sade's pornography, Carter makes an implicit comparison between fairy tales and pornography: "the moral of the fairy tale about the perfect woman" is that "[t]o exist in the passive case is to die in the passive case—that is, to be killed" (77). This assertion comes from her discussion of Sade's *Justine* and so points to a common trope of both classic fairy tales of the Perrault variety and the bulk of pornography: depicting and therefore defining women as passive sexual objects and/or commodities to be bought. By combining elements of a classic fairy tale narrative with elements from a pseudo–Sadeian pornographic tale, the title story of Carter's *The Bloody Chamber* also suggests that the two genres have thematic and ideological similarities.

"The Bloody Chamber" (and other stories in that collection) claims the implicit presence of pornographic and sado-masochistic elements in traditional fairy tales by making them explicit. Carter's Bluebeard (or the "Marquis" as he is called here, linking him to Sade) is not only a punishing, tyrannical husband, but a libertine: his library consists of rare volumes of pornographic literature; his private, "off-limits" room is stocked with instruments of sexual torture; and he takes sadistic pleasure in consummating his marriage with his virgin bride. To him, his bride (who narrates the story) is a sexualized commodity: "I saw him watching me in the gilded mirrors with the assessing eye of a connoisseur inspecting horseflesh, or even a housewife in the market, inspecting cuts on the slab" (*BC* 11). Later, describing his seduction of her, she comments: "He in his London tailoring; she, bare as a lamb chop. Most pornographic of all confrontations. And so my *purchaser* unwrapped his *bargain*" (15, my emphases). It is important to note here that Carter draws explicit attention to the pornographic subtext of this scene for in doing so she suggests that one of the principal effects of pornography is that it depicts human beings (usually women) as commodities and so perpetuates what is already a culturally pervasive androcentric idea. In addition, the language choices of the Marquis's bride are strangely disembodied. By referring to herself in the third-person she conveys the sense that her body is no longer her own or even a human body: it is his "bargain" or "purchase." This, in conjunction with Carter's representation of the Marquis as a financial tycoon, suggests that this tale should be read in part as a critique of the entangling of economics and sex in capitalist culture, especially within the institution of marriage.[12]

Carter's *critique* of pornography, then, is as much a part of her work as her advocacy of the progressive or liberatory potential of pornography. Many commentaries on Carter's approach to pornography oversimplify her position. Like any genre, pornography can serve different interests, including feminist ones. It is the uses to which pornography is put and the contexts in which it is read or received that can prove either liberatory or confining. So "The Bloody Chamber" is not about the "evils" of pornography (or fairy tales) as such. It is a critique of one tradition of ideological conventions in these genres—conventions which assume and even valorize female passivity, especially with regards to sexuality and desire.

"Moral Pornography" and the Anti-Pornography Movement

"The Bloody Chamber" is Carter's final fiction to prominently thematize pornography and incorporate its generic features. In combination with *The Sadeian Woman*, it is the culmination of her fascination with the genre that dominated her work in the 1970s. Carter's ideas about pornography made her relationship with other prominent feminists a vexed one. The burgeoning women's liberation movement in the 1960s and 70s sought to correct the myths associated with femininity which have accrued through depictions of women in various influential discourses: myths, for example, that linked virtue to virginity (as in the Christian archetype of the Virgin Mary), charm and attractiveness to suffering (as in the Marilyn Monroe–style Hollywood icon), femaleness to "lack" (as in psychoanalysis' Oedipus Complex), and sexual agency to whorishness (as in pornography). But whereas the women's movement was able to unite behind the project of demythologizing the majority of such representations, pornography has proved an ongoing source of division among feminists.[13]

Since the late seventies, the most publicly visible forms of feminist action in both the U.S. and Britain have centered on pornography.[14] More than just a convenient focus for all the injustices that women suffer, pornography is a political rallying point that can be identified as vivid evidence of those injustices. Andrea Dworkin and Catherine MacKinnon— the most prominent feminist anti-pornography campaigners—argue that pornography is the primary cause and manifestation of male dominance, misogyny, and women's victimization and objectification.[15] Ann Snitow, however, argues that the focus on anti-pornography campaigning has led to a re-direction of the feminist movement away from the struggle for sexual and economic equality and child-care reform towards "an emphasis on how women are victimized, how all heterosexual sex is, to some degree, forced sex, how rape and assault are the central facts of women's sexual life and central metaphors for women's situation in general" (Ellis 11).[16] In her essay "Feminist Fundamentalism: The Shifting Politics of Sex and Censorship," Elizabeth Wilson goes a step further, suggesting that the antiporn movement is a new manifestation of fundamentalism: "To have made pornography both the main cause of women's oppression and its main form of expression is to have wiped out almost the whole of the feminist agenda, and to have created a new moral purity movement for our new (authoritarian) times" (Segal and McIntosh 15–28: 28).

At roughly the same historical moment as the antiporn campaign was beginning to dominate the feminist agenda, Angela Carter published *The Sadeian Woman* (1978). In it, Carter proposed the radical idea of the "moral pornographer": an artist who "might use pornography as a critique of current relations between the sexes" (19). Today, despite wide-ranging critiques of the anti-pornography dominance of feminist agendas, the false equation of feminism, antiporn agendas, and "male-bashing" is so common that Carter's early proposal of pornography's potential to be critical of gender relations seems even more radical than when it was first published.

Carter derived her idea of the "moral pornographer" from her reading of Sade. She values his unrestricted disclosure of sexual power dynamics and reads him as a satirist who "describes sexual relations in the context of an unfree society as the expression of pure tyranny, usually by men upon women" (*SW* 24). Sade makes an interesting foil for Perrault. Whereas the latter was concerned with scripting tales that instruct in the "proper" behavior—especially sexual—for women, Carter perceives the former as having irreverently challenged the received notions about what constitutes "proper" and "improper" sexual behavior which were so sacred to that era of French history.

In contrast to Sade's pornography, Carter critiques quotidian pornography as a genre which depicts and perpetuates "mythic" versions of femininity (and masculinity):

> Since all pornography derives directly from myth, it follows that its heroes and heroines [...] are mythic abstractions. [...] Any glimpse of a real man or a real woman is absent from these representations of the archetypal male and female. [...] [P]ornography reinforces the archetype of [women's] negativity and [...] it does so simply because most pornography remains in the service of the status quo [6, 16–17].

For Carter, Sade certainly portrays mythic notions of femininity, but he does so in large part to satirize the ideological assumptions underlying them. She argues that Sade's Justine—the archetypical suffering woman— suffers principally because of her "virtuous" insistence on the preservation of her virginity despite her multiple brutal rapes. Obviously, Carter's reading is problematic in that it at times seems to suggest that Justine should enjoy the abuse she suffers,[17] but what she reads as important in

Sade's representation of Justine is his satire of the male-authored myth which insists that a woman's value is dependent on her virginity.

Even more importantly for Carter, Sade challenges archetypical models of femaleness by portraying antithetical mythic models, that is, "Sadeian Women," or "women as beings of power" (*SW* 36) like Juliette and Durand. Such transgressive women, Carter interprets, wield power by actively "fucking" and thereby overturning the "normal" dynamic of sexual relations:

> Women do not normally fuck in the active sense. They are fucked in the passive tense and hence automatically fucked-up, done over, undone. Whatever else he says or does not say, Sade declares himself unequivocally for the right of women to fuck. [...] [Sade] urges women to fuck as actively as they are able, so that powered by their enormous and hitherto untapped sexual energy they will then be able to fuck their way into history and, in doing so, change it [27].

These are provocative claims, but Carter admires Sade for his uncompromised flouting of so many of the institutions, virtues, ideals, and taboos of a theistic, androcentric world. She reads Sade's libertines as desacralizing crusaders who "turn the Blessed Virgin over on her belly and sodomise her" and debunk the notion that "sex is sanctified only in the service of reproduction" (76). Carter celebrates their desacralization of the bourgeois sexual ideals of chastity and purity. Similarly, the libertines defy the ideal of feminine physical beauty by taking pleasure in its opposite — excessive ugliness. "[N]onsense! cry the libertines" (76) and this might be considered Carter's rallying cry as well.[18]

The language, also, of the above passage emphasizes Carter's irreverence towards androcentric social conventions. "Fuck," she implies, is a masculine word about masculine activity — sexual or otherwise. It functions as a pervasive social metaphor for action, and in an androcentric world it is inevitably women who are the implied recipients of the word and all of its connotations. With her aggressive appropriation of this masculine discourse, Carter upsets the bourgeois ideal of women as demure drawing-room objects and asserts their right to be part of the culture of "fucking" — the society of activity — and shape history in the active sense.

As might be expected, Carter's interpretation of Sade has been a major source of contention for antiporn feminists such as Susanne Kappeler, Susan Brownmiller, Susan Griffin, and Andrea Dworkin, whose writings on pornography are implicitly, and occasionally explicitly, in dialogue with Carter. Nevertheless, Carter's relationship with them is complex, full of curiously overlapping sympathies which neither Carter nor her interlocutors would be (or would have been) likely to recognize or admit. Carter clearly abhors the predominance of the "woman as victim" archetype which Dworkin and Catherine MacKinnon purposefully perpetuate; however, there are a few striking similarities in their ideas. For example, Andrea Dworkin, whose *Pornography: Men Possessing Women* is an implicit denunciation of Carter's *Sadeian Woman*,[19] shares her anti-mythologizing agenda and concerns about the trend among some feminists to want to replace patriarchy with matriarchy (Dworkin, *Letters* 110–116).[20] And, like Carter, Dworkin views sex in terms of a power struggle between the sexes: "Fucking is the means by which the male colonializes [sic] the female. [...] [I]t is regarded as an act of possession" (119).

What I find hypocritical, however, is that Dworkin, like Carter, uses language, scenarios, and themes in her own fiction that could be (and have been[21]) construed as pornographic. Her novel *Mercy*, for example, which describes a woman's physical/sexual suffering in explicit detail, might easily be classified as Carter's brand of "moral pornography," but Dworkin would no doubt consider it as belonging to a genre of realism rather than pornography. For Dworkin, the label "pornography" automatically implies an exploitative, misogynistic authorship, whereas Carter treats the genre as historically dominated by misogyny but not essentially tied to it. Similar to fairy tales, in which sexist depictions of women are often seen as intrinsic to the form, Dworkin argues that pornography inevitably represents women as sexual objects in subservient or subordinate positions to men and so is inherently degrading towards women. While sexist conventions are dominant in these genres, recent genre theory disputes the idea that genres are *intrinsically* tied to specific ideological goals (Cohen, "History and Genre" 209). Carter's fiction and her discussion of pornography in *The Sadeian Woman* supports this notion. The points of contention for the antiporn camp, then, are Carter's propositions that pornography, even in its most violent and misogynistic forms, always has something to teach us about sexual power relations and the cultural construction of gender; and that pornography can be used to present alternative images of sexual empowerment for women.

Despite some similarities between Carter and the antiporn feminists, then, one ought not underestimate their differences. Catherine MacKinnon, who views pornography as "constructing and performative rather than merely referential or connotative" (*Only Words* 21), takes it as a given that the use of pornography leads directly to the forceful re-enactment of the scenarios it presents. Carter too views pornography as "constructing and performative," but sees in that the potential to revise the traditional message of male dominance which pornographic scenarios often convey.

Carter doesn't want a simplistic inversion of the current power disparity between men and women. Rather, she wants to protest the naturalization—through genres like pornography—of sexual inequalities. If women can achieve autonomy with their sexuality and their sexual relations, Carter suggests, then equality can be achieved in economic and other spheres of society.

To understand Carter's concept of a moral pornographer, then, one has to be willing to see pornography as having the potential to criticize as well as reinforce sexist ideals. It is this view that Susanne Kappeler, for example, cannot tolerate, arguing that pornography informs actual sexual practices in the most causally direct manner (1–4).[22] Kappeler, MacKinnon, and Dworkin do not consider that pornography can be (and in most cases is) non-violent; they seem unwilling to consider pornography as anything other than mimetic and prescriptive.[23] My purpose in these comparisons is not to dismiss the concerns of the antiporn feminists.[24] Their goal to prevent the exploitation of women is certainly no different than that of other subgroups of feminism. However, their focus on pornography as the principal cause and manifestation of women's oppression is misguided (see Strossen, Ellis, Williams, and Segal and McIntosh). There are many genres, including pornography, that subordinate and demean women through their representations. But since gender roles are naturalized in artistic, literary, and other representational genres, critical readings and rewritings of genre present the opportunity to challenge those roles— to show their androcentrism. According to Linda Hutcheon, postmodern writers such as Carter seek to "point out that those entities that we unthinkingly experience as 'natural' [...] are in fact 'cultural'; made by us, not given to us" (*Politics* 2). A "moral pornographer," then, would use pornographic forms, language, and other conventions to "de-naturalize" (3) commonly held values about sex and gender.

Gender Archetypes

Carter's interest in pornography can partly be understood by the fact that, similar to fairy tales, pornography offers archetypes for sexual behavior and sexual "ideals," especially with regards to women. As I have already discussed, the facility with which Perrault's tales presented androcentric bourgeois values as universal meant that fairy tales were received as myth. Pornography also perpetuates mythic ideals by depicting gender archetypes. Carter protests androcentric sexual ideals by rewriting the scripts for archetypal female figures.

In raising the issue of archetypes, I am not referring to the Jungian notion of hypothetical figures in the "collective unconscious" of societies and cultures, but to the popular figures of myth and fairy tale and other genres widely disseminated in Western culture. As Jack Zipes writes of fairy tales: "their 'universality' has more to do with the specific manner in which they were constructed historically as mythic constellations than with common psychic processes of a collective unconscious" (*Fairy Tale as Myth* 19). It is the assumed universality of pornographic and classic fairy tale archetypes that Carter tries to debunk in her writing by always making us conscious of the artifice behind such constructions.

Gender norms are constructed and disseminated through sources such as myth, fairy tales, religion, psychoanalysis, and Hollywood cinema. These sources proffer a common cultural base of archetypical figures which provide authoritative models for gendered behavior. For Luce Irigaray, there are three central female archetypes which define and limit women's social behavior:

> *Mother, virgin, prostitute: these are the social roles imposed on women.* The characteristics of (so-called) feminine sexuality derive from them: the valorization of reproduction and nursing; faithfulness; modesty, ignorance of and even lack of interest in sexual pleasure; a passive acceptance of man's "activity"; seductiveness [186–87].

Scholars contributing to *Feminist Archetypal Theory* (Lauter and Rupprecht) argue that such archetypes are cultural constructs which *prescribe* and reinforce stereotypical gender roles and behavior rather than "innate" human categories which *describe* some putatively universal reality (as in Jungian archetypal theory). In *The Sadeian Woman*, Carter forcefully announces that archetypal depictions of femininity are the target of her critique as well: "All the mythic versions of women, from the myth of the redeeming purity of the virgin to that of the healing, reconciling mother, are consolatory nonsenses" (5).

In Sade's *Justine*, Carter sees a re-manifestation of the "holy virgin," while Juliette is the "profane whore" (101). The antiporn feminists perceive women represented in pornography as Justine-figures—women for whom suffering is made (in the pornographic context) to seem "natural."[25] It is this Justine archetype that Carter is most critical of in her analysis of Sade, suggesting that women mustn't give in to the idea of themselves as victims. While Justine embodies victimhood—the archetype which the antiporn feminists actively encourage—Juliette, in Carter's opinion, does not simply act out the role of the archetypical prostitute; rather, she is a "blasphemous guerilla of demystification" (105). Defying objectification, Juliette becomes an autonomous sexual being. In doing so, "she rids herself of some of the more crippling aspects of femininity" (79). Juliette achieves her autonomy because she is able to become sexually and economically exploitative: like men, she "fucks." True, she participates in many horrifying acts of sexual violence and economic crime, but Carter is not suggesting that women literally adopt Juliette's methods. Carter characterizes Juliette as empowered but also as another source of tyranny. "I do not think I want Juliette to renew my world," Carter writes, "but, her work of destruction complete, she will [...] have removed a repressive and authoritarian superstructure that has prevented a good deal of the work of renewal" (111).

Juliette's importance for Carter, then, is as an iconoclast. Her own fiction is populated by a variety of contemporary Juliettes—characters who are not quite so violent or criminal as Sade's Juliette, but who are nevertheless iconoclastic and break the molds of prescribed gender behavior. The female protagonists of later works like *Nights at the Circus* and *Wise Children* are obviously exemplary in this regard, but it is in *The Bloody Chamber* and Carter's earlier work that she was most radical and challenging with her depictions and critiques of femininity (and masculinity). It is in her earlier fiction too that she puts her theories about "moral pornography" into practice.

Revealing the Artifice of Femininity

Although the Marquis de Sade is Carter's historical model for the writer who comes closest to her paradigm of the "moral pornographer," her own fiction evolved from this concept. *The Passion of New Eve* (1977), written around the same time as *The Sadeian Woman*, is an explicit attempt to write "moral pornography." In *The Passion of New Eve*, Carter uses pornographic conventions to rewrite archetypical representations of Woman as Mother, Nature, Biblical Eve, sex symbol or screen icon, profane whore, and sacred virgin, as well as the sources of these archetypes (e.g. psychoanalysis, religion, Hollywood). As Nicole Ward Jouve remarks, Carter perceived these incarnations of womanhood as mere stage machinery: "She finds ropes and pulleys, props, make-up, dye, sequins, where others saw gods, virgin mothers, stars, and angels" (158). Jouve's reference to theatricality is an important one, for if these paradigmatic figures of femininity are revealed to be performances or artifice, then those performances can be changed.[26]

An early scene in *New Eve* imports narrative elements from a clichéd

pornographic pursuit scene.[27] Leilah, an exotic dancer dressed in fetishis-
tic heels and crotchless panties, leads Evelyn, a young English misogynist
newly arrived in America, on an erotic chase through a near-future New
York immersed in dystopian chaos. In a graphic sexual depiction, Carter
parodies pornographic language, critiquing the essentialism of pornography which symbolically reduces people to genitalia. When Evelyn and
Leilah are at the climax of their pursuit, Evelyn comments:

> All my existence was now gone away into my tumescence; I was nothing
> but cock and I dropped down upon her like, I suppose, a bird of prey,
> although my prey, throughout the pursuit, had played the hunter. My
> full-fleshed and voracious beak tore open the poisoned wound of love
> between her thighs [25].

There is a heightened quality to the language here that imitates (albeit at
a more sophisticated level than most) pornographic literature. Perhaps the
most recognizable language convention of pornographic literature, whether
of the "lowbrow" or "highbrow" variety, is to substitute a variety of metaphors for parts of the body. Here Carter does the same, but with metaphors
that draw attention to the dehumanizing facets of a sexual act in which
the participants are playing out a violent sexist fantasy. The aggressive-
ness of the language Evelyn employs to narrate the event reveals a mind
dominated by an association of sex and violence: thus, he *tears* into her
voraciously. Evelyn's violent desire deforms both of them so that, for that
moment, they *become* the metaphors used to describe them. They have
become grotesque, inhuman: he is a "bird of prey" whose human body is
gone, leaving only his penis depicted as a vicious animal—a "cock" in two
senses; and she is reduced to a "poisoned wound," echoing the myth of
God's blood vengeance on Eve.[28]

The fact that Leilah initiates this pursuit and encourages it by drop-
ping her dress and then her underwear for Evelyn to pick up at first seems
problematic for reading this scene as critical of rather than complicit with
sexist representations. On the one hand, her initiation of sex in this instance
and others indicates a strong sexual autonomy. On the other hand, she
seems trapped in a view of herself as a sexual object—a view perpetuated
by the sex work she performs.

Her status as an object is evident in her nightly ritualistic cosmetic
preparations. Standing before a mirror, she creates the "edifice" (29) of
her femininity from a vast "assemblage of [...] paraphernalia that only
emphasized the black plush flanks and crimson slit beneath" (30). Leilah
paints both her face and body, reifying a male libidinal fantasy—the archetypical porn model who exists solely for a man's pleasure and is cosmet-

ically enhanced and posed to draw attention to her genitalia. She conforms to the conventional portrayal of women in heterosexual, androcentric pornography and becomes, in Luce Irigaray's comparable terms, an "obliging prop for the enactment of man's fantasies" (25). Irigaray elaborates on this by arguing, as Carter might, that women's bodies are commodities which must conform to social expectations: "Participation in society requires that the [female] body submit itself to a specularization [...] that transforms it into [...] a 'likeness' with reference to an authoritative model" (179–80). In this case, Leilah imitates the "authoritative model" of the porn icon. Thus, when Evelyn comments that he "never knew a girl more a slave to style" (*PNE* 31), he may mean to be hyperbolic, but he is in fact merely stating it as it is. Leilah is literally enslaved to style: she is meticulous about embodying male pornographic fantasies, and the image of herself as an object in the mirror holds her captive. The fact that she is black further emphasizes her position as an exotic, enthralled woman.

Despite this, Leilah cannot be viewed solely as a victim of pornography and prostitution. She is not entirely the "born victim" that Evelyn perceives her to be (28). By leading the chase, Leilah presents herself as a sexual subject. Similarly, Leilah later exhibits aggressive sexual agency: "she would clamber on top of me [...] and *thrust* my limp cock inside herself. [...] Waking just before she *tore* the orgasm from me, I would [...] remember the myth of the succubus" (27, my emphases). Here Carter, like Sade, affirms women's right to "fuck"—that is, to be sexual agents and consequently to exercise power. But Carter goes on to suggest that in a male-dominated world there is inevitably a price that women have to pay for exercising sexual autonomy: the climax of the pursuit scene is described as a brutal domination of Leilah by Evelyn and, subsequently, Evelyn punishes Leilah regularly by tying her to the bed and beating her with a belt. They play out a cycle of sadomasochistic power reversals in which Leilah exhibits sexual desire and initiative and Evelyn punishes her, presumably for transgressing traditional sexual roles.

Thus, although Leilah exhibits some sexual agency, she is not a "Sadeian Woman" such as Juliette. Her acts of sexual aggression meet with violent, misogynist retaliation in which Evelyn re-establishes his dominance by beating and penetrating her. Ultimately, Leilah remains trapped in the role of sexual object—"the woman watching herself being watched" (30)—prescribed by the pornographic archetype of womanhood. At this stage of the story, Leilah is more Justine than Juliette, though later she reappears radically transformed and empowered.

It would be naive to read this portrayal of Leilah as somehow merely replicating the power inequities represented in the bulk of pornography.[29]

Carter's writing is highly self-conscious and ironic in such a way that it is perpetually commenting on the nature of the sexual relations being depicted. And if there is any doubt as to the critical thrust of Carter's writing, it quickly becomes evident that Evelyn's mistreatment of Leilah is to be severely paid for: he himself is to become the subject of all the abuses (and more) which he has previously been the instigator of.

This reversal begins in "Beulah," a womb-like underground city housing a women's resistance group, where Evelyn is forcefully castrated, surgically sex-changed, and subsequently re-programmed as a woman complete with a "maternal impulse." On the run from Leilah after she has a nearly fatal encounter with a back-alley abortionist, he is captured in the desert and presented to "Mother," the matriarch of the women's group. Mother is one of Carter's most brilliant grotesque figures. She has surgically altered herself to incarnate a mythic and *deformed* notion of motherhood. Described in gargantuan terms, Mother is "a sacred monster [...] personified and self-fulfilling fertility. [...] [B]reasted like a sow—she possessed two tiers of nipples. [...] Her ponderous feet were heavy enough to serve as illustrations for gravity" (59). Carter emphasizes the grotesqueness and artificiality of Mother in part to draw attention to the artificiality of the figure she replaces—the traditional white male, patriarchal, bearded, and vengeful god of Judaism and Christianity. Of course, Carter is not actually trying to write a new theology. Mother is an ironic figure who represents a warning against the dangers of merely inverting patriarchal myths, a point Carter makes explicit in *The Sadeian Woman* when she declares that "Mother goddesses are just as silly a notion as father gods" (5).

Mother, then, is a parody of the maternal archetype and how warped the *concept* of motherhood has become, not only in androcentric discourses like psychoanalysis, but in some feminist circles. Reclaiming the maternal archetype as the primary emblem for women's political emancipation, Carter believes, is a particularly seductive impulse since it does represent the major biological function that men can never perform but have sought to regulate throughout history. But, warns Carter,

> The theory of maternal superiority is one of the most damaging of all
> consolatory fictions and women themselves cannot leave it alone,
> although it springs from the timeless, placeless, fantasy land of arche-
> types where all the embodiments of biological supremacy live. It puts
> those women who wholeheartedly subscribe to it in voluntary exile from
> the historic world, this world [...] where actions achieve effects and my
> fertility is governed by my diet, the age at which I reached puberty, my
> bodily juices, my decisions—not by benevolent magics [SW 106–7].

Carter's comments here are aimed at sacralized fantasies of a protective, conciliatory, "all-affirming" mother such as those offered by Cixous and Kristeva.[30] Mother in *New Eve* is more akin to Carter's description of Sade's Durand: "she is the omnipotent mother of early childhood who gave and withheld love and nourishment at whim. [...] The cruel mother, huge as a giantess, the punishment giver, the one who makes you cry" (*SW* 114). Mother, like Durand, represents an "anti-myth of mothering" (113), a "phallic mother." In one scene which showcases Carter at her most jubilantly parodic, Mother declares "I am the Great Parricide, I am the Castratrix of the Phallocentric Universe" (*PNE* 67).

Hyperbolic pronouncements like this one, coupled with the grotesque presentation of Mother, make it apparent that Carter is also targeting Freud, who promoted many of the most problematic myths regarding sexuality and gender roles. Freud's notion of the Oedipal Complex, especially, is one of the most influential narratives about "normal" and "deviant" sexuality in modern history. Carter rewrites this archetypical tale of incest, changing its genre from tragedy to outrageous comedy, in order to parody some of the more androcentric facets of psychoanalysis and undermine the authority of psychoanalysis by calling attention to its foundations in literary motifs. Against a background of women chanting the names of female deities and mythic figures, Evelyn is raped by Mother and so forced to re-enact the Oedipal transgression. Sophia, one of his captors, adjures him:

> "Kill your father! Sleep with your mother! Burst through all the interdictions!" [...]
> "Reintegrate the primal form!" she urged me.
> "Reintegrate the primal form!" shrieked Mother.[...]
> I caught one glimpse of her gaping vagina as I went down; it looked like the crater of a volcano on the point of eruption. [...] Then her Virginia-smoked ham of a fist grasped my shrinking sex; when it went all the way in, Mother howled and so did I.
> So I was unceremoniously raped [64].

The massive irony of the last line (with a chorus chanting in the background, what could be more "ceremonious"?) calls attention to the ritualistic elements in this passage, highlighting the fact that the inhabitants of Beulah have incorporated motifs from psychoanalytic theory into their theology. The voguish uses of psychoanalysis by many feminist theorists is clearly something Carter is suspicious of, and so the aggressively hyperbolic language of the passage (such as the entreaties to "Reintegrate the primal form!") ridicules this trend. Mother inverts psychoanalytic themes to put the power in women's hands: Evelyn's "shrinking" penis is divested of all the symbolic power attributed to it in psychoanalysis while Mother's "gaping" vagina is "erupting" with power. But the sexual inequalities which are evident throughout Freudian theory remain. That patriarchy should be replaced by matriarchy is, as Carter suggests, a "consolatory nonsense." So Carter desacralizes the fantasy of a matriarchal god by dramatizing its consequences in the form of an extended joke in which the maternal figure is grotesquely misshapen and merely attempts to rewrite psychoanalytic motifs to her own advantage.

Mother also falls prey to inverting androcentric ideals when she attempts to rewrite Old Testament mythology by "trimming" Evelyn to Eve. Evelyn's body becomes the text on which Mother will inscribe a new story. He is in part to be reconstructed as a new Virgin Mary archetype; that is, he is to be impregnated with his own sperm to produce the "Messiah" of a new matriarchal world order to overthrow the old patriarchal one. Mother's mistake, however, is that by constructing a "New Eve" she is doing nothing more than re-creating the original archetype of the patriarchal Old Testament myth. She does not "subvert" the dominant paradigm; she merely attempts to invert it.

Mother plays even more readily into sexist gender values when she resorts to androcentric images of maternity and femininity to "program" Eve with a new feminine, maternal subjectivity. Eve is exposed to Hollywood movies featuring Tristessa—a female screen icon reminiscent of Marilyn Monroe (whom Evelyn fixated on as an adolescent), Western European portraits of the Virgin and Child, slides of suckling mammals and "non-phallic imagery such as sea-anemones opening and closing," and audio tapes of gurgling babies and contented mothers (*PNE* 72).[31] It is also critically important that Eve's body is constructed to fit "the physical nature of an ideal woman drawn from a protracted study of the media" (78). Eve assesses her new self in the mirror: "They had turned me into the *Playboy* centerfold. I was the object of all the unfocused desires that had ever existed in my own head" (75). Like Leilah, she has become a pornographic archetype—a "woman watching herself being watched" (30). Ironically, however, she still possesses a man's libidinal mindset, causing the "cock in [her] head" to "[twitch] at the sight of" herself (75). This hilarious observation heightens our awareness of the artificiality of pornographic icons: Eve's new archetypical physique is as much an artifice—as much a generic convention—as that of the porn centerfold, a theatricality whose effect and coherence depend on lighting, make-up, set, positioning, air-brushing, and other illusionary techniques. And it produces the expected, programmed effect: arousal for the male viewer.

It might seem that Mother's strategy is akin to that of a postmodern writer. Eve is the product of a "bricolage" of myths derived from psychoanalysis, Old and New Testament scripture, pornography, and Hollywood film. Mother takes motifs from these sources and attempts to rewrite them from a feminist perspective to give women the power. But she fails because she is still drawing on and therefore validating androcentric source material. She creates a fundamentalist religion out of her version of feminism, but this is hardly a victory for sexual equality. Her failure is deliberate, however, for it is Mother and her fanatical attempt to rewrite patriarchy as matriarchy that is the target of Carter's ridicule in this section of the novel. Carter's parody desacralizes systems of social organization based on sexual inequality whether they are androcentric or gynocentric. As an alternative to Mother's inversion of patriarchy, Carter will eventually lead us towards imagining a world without gender hierarchies.

Carter shifts her focus to critique a masculine archetype when, after an escape from Beulah, Eve is captured by the mad "poet" Zero, initiated into her womanhood by being raped, and made one of his harem of wives. A foil for Mother, Zero is a one-eyed, one-legged desert patriarch—in essence, a personified penis—who has convinced his harem that his sexual attentions are necessary for their continued health. His wives are reduced to unindividuated combatants for equal access to his "elixium vitae" (92)—i.e. his semen. Sex with Zero, then, is literally the means of their subordination. Again, the scenario draws on and refers to the tropes of pornography: Carter depicts Zero's wives as masochistic sex objects—willing, submissive, "wanting it," even "needing it"; they are archetypical figures of heterosexual, androcentric pornography. They accept Zero unquestioningly as a godhead, and, as with Mother's Beulah, their community is a kind of fundamentalist cult—in this case structured as an androcentric pornotopia. And Carter does not shy away from critiquing the link between some pornographic ideas and physical violence: Zero's wives are the object of much physical abuse, including having had their front teeth knocked out to prevent nicks to Zero's penis while performing oral sex. This pornotopia, then, is maintained by a violent enslavement and Carter's emphasis on this highlights the link between sexual/physical cruelty and male social dominance.

Zero not only physically abuses his wives but he deprives them of the capacity to communicate. Describing the linguistic order of this micropatriarchy, Eve tells us that Zero

> would bark, or grunt, or squeak, or mew at us because he only used the language of the animals towards his wives. [...] [H]e would savage [...]

offender[s] unmercifully with his bullwhip. So our first words every morning were spoken in a language we ourselves could not understand; but he could. Or so he claimed, and, because he ruled the roost and his word was law, it came to the same thing [96–7].

Zero speaks a different language, a language that imitates the sounds of animals and so automatically degrades those to whom it is directed—his wives. By forcing them to use it, despite their incapacity to understand it or express meaning in it, Zero reinforces their status as animals rather than people. Zero's wives (including Eve) produce meaning by uttering signifying noises but they have no access to that meaning themselves and so must resort to whispering to each other in secret, afraid of being detected and punished for transgressing Zero's law. Here again Carter's fictional society makes explicit the radically unequal distribution of power among men and women. Luce Irigaray suggests that access (or lack thereof) to language—the means of signification—is a key factor in the social gender power imbalance: "Women, animals endowed with speech like men, assure the possibility of the use and circulation of the symbolic without being recipients of it. Their nonaccess to the symbolic is what has established the social order" (189).[32] Irigaray's comments suggest that Zero's power is predicated on his ability to exclude his harem from speech. Without language, there can be no autonomy of thought or action: they remain enslaved and utterly dependent on him. In her essay "Notes From the Front Line," Carter suggests that language itself is androcentric and leads women, including herself, to unconsciously "posit a male point of view as a general one" (71). Language, she writes, "is power, life and the instrument of culture, the instrument of domination and liberation" (77). It is for this reason, she asserts, that "it is so enormously important for women to write fiction *as* women—it is part of the slow process of decolonialising our language and our basic habits of thought" (75).

Just as Zero denies his wives the capacity to communicate anything that might express individuality, he denies them individuality in appearance: their behavior, their hair, and their dress—either naked except for dungarees or, for ritual poetry recitations, "dressed up, or undressed, in the style of high pornography" (*PNE* 103)—are all identical, all designed to meet Zero's desire. Similarly, their backgrounds are expeditiously summarized as that of archetypically abused women: "All the girls had the same dreary biographies; broken homes, remand homes, parole officers, maternal deprivation, inadequate father figures, drugs, pimps, bad news. They were case histories, rather than women" (99). Eve mimics the experience of these women by fabricating an autobiography that conforms to the conventions of such "case histories": "a cruel mother who kept me locked in the coal-shed, a lustful step-father" (87). Disguising herself with this narrative, Eve becomes a kind of undercover chronicler of their experience.

Eve's sexual interactions with Zero put her on the receiving end of the violence she (as Evelyn) enacted on Leilah. Sex with Zero is brutal and violent, described in metaphors allusive of Sade: "I was in no way prepared for the pain; his body was an anonymous instrument of torture, mine my own rack. [...] He entered me like the vandals attacking Rome" (88, 91). After raping her a second time, Zero announces that she is now his eighth wife, forcing Eve into a situation tantamount to Sade's Justine— the virgin archetype made unwilling whore.[33] The sexual abuse Eve suffers at Zero's hands completes her programming as a "woman": "Zero turned me into a woman. More. His peremptory prick turned me into a savage woman" (107–8). The implication here is that to be a woman is to be the object of male sexual violence. Thus, Carter draws attention to the problem of sexual violence—either in the "real" world or in representations of women such as those of pornography—as a factor often contributing to the development of women's personhood.

With an exuberant lack of subtlety, Carter mocks the patriarchal archetype by naming its one-eyed, one-legged embodiment "Zero," drawing attention to his infertility and symbolic impotence. Zero attributes his infertility to Carter's fictional screen icon, Tristessa. Tristessa—a Marilyn Monroe–style actress who is famous for her masochistic depictions of Madeline Usher, Desdemona, and Catherine Earnshaw—is portrayed as a descendent of Sade's Justine, the "mythically suffering blonde" (*SW* 102). Combining the appeal of sex symbol and female masochist, she is another incarnation of male sexual fantasies. In Tristessa, Carter finds a potent image for the problematic link between male desire and female suffering—a link perpetuated in pornography and Hollywood cinema. For Evelyn especially, Tristessa was yet another pornographic archetype, the object of his sadistic sexual fantasies: as a youth he "dreamed of meeting Tristessa, she stark naked, tied, perhaps to a tree in a midnight forest under the wheeling stars" (7); and even the night before he arrives in New York he goes to see an old film of *Wuthering Heights* and, moved by the spectacle of Tristessa's suffering as Catherine Earnshaw, pays her "a little tribute of spermatazoa" (5). In Zero's monomaniacal imagination, however, this archetypal object of the "male gaze" bites back: Tristessa transcends the cinema screen and "her eyes [consume] him in a ghastly epiphany" (104). The "male gaze" which, in Laura Mulvey's discussion of cinema, tends to view women as passive sexual objects (19) is turned with searing effect back at the gazer, thwarting one of the traditional functions of this genre of film—to titil-late male viewers with the spectacle of female suffering.

Given new insight by her trans-gendered status, Eve becomes a per-ceptive reader of such genre conventions. She gains a critical distance from her previous position as a male consumer of female masochistic images and notes that, like the porn model whose personhood or self "is reduced to its formal [sexual/genital] elements" (*SW* 4), Tristessa has "no ontologi-cal status; only an iconographic one" (*PNE* 129). A "high-class" version of Leilah, Tristessa employs the theatrical tools of artifice (i.e. cosmetics and costumery) in conjunction with her characteristic display of maso-chism to simulate a masculine ideal of femininity. This artifice is literally torn away when Zero cuts through her g-string to reveal that Tristessa is a man in drag. It is one of the more dramatic, humorous, and critically incisive moments in Carter's fiction. Tristessa's artifice flouts hetero-nor-mative, androcentric gender norms: this idealized incarnation of "femi-ninity" is revealed to be a theatrical illusion, one which fools heterosexual men into betraying the sexual orientation that is so critical to their self-identity.

Carter's revelation of Tristessa's transvestitism again dramatizes her idea of gender as artifice and performance. Alterations to the surface of the body produce what is assumed to be a universal essence—femininity or masculinity—but this scene asks us to question the relation between appearance and essence. Judith Butler put it into theoretical terms years after Carter dramatized it: "Just as bodily surfaces are enacted *as* the nat-ural, so these surfaces can become the site of a [...] denaturalized perform-ance that reveals the performative status of the natural itself" (146). Tristessa's revelation results in exactly the kind of "denaturalizing" effect that Butler imagines: the "loss of gender norms [...] depriv[es] the nat-uralizing narratives of compulsory heterosexuality of their central protag-onists: 'man' and 'woman'" (146). In other words, Carter purposefully departs from narrative conventions which clearly delineate and maintain masculinity and femininity as discrete concepts defined in opposition to each other. With the explicit examples of Leilah, Tristessa, and Eve *per-forming* gender, Carter, pre-dating Butler's idea that gender performances are a compulsory facet of human behavior, demonstrates that gender is an "act."[34]

Although the gender transgressions of Carter's characters, like those of Winterson's, challenge traditional concepts of "masculinity" and "fem-ininity," the effects of androcentric norms are still evident: Eve, Leilah, and Tristessa all play the role of "Woman" according to a set of dominant cultural expectations, and the common defining feature of their experience as women is suffering. Thus, Eve comes to the realization that "femininity" is an amalgamation of male-authored conventions to which women feel compelled to conform throughout their lives: "although I was a woman, I was now also passing for a woman, but, then, many women born spend their whole lives in just such imitations" (*PNE* 101). But Carter's female characters, especially in her later work, do not remain in such confining roles. Like Winterson's female protagonists, they set out on their own, determine their own destinies, and defy social expectations.

Eve's ability to "read" or interpret and demystify gender increases as she gains experience. A particularly significant experience is her sexual union with Tristessa. Having escaped from Zero, Tristessa and Eve form a transgressive figure which defies the norms and categories of heterosexist society: "I know who we are," says Eve, "we are Tiresias. [...] [O]ut of these fathomless kisses and our interpenetrating, undifferentiated sex, we had made the great Platonic hermaphrodite together, the whole and perfect being" (*PNE* 146, 148). As Tiresias—the blind prophet of Greek myth who illicitly obtained knowledge of male *and* female sexuality—Eve and Tristessa represent a synthesis of polar modes of being: "masculine" (phallic) and "feminine" or aggressive and submissive. Carter is not literally proposing that hermaphroditism is a prerequisite for liberated sexuality; she is presenting a fantasy image of a sexual union in which the participants have transcended the limiting gender values that pervade our theistic, androcentric world. The transcendence of this moment gestures towards hope, a hope that Carter finds lacking in Sade's transgressive writings (*SW* 129). But the legend of Tiresias' blinding (whether by Athene because he saw her bathing or by Hera because he sided with Zeus on the question of whether men or women derive more pleasure from love) foreshadows a necessary fall from their utopian union. Like Tiresias, they must be punished for having obtained a forbidden knowledge of sexuality and pleasure. The transcendental moment is checked by a starker social reality when an ad hoc militia of fundamentalist Christian boys tear them apart and execute Tristessa. The fact that these boys are Christian fundamentalists further implicates religion as a damaging source of intolerance with regards to human diversity, as we've already seen in the fiction and lives of Rushdie and Winterson.

While Eve and Tristessa are together, however, another important critique of gender takes place. They both abandon the performance of masculinity and femininity and Eve's experience of sexual pleasure precipitates an epiphany regarding the arbitrariness of gender: "Masculine and feminine are correlatives which involve one another. I am sure of that—the quality and its negation are locked in necessity. But what the nature of the masculine and the nature of feminine might be, whether they involve male and female [...] that I do not know" (*PNE* 149–50). In a sense, this sums up the point of all of this novel's sexually explicit depictions: to express skepticism about the presumed link between biology and gender. Seventies' feminism, like feminism today, was in part divided by the debate over whether gender is the product of "nature" or "nurture." Carter is careful in the above passage not to completely dismiss a possible connection between the gender and innate, biological factors, but it is clear that she repudiates the once-dominant notion that biology is entirely responsible for how gender is expressed in human society. This matter requires further investigation on a number of disciplinary fronts, but one of Carter's main objectives with her "moral pornography" is to promote the idea that a variety of social and cultural factors contribute significantly, and perhaps entirely, to the determination of gender traits: gender is a learned behavior and an artifice. To understand this point of view creates the possibility for change in received gender roles and relations between men and women, and it has the potential to benefit humanity as a whole by enabling both women and men to participate in society in ways that were previously deemed taboo.

The finale of the novel reunites Eve with Leilah who is now part of the women's resistance and (significantly) calling herself Lilith.[35] She gives Eve the news that "Mother has voluntarily resigned from the god-head" and "retired to a cave by the sea for the duration of the hostilities" (174). With a masterstroke of comic irony, Carter confines Mother to a "cave beyond consciousness" (184)—the mystical womb central to Freudian psychoanalysis and its later feminist revisions. The goddess, if not dead, as Carter wishes in *The Sadeian Woman*, is at least in hibernation. Desacralizing myths of deities, heaven, and eternity is fundamental to Carter's objectives:

> with the imaginary construct of the goddess, dies the notion of eternity, whose place on this earth was her womb. [...] There is no way out of time. We must learn to live in this world [...] because it is the only world we will ever know. [...] I think this is why so many people find the idea of the emancipation of women frightening. It represents the final secularisation of mankind [*SW* 110].

Whereas Rushdie, Barnes, and Winterson are, like Carter, deeply critical of religion in their fiction, only Carter boldly announces her desire to see an atheistic world. To entirely give up our religious myths, Carter suggests, would mean giving up once and for all the institutions that uphold male social dominance. It is for this reason that Carter is relentless in her attack on religious and pseudo-religious figures. Nicole Ward Jouve writes that in *New Eve* Carter "hunted the [maternal] archetype down to extinction" (157). It is a dramatic assessment which gets at the root of what Carter is attempting in all of her writings: to eradicate myths and archetypes which define social roles and limit human potential by attributing essential qualities to people based upon their gender.[36] Like Sade's libertines, Carter cries "nonsense!" (*SW* 76) in the face of received social and religious values.

Along with Mother, the rest of the archetypes have become redundant, as Lilith/Leilah notes:

> when there was a consensus agreement on the nature of the symbolic manifestations of the spirit, no doubt Divine Virgins, Sacred Harlots and Virgin Mothers served a useful function; but the gods are all dead, there's a good deal of redundancy in the spirit world [*PNE* 175].

Nowhere is the desacralizing thrust of Carter's fiction more explicit. Carter speculates that dispensing with this pantheon of deified archetypes would result in a liberatory social destabilization: Eve and Lilith arrive at an apocalyptic California riven by a civil war that has destroyed Hollywood, the most influential source of American myths. The old society is being torn down, presenting revolutionary opportunities not just for women but for Blacks and other disempowered freedom-fighting groups as well.

By the seacoast they encounter a mad old woman sitting in a wicker chair. Her face is "magnificently painted" (177) and she is burlesquely costumed in a two-piece bathing suit, stole, and high-heeled sandals. The burlesque aspects of her appearance again suggest a pornographic and performative embodiment of femininity. With her theatrically heavy make-up and costume, Carter depicts her as an old performance artist— the quintessential performer of femininity—in her twilight. The artifice of femininity remains, but the overall effect is eroded as the decaying underside shows through: her face is dirty, "her flesh [...] wrinkled and ravaged and sagged from her bones," and the polish on her six-inch fingernails is "badly chipped and scratched" (177). The garishness of her appearance augurs the dying days of this constraining version of femininity.

Looking at this decaying archetypical figure, Eve asks herself, "how would the old ones fare, in the post-apocalyptic world?" (178). In Carter's scenario, the apocalypse constitutes the end of one iconography or set of expectations for the performance of gender and the birth of another, formerly repressed one: Lilith and Tiresias—irreverent, disobedient, and marginal figures in myth—will ascend to central positions in the new order. Having found both sexes so constricted by archetypal expectations, Carter's protagonist transcends the limits of gender and is reborn, expelled from Mother's womb-like cave by the seashore as the "apotheosis of Tiresias" (186). Carter is hostile to myth as we know it but ironically delights in scripting new mythologies by salvaging marginal mythic figures like Tiresias. As an incarnation of Tiresias, *New* Eve manifests a new kind of liberated personhood or subjectivity which combines the knowledge of what it is to be male and female. Prefiguring Barnes's Kath Ferris in *A History of the World* and Winterson's coterie of women rebels in *Boating for Beginners*, Eve sets sail in a small boat with her unborn child (conceived in the desert with Tristessa) to begin a new world. Though formed from a melting pot of female archetypes, Eve emerges as a radically new and socially disruptive icon—a deviant from what is widely considered to be "natural"—and heralds a "new" era.

The Uses of Pornography

Linda Williams, who defines genre as a problem-solving technique,[37] asserts that male-authored heterosexual

> pornography is a speculation about pleasure that begins, as does Tiresias, from a phallic perspective, journeys to the unseen world of the sexual other, and returns to tell the story. An ideal of bisexuality drives the quest for the knowledge of the pleasure of the other: that one sex can journey to the unknown other and return, satiated with knowledge and pleasure, to the security of the "self" [279].

The Passion of New Eve follows this path but not with the purpose of uncovering the "secrets" of female pleasure for the male reader. It begins from Evelyn's "phallic"/male perspective and journeys to a female perspective to tell a story not principally of pleasure (though there is an important moment of this with Tristessa) but of pain. "Moral pornography" represents a conceptual change in pornography as a genre. It is not a fantasy depiction of women performing sex for the titillation of male viewers or readers; instead, it is aimed at demonstrating the real problems of life as a woman in a male-dominated society and culture. And for Eve/lyn, importantly, there is no return to the "security" of masculinity.

Williams also notes that "Pornography as a genre wants to be about sex. On close inspections, however, it always proves to be more about gender" (267). This is the assumption that underlies Carter's concept of moral pornography. Her fiction purposefully employs the conventions of pornographic literature to critique traditional ideas about gender. One by

one, Carter evokes, rewrites, and so dispenses with the old gender archetypes: "Mother" retires to a "cave beyond consciousness" and expels New
Eve from that haven, Leilah is reborn as Lilith, and Zero is nullified. *The
Passion of New Eve* dramatizes an apocalyptic end for many of the myths
related to gender which have historically limited human, especially women's,
potential.

Speculative-Fiction and the Gothic

I have not yet explicitly drawn attention to Carter's use of conventions drawn from speculative-fiction[38] and gothic fiction, though these are
evident in *The Bloody Chamber*, *The Passion of New Eve*, and other works.
Until the 1970s, speculative or science fiction, in both its pulp and more
"mainstream" manifestations, was almost exclusively a male-authored
and notoriously sexist genre, often merely replicating the fairy tale paradigm of man as heroic savior and woman as helpless damsel-in-distress.
Although Charlotte Perkins Gilman's *Herland* (1915), which depicts a
utopian world inhabited solely by women, set an important precedent for
feminist uses of speculative-fiction,[39] and although a few women wrote
science fiction under pseudonyms (for example, C. L. Moore) during the
1930s–1960s era of popular pulp science fiction, it was not until the late
sixties and early seventies that a significant number of women writers began
to adopt conventions from science fiction, fantasy, and dystopian fiction
to portray the experiences of women in androcentric society. According
to Sarah Lefanu, women writers finally turned to speculative-fiction because
of its capacity to make readers examine the "social and sexual hierarchies
of the contemporary world [...] through the process of 'estrangement,'
thus challenging normative ideas of gender roles" (21–22).

As with fairy tales (which are related to other fantasy sub-genres),
women writers including Doris Lessing, Alice Sheldon (a.k.a. James Tiptree, Jr.), Margaret Atwood, Suzy McKee Charnas, Ursula Le Guin, Joanna
Russ, Marge Piercy, and Angela Carter took a genre that was traditionally
dominated by male writers and characterized by sexist tropes, and made
it work for feminist ends.[40] Today, writers like Octavia Butler, Pamela Sargent, Ursula Le Guin, Lisa Tuttle, Sheri Tepper, Pat Cadigan, Suzette Elgin,
Fay Weldon, and Candas Jane Dorsey are producing the most topical and
exciting work in the genre.[41] Carter was one of the pioneers in this feminist adoption of speculative-fiction; her work in this genre, which helped
pave the way for these other writers,[42] is primarily dystopian. *The Passion
of New Eve*—set in a near-future of chaos and social disintegration—was

actually her final dystopian work. It was preceded by *The Infernal Desire Machines of Doctor Hoffman* in 1972 and *Heroes and Villains* in 1969.

Heroes and Villains, a novel which mixes genre conventions from post-apocalyptic dystopian fiction, fairy tales, and the gothic is one of Carter's darker looks at myth, gender relations, and human social structure. By the time it was published, the post-apocalyptic dystopia was a well-established and popular sub-genre of speculative-fiction.[43] In the years following World War II, writers generally employed the post-apocalyptic genre to protest the threat of nuclear Armageddon and articulate fears fed by historical crises like Hiroshima, the Cold War, and the Bay of Pigs.[44] But the post-apocalyptic tale is also well-suited to exploring the myths and institutions which uphold human social structure. For example, although Carter's *Heroes and Villains* arises out of the global anxieties of the fifties and sixties Cold War era, it is not primarily a warning tale against Armageddon. Rather, its focus is on speculating what shape society might take if given the chance to reinvent itself.

It is this kind of speculative flexibility that has made dystopian fiction (and speculative-fiction more widely) so appealing to many contemporary women writers. Margaret Atwood's *The Handmaid's Tale*, for example, responds to the abortion debates and the rise of the Moral Majority in the 1980s, protesting the threat to women's right to control their own bodies by dramatizing a scenario in which women's lack of control is integral to the political, familial, and religious structures of society. The dystopian society depicted by Atwood is a fundamentalist, totalitarian one. Like virtually all fundamentalist communities, it is a male-dominated one, and Atwood's novel expresses outrage at the presumption of men who would dictate what women can do with their bodies.

Heroes and Villains shares similar concerns about potential future manifestations of fundamentalism and totalitarianism. Set in a hypothetical post-nuclear-war future, human society is segregated into three groups: the rationalistic Professors who live in walled and guarded agricultural communities; the nomadic Barbarians who inhabit the forests and raid the Professors' communities for resources; and the Out People—aggressive, mutated victims of the nuclear holocaust. This post-apocalyptic social setting provides a stage for an investigation of the myths that bind social groups.

Carter's interest in fairy tales is evident even in this early work. Marianne, the protagonist, is the daughter of a Professor of History. From the beginning, Carter portrays her as a rebellious child who lacks decorum. Her nurse attempts to coax her into behaving properly with frightening tidbits of mythic lore characteristic of fairy tales: "If you're not a good little girl, the Barbarians will eat you. [...] They wrap little girls in clay [...] bake them in the fire and gobble them up with salt. They relish tender little girls" (*HV* 2). But Marianne fails to be "good" and her nurse locks her away in a "white tower" for "bothering and pestering everybody, stealing scraps of uncooked dough and [...] indulging her spitefulness" (3). From the tower, she watches helplessly as a tribe of Barbarians raid her community and a Barbarian boy kills her brother in hand-to-hand combat.

Like the archetypical fairy tale heroine, Marianne is confined by physical strictures: a garrisoned town wall, an austere tower, and—that convention most typical of fairy tales—a treacherous forest. Unlike naive Little Red Riding Hood or Hansel and Gretel, however, she is savvy to the forest's dangers:

> She learned to beware of the ugly plants covered with razor-sharp thorns [...] and never even to touch the green and purple berries swarming with iridescent flies [...] for the noxious sap burned the fingers. She knew how brambles sometimes masked the mouths of bottomless vents in the ground [7–8].

No passive fairy tale heroine, Marianne ventures the ruins of a city destroyed in the war, and when she is sixteen she flees the Professors' community. Ten years after her brother's death, when the same group of Barbarians attack, she helps one of them to escape and joins their tribe.

The Professors' society is characterized by a predominance of academic discourses that preach restraint, repression, and Enlightenment rationality. The Professors, who appear to be exclusively men, possess an abundance of discourses to taxonomize and analyze information, but they are themselves drab, lifeless, cold, and clinical. Typical of postmodern literature, this novel negatively portrays the Enlightenment ideals embraced by their overly rationalistic society. The Professors have lost any connection they once may have had with the living world. They have sunk into stasis and become mere museum keepers for ideas and branches of study no longer applicable in the post-apocalyptic world. When asked about the novel during a videotaped interview with Lisa Appignanesi, Carter commented that "The people who are sitting there in their bunkers are the ones whose imaginations are too impoverished to imagine what the world is going to be like afterwards."

In portraying the professorial community as so obviously myopic about the world beyond what they can glean from their books, Carter mocks the sterility of the academy (the British academy in particular), an institution which she and many others have perceived to be an exclusive club for middle- and upper-class, white Anglo-Saxon Protestant men. In British university English departments, she has commented,

> Middle-aged men [...] teach WASP texts from a WASP perspective. The books are written on the whole by male white Anglo-Saxon Protestants, and they are taught by them, and they are written for an audience of them. [...] The way that one is taught English literature in Britain leaves out almost everybody in Britain [Goldsworthy 9].

It would not be an unwarranted leap to suggest that Carter views the British academy—at least in its traditional Oxbridge form—as a kind of cult or even fundamentalist institution whose priesthood (the dons) worship the ancient knowledge of male scholars. Their real pedagogical function in passing on this knowledge was/is to perpetuate the British class system by reinforcing the sense of elitist separatism among the university's upper-class male students. *Heroes and Villains* echoes and parodies this tradition. In erecting walls around their community and employing a Soldier class to protect those boundaries (an arrangement evocative of the Oxford and Cambridge campuses which are "policed" by porters), the Professors of *Heroes and Villains* have shut themselves off from the possibility of directly interacting with the world and having new experiences. As a result, they stagnate, grow old and die, or go insane and commit suicide.

In contrast, the Barbarians are colorful, exotic, and fecund. They are adapting to the new world, even if that adaptation takes the form of a "regression" into a tribal, nomadic society. Marianne, who has inherited the detached, analytical attitude held by the Professors, acts as an anthropological emissary and categorizes the social relations in the tribe as she is integrated into the Barbarian community. She finds "evidence of a Barbarian snobbery," noting that Jewel, the man whom she helped escape, is one of the community's aristocrats (40), while she slots Mrs. Green, Jewel's foster mother and another defector from the Professors' community, into the position of "housekeeper or, perhaps, more properly, some kind of domestic matriarch" (43).

With Marianne's defection to the Barbarian community, the novel adopts a number of gothic conventions. Normally, we associate the gothic with enclosed, forbidden places, dungeons, torture-chambers, sexual danger, ghosts, and creatures such as Frankenstein's monster or Count Dracula who defy the laws of nature. Carter made use of all of these conventions, but the real allure of the genre for her was in its parodic, critical potential. She announces her gothic intentions for *Heroes and Villains* with an epigraph taken from Leslie Fielder's *Love and Death in the American Novel*: "The Gothic mode is essentially a form of parody, a way of assailing clichés by exaggerating them to the limit of grotesqueness." In essence, the gothic is a genre about transgressing taboos and therefore has an affinity with postmodern techniques. In Carter's own words, gothic fiction ignores "the value systems of our institutions" and deals "entirely with the profane." Its "characters and events are exaggerated beyond reality, to become symbols, ideas, passions." Its "style will tend to be ornate, unnatural—and thus operate against the perennial human desire to believe the word as fact." The gothic "retains a singular moral function—that of provoking unease" (Afterword, *Fireworks* 122).

Foremost among the anxiety provoking depictions in *Heroes and Villains* is the decaying country mansion which the Barbarians have inhabited. The occupancy of this house—once the symbol of rigid British social hierarchy, aristocratic dominance, and civilité—by the ghoulish Barbarians confronts the middle-class reader with an uncanny image, threatening the securities synonymous with pre-war, imperial, classist Britain. Gothic tales, Chris Baldick writes, offend "classical tastes and rational principles" (xiii). This offense to classical taste is immediately apparent as Marianne tours the sprawling, crumbling mansion. No doubt once the country home of aristocrats, it is being reclaimed by the forest and the Barbarians:

> Wholly abandoned to decay, baroque stonework of the late Jacobean period, Gothic turrets murmurous with birds and pathetic elegance of Palladian pillared façades weathered indiscriminately together towards irreducible rubble. The forest perched upon the tumbled roofs in the shapes of yellow and purple weeds rooted in the gapped tiles, besides a few small trees and bushes. The windows gaped or sprouted internal foliage, as if the forest were as well already camped inside, there gathering strength for a green eruption which would one day burst the walls sky high back to nature. [...] Everywhere she looked there were men, women, children and horses. A few half-naked children sat on the banks of the river and fished. Mangy dogs scavenged in an enormous midden of bones and liquid dung which spread out from the side of the house like a huge stain [*HV* 31–32].

Marianne goes on to witness copious public displays of urination, defecation, vomiting, and sexuality, a stark departure from the contained, controlled, and relatively lifeless community of Professors—the symbolic remnant of a once rationalistic, hierarchical, Enlightenment-inspired British society. The passage above presents a lush image of decay; the language is breath-taking in its ornateness. It is also uncanny, for this house, in its advanced state of deterioration, is a metaphor for the contemporary decline of classical British society, extrapolated into the future. What Britain has built in the name of "civilization," this passage implies, will fall into "Barbarism." As Matthew Arnold predicted, culture will become anarchy. And reason will become unreason, or perhaps Carter's point is that it always has been.

Heroes and Villains dramatizes many of the concerns Carter explicitly addressed later in *The Sadeian Woman*. Foremost among these is her atheistic agenda. The architect of the Barbarian society's cultural codes is Donally, a renegade Professor. Donally is a postmodern/post-apocalyptic version of the menacing figures central to early gothic tales which are "peopled by scheming Franciscan poisoners, depraved abbesses, fearsome Inquisitors, and diabolical murderers [...] plotting against helpless maidens who have been forced against their wills into the hypocrisies of a conventual regime" (Baldick xiv). Whereas his professorial colleagues are content to sit back and passively observe, catalogue, and theorize about things in the world around them, Donally thirsts for activity and feels compelled to put theory into practice. He hypothesizes that "Power is forced to display persuasive force" (*HV* 111),[45] and sets out to use the Barbarians in an "experiment" that could "prove" his theory. To that end, he plots to poison Jewel, his protégé; he keeps his "half-wit" son chained naked to a pole in the middle of the compound; and he kills a little girl by tattooing her with tiger stripes. In addition to these sadistic acts, he disseminates old world myths in the new world. Donally is the tribe's "shaman"; he is storyteller, religious official, and advisor to Jewel, who acts as the tribe's king. He engineers a social collective with the aid of those narratives that have proved most efficacious in the past for establishing power structures, namely religious ones.

The Barbarian community is rife with religious superstition, iconography, and gestures which are mostly derived from Jewish and Christian traditions. Donally fosters this by exhibiting a venomous viper, held in a cage, as a deific symbol of power for the Barbarians to fear. The image of the snake features prominently in another of his creations: on Jewel's back he has tattooed his masterpiece—a portrait of Eve tempting Adam with the apple. Further, when Marianne first arrives at their encampment, Jewel's cousin Annie greets her with superstitious fear, making a gesture to ward off the "evil-eye," a gesture we later learn is the sign of the cross. The rest of the tribe treats Marianne with similar suspicion. Donally, however, welcomes her as the missing figure in the mythos he is trying to script. He calls her "Our lady of the wilderness [...] The Virgin of the Swamp" (50) and wants to cast her as the "holy image" (50) of his new religion. "It seemed to me that the collapse of civilization in the form that intellectuals such as ourselves understood it might be as good a time as any for crafting a new religion," he explains to her. "I still use most of the forms of the Church of England. I find they're infinitely adaptable. Religion is a device for instituting the sense of a privileged group, you understand" (63). This is the kind of self-conscious attempt to desacralize myths and their social functions that Carter later announced in her essay "Notes From the Front Line" was her life's work. Religion is certainly one of the more potent "social fictions that regulate our lives" ("Notes" 70).

The speculative-fiction frame of the novel motivates a metaphysical discussion between Marianne and Donally about the social utility of religion and God: "God died, of course," Donally tells Marianne at one point. "Quite early. Do you think we should resurrect him, do you think we need him in this hypothetical landscape of ruin and forest [...]?" (*HV* 93) "God," Donally implies, is merely a useful tool for social control. By depicting Donally's conscious attempt to institute religion as a pragmatic justification for social hierarchy, Carter desacralizes God and religion in general. Like Mother or Zero, Donally draws on a "bricolage" of sources to invent a religion which is designed to ensure his ongoing hegemony: just as the Professors are a kind of select clergy, Donally fashions himself as the high priest of the religion he institutes among the Barbarians.

Marianne's wedding to Jewel is another element of Donally's plan to solidify his hold on power. It is a gothic piece of theatre meant to bind the community through religious ritual. Marriage is the idealized goal of fairy tales in Perrault's tradition, and it is also the socially sanctioned climax of romance narratives. Its achievement in these genres of fiction instills the ideology that marriage, in which the woman is expected to willingly give up her independence to a man, is the desired end of social maturity. Carter gothicizes the wedding of Marianne and Jewel to parody its cultural significance. From an ancient chest, Mrs. Green uncarths a horrid, decaying wedding dress for Marianne:

> The dress had a satin bodice, now fissured with innumerable fine cracks; long, tight, white sleeves that came to a point over the backs of the hands and an endless skirt of time-yellowed tulle. There was a vast acreage of net veil and a small garland of artificial pearls. Most of the pearl coating had detached itself from the surfaces so they were now only little globes of white glass. [...] Marianne screwed up a handful of the hem and watched the fabric shiver to dust between her fingers. [...] There were shadows of mildew in every fold of the voluminous skirt and all smelled musty and stale [67–68].

Carter expansively describes every decaying facet of the dress to emphasize the limitations for women it represents—limitations Donally plans to reaffirm by forcing Marianne to wear it. Like the crumbling country house, it is an artifact of a past era, an icon of an extinct social order which Donally intends to resurrect in a distorted form. Carter's language aggressively attacks the dress's social significance, comparing it to a dormant plague virus which "might survive for years under the briars of a dead city, nesting invisibly in the contents of just such a Pandora's box as this metal chest" (68). Marianne perceives the dress as a scourge of the past and recoils from it. It becomes, for her, "an image of terror" (68) as she realizes that it was once worn for a proper, "old style" (69) wedding. Hers is to be a perverted mockery of that past ideal.

Donally's goal is to create a dramatic spectacle of magnificent proportions, akin to a fairy tale royal wedding which, along the lines suggested by Benedict Anderson's description of "imagining" a nation, helps to create a cultural unity among the spectators. But if this is a fairy tale wedding of maiden and prince, the post-apocalyptic and gothic context makes all of its components seem anachronistic and grotesque. Not only is Marianne ludicrously arrayed, but so is Jewel:

> Jewel had on a stiff coat of scarlet interwoven with gold thread, perhaps once a bishop's possession; he was as strangely magnificent as an Antediluvian king or a pre–Adamite sultan. [...] He was like a work of art, as if created, not begotten, a fantastic dandy of the void whose true nature had been entirely subsumed to the alien and terrible beauty of a rhetorical gesture. His appearance was abstracted from his body, and he was willfully reduced to sign language. He had become the sign of an idea of a hero; and she herself had been forced to impersonate the sign of a memory of a bride [71–72].

Carter's attention here to the cultural significance of their dress is a typical convention of her fiction. Like New Eve, Leilah, or Tristessa, Jewel and Marianne are "reduced to sign language" through the artifice of their dress. They are abstract ideas of "man" and "woman" or "hero" and "bride" made manifest. In their costumery, both Jewel and Marianne are "rhetorical gesture[s]"—conventions of genres like fairy tales and romance which instill androcentric, bourgeois ideals by marrying the hero to a subservient, virtuous, and virginal bride. But in this instance they are parodies of such bourgeois figures, forced to play these roles to create an impressive spectacle that will solidify Donally's rule. They both abhor the charade, but for Marianne it is particularly repellent as it is an attempt to make her Jewel's property and thereby provide a model for the "proper" gender hierarchy.

Carter uses this opportunity to critique some of the traditional cultural significances of marriage. She views marriage and religion as interrelated social institutions which historically have been damaging, particularly to women. For Carter, marriage, especially as it is presented in genres like fairy tale and romance, is traditionally an obstacle to women's independence—financial, sexual, and otherwise (*SW* 59). The marriage of Marianne and Jewel is a parody of bourgeois ideals embodied in such fictions. In the idealized tale, the story ends with the "happily ever after" convention once hero and heroine are united. This tale concludes differently. Like New Eve, Marianne is forced to play an archetypical "feminine" role—the virginal bride. Though outwardly she complies, internally she remains defiant and plans her rebellion: she assumes the stance of a "mute, furious doll which allow[s] itself to be totally engulfed," but "her ruling passion [is] always anger rather than fear" (*HV* 69). Although she plays the part of "mute [...] doll" for the ceremony, she is not content to remain silent or passive as convention dictates. She rebels by becoming an active sexual partner and through other defiant acts: she has sex with Donally's "half-wit" son, and she refuses to obey Jewel's command to "go in the cart with Mrs. Green, like a bloody lady" (97) when the tribe later migrates to the sea.

The wedding ceremony itself mocks bourgeois tradition and values. Donally mixes ritualistic traditions, deriving the words from the *Book of Common Prayer*; incorporating a blood-bonding ritual; and, finally, throwing himself down, feigning spiritual possession:

> He rolled and tossed like a tumultuous river, blowing out an incoherent spume of sound. The tribe pressed back against the walls to allow him room. Many children burst into tears while their parents stared from eyes round with fright and awe. The fit encompassed as many baroque variations as if he were playing the organ and lasted until the candles were half burned down [73].

There is little comedy in this novel, but the image of Donally enacting a fit is funny in Carter's jubilantly perverse way. Humor like this is incisive and critical, pummeling the artifice and absurdity of superstition and religious systems.

The dramatic apex of Carter's work often features a revelation and destruction of artifice. In *The Passion of New Eve*, for example, Tristessa reveals his transvestitism and is then shot for betraying gender norms. In Carter's second novel, *The Magic Toyshop*, an oppressive patriarch, Uncle Philip, forces his niece Melanie to perform in a puppet-show reenactment of the rape of Leda by the Swan. Philip's son, Finn, who has also been abused by his father, exacts vengeance by chopping up and burying the wooden swan, thus dispensing with the artificial symbol of Philip's phallic rule. Similarly, towards the end of *Heroes and Villains*, Carter pulls up the curtain on Donally's little play. After Jewel exiles Donally from the tribe, he takes the iconic snake from its cage, cuts it open before the tribe, and sawdust spills out. It is a theatrical prop, a mythical symbol of power which Jewel reveals to be hollow and toothless. Consequently, Donally is exposed and discredited.

Another prominent convention of Carter's has her female characters reborn as strong, independent, and rebellious. In *The Passion of New Eve*, abused Leilah is transformed into the empowered Lilith, and New Eve herself escapes the degradations she suffered from Zero to be "reborn" as the "apotheosis of Tiresias" and sail off into the ocean on her own. Aunt Margaret, the long-suffering, mute wife of Uncle Philip in *The Magic Toyshop*, regains her voice by defying Philip and consummating her incestuous love with her brother Francis. Marianne is strong-willed and rebellious from the start of *Heroes and Villains*, but her experiences with the Barbarians, particularly her sexual experiences, awaken her to her untapped potential.

Throughout her work, Carter portrays sex primarily as a tool of power, power that women can tap into by making use of their sexuality, as when she advocated for women's potential to "fuck their way into history and, in doing so, change it" (*SW* 27). Though it does not explicitly use pornographic conventions in the way that many of Carter's other fictions do, *Heroes and Villains* does explore sexual themes. Gothic fiction, like pornography—a genre with which it frequently cohabits (as in Sade or Bataille)—is often about sex and teaches gender values. Typically in gothic fiction the heroine is in danger, usually of a sexualized nature, and must be protected, thus reinforcing the idea of women's dependence on men. In *Heroes and Villains*, Marianne at first needs male protection but then becomes a powerful force in her own right by capitalizing on the tribe's vulnerability to myth. When Marianne first arrives at the Barbarian encampment, Jewel's brothers try to rape her, apparently in order to tame the threat she represents to them as an outsider. In what Carter would have considered an admirable display of self-possession, Marianne faces the threat without fear, "only very angry indeed," but is saved at the last moment by Donally who manufactures a convenient myth to control the brothers through their fear: "They're brave, grant them that," he says. "It's a well-known fact that Professor women sprout sharp teeth in their private parts, to bite off the genitalia of young men" (49). But she is not saved from suffering the same abuse by Jewel. She flees the Barbarians only to be chased down by him and raped. Explaining why he did it, he tells her: "Swallow you up and incorporate you, see. Dr Donally says. Social psychology. I've nailed you on necessity, you poor bitch" (56). Carter depicts sex and marriage as acts often undertaken to tame radical female potential. With the Adam and Eve tableau inscribed on Jewel's back, Carter implies that the rape is Jewel's attempt to thwart the archetypical threat of female sexuality.

Later, after they are married, their sexual relations take on other significances. Like many of Carter's other heroines, Marianne learns to be sexually active, to seek pleasure in flesh. When Jewel makes it clear that he is determined to impregnate her, however, this new found pleasure is spoiled: "The idea of pleasure died now she realized pleasure was ancillary to procreation" (91). Jewel articulates his intent with hostility, growling at her: "Conceive, you bitch, conceive" (90). When she asks him why, he gives her a list of reasons:

> Dynastically [...] It's a patriarchal system. I need a son, don't I, to dig my grave when I'm gone. A son to ensure my status. [...] Politically. To maintain my status. [...] Revenge [...] Shoving a little me up you, a little me all furred, plaited and bristling with knives [90].

These are the values which motivate the conventional "demon-lover" of gothic fiction: dynasty, politics, and revenge.[46] Sex, Marianne learns, can never simply be about pleasure. It is tainted by androcentric values and the struggle for power.

A Fairy Tale Ending?

Heroes and Villains is a more despairing book, I think, than *The Passion of New Eve* and Carter's later work. *Nights at the Circus*, Carter's penultimate novel, features a "fairy tale" happy-ending—the reunion of the mythologically winged Fevvers with Jack Walser. "The Bloody Chamber" and other stories in that collection celebrate the ingenuity, independence, and power of women. And *The Passion of New Eve*, with pregnant Eve sailing off into the sea, at least suggests the possibility of a new beginning. But Carter's vision is usually much darker in her early work. The end of her first novel, *Shadow Dance*, for example, has the masochistic Ghislaine return to the crazed and sadistic Honeybuzzard who monstrously disfigured her by cutting up her beautiful face. She tells him: "you are my master, do what you like with me" (166), whereupon, Sadeian like, he rapes and murders her on a crucifix in a basement room lit by hundreds of candles. Subsequently, Morris, Honeybuzzard's tortured friend who has also suffered abuse by him, chooses to return to him rather than help turn him into the authorities.

The end of *Heroes and Villains* is similarly stark. Marianne is ready to take her place as the head of the tribe's mythology. When Jewel is shot and killed by the Soldiers (the military class in the Professors' community), she announces to Donally's son that she will be "the tiger lady and rule them with a rod of iron" (150). This final image is a bleak one. Though she can no longer be subjected to the violence and degradation forced on her by Jewel and Donally, she seems to have internalized the latter's methods, intending to adopt his policy of absolute rule. What kind of fairy tale is it that ends with the heroine staring out into the future, declaring that she will rule the community "with a rod of iron"? The implication is that she will become a "mother goddess," which, to Carter, we recall, is just as "silly [and dangerous] a notion as father gods" (*SW* 5). Like New Eve, Marianne is pregnant. However, whereas New Eve's pregnancy is the product of a loving union which defied gender norms, Marianne's baby is a product of gender conflict and a treacherous affair. Jewel, we remember, has tried to exact "revenge" by "Shoving a little me up [her]." Figuratively, she is pregnant with the tribe's future and expects that future, like the baby, to be monstrous (*HV* 90). Though the ending is ambiguously open-ended, she seems ready to take up Donally's methods. To replace the snake, she will become the "tiger lady," a dystopic inversion of Plato's Philosopher King.

One of the functions of the post-apocalyptic tale is to speculate on how society will re-organize itself after global destruction. *Heroes and Villains* poses the appalling scenario that the oppressive myths of human society will find new prophets in a post-apocalyptic era. Consistent with traditional gothic form, the tyrannies and superstitions of the past return to haunt the present. Carter's mix of speculative-fiction and the gothic is interesting for it reveals a striking similarity in the two genres despite what may seem obvious differences. Both genres comment on the present and express fears and anxieties about human history: the latter does so by looking at the past while the former does so by imagining the future. Post-apocalyptic fiction explores fears about the future—that our present course will lead us to a disaster and may prevent us from having any future at all. Gothic fiction confronts fears about the past—that we have not and will never be able to rid ourselves of its worst horrors. In knitting these two genres together, Carter suggests a truly nightmarish scenario: that the future may be dominated by all that is "monstrous" about the past.

CHAPTER FIVE

Failing to Observe Decorum

The four seasons are meant to correspond to the four principal literary genres. That is to say, summer, autumn, winter and spring are meant to correspond (and here I list them hierarchically) to tragedy, romance, comedy and satire. [...]

It's obvious, really. Once you've got comedy and tragedy right, the others follow.

Summer: romance. Journeys, quests, magic, talking animals, damsels in distress.

Autumn: tragedy. Isolation and decline, fatal flaws and falls, the throes of heroes.

Winter: satire. Anti-utopias, inverted worlds, the embrace of the tundra: the embrace of wintry thoughts.

Spring: comedy. Weddings, apple blossom, maypoles, no more misunderstandings—away with the old, on with the new.

We keep waiting for something to go wrong with the seasons. But something has already gone wrong with the genres. They have all bled into one another. Decorum is no longer observed [Martin Amis, *The Information* 35].

No, decorum with regards to such traditional genre boundaries is not frequently observed today. And—Egads!—how very un–British to fail to observe decorum. But that is mere stereotype of stiff upper-lip Britishness. Social and cultural irreverence has always been integral to the British, especially those Britons who are not in the ruling classes. And there is a long tradition in Britain of maverick writers who have balked at social conventions by purposefully transgressing the conventional expectations for literary genres. To return to the example with which I began this study, the finale of John Gay's *The Beggar's Opera*: the exchange between the Player and the Beggar mocks the idea that generic boundaries—in this case, between opera and tragedy—must not be crossed. Like the stereotype of the Hollywood producer insisting on a screenplay rewrite so that a film will meet the formal expectation of having a happy ending which reunites hero and heroine, the Player insists that Macheath's execution must be rescinded as it would thwart the expectation for a happy outcome in the opera form: "All this we must do," says the Player, "to comply with the taste of the town" (Hampden 158). Framed in this way, adherence to generic expectations is a matter of "decorum," but Gay mocks this notion to expose it as an absurdity which simplifies life's complexities so that an economically and politically privileged class can more easily consume their entertainment without having it challenge their social dominance.

Contemporary or "postmodern" writers such as Rushdie, Barnes, Winterson, and Carter carry on the indecorous spirit of Gay's mockery and transgression of generic expectations. Actually, they are far more than simply "indecorous." They are proudly, uncompromisingly outrageous. The energy of their work—their experimental spirit towards genre; their aggressive use of language; their grotesque and parodic representations of ignorant, tyrannical figures; their sheer frustration and even fury with the way things are—is fiercely defiant. They are often comparable to Carter's description of Sade's libertines—figures who "turn the Blessed Virgin over on her belly and sodomise her" (*SW* 76)—in that they are crusaders out to desacralize the ideas that sustain prejudice and conflict between people of different races, nationalities, genders, and sexual orientations.

Like Gay, contemporary writers such as Rushdie, Barnes, Winterson, Carter, and others in Britain and elsewhere foreground their deviations from traditional literary genre boundaries and conventions. The idea of genres as self-contained categories is an academic convention upheld by an ahistorical view of literary history. The ahistorical model of generic classification, first posed by Aristotle and given modern prominence by structuralists such as Northrop Frye, does not take into consideration that genres are always changing—that each text in a genre contributes to that process of constant change. According to Ralph Cohen, Frye's concept of the romance genre, for example, "is committed to the view that its features, however drawn from different times, are divisible into the basic structure" ("Afterword" 271). The theory of genre underlying this view, Cohen asserts, "is not interested in explaining why literary conventions arise or decline, why genres are constituted as they are, when they are" (271). A more useful approach to genre discusses how and why changes in literary form are connected to specific historical, social, cultural, and ideological changes.

In one of Ralph Cohen's examples of generic change, he notes an "ideological shift" (274) between the original "Ballad of George Barnwell" in 1624 and its subsequent rewritings as a prose fiction, a play, a revised ballad (by Bishop Percy), and part of a novel (Thomas Skinner Surr's *Barnwell* [1798]). The prose fiction shifts the focus away from Barnwell, a merchant's apprentice, and concentrates on the character of the harlot who seduces Barnwell to rob his master and murder his rich uncle, thus conveying a form of "antifeminism" ("History and Genre" 215). The tale was further changed when George Lillo refashioned it into the tragedy *The London Merchant* which was produced in 1731. The original ballad is considered a "vulgar" work which "outlines the consequences of sensual indulgence" while the latter form requires that "the characters be elevated and the problems become affairs of state" ("Afterword" 273). At the same time, this play affected the evolution of the tragedy genre, initiating what Cohen calls the "domestic" tragedy, by opening the form to "include common people and the events in which they were involved" ("History and Genre" 215). As a result, the tragedy "focuses on class changes and the moral responsibility that accompanies such changes" ("Afterword" 275). Bishop Percy's revision of the ballad altered the lewdness and bawdiness of the tale and imposed on it "the standards of decorum and correctness practiced by established eighteenth-century poets" ("History and Genre" 216). Such shifts in genre, Cohen notes, make possible "the recognition of historical changes in attitude—to merchant, merchant's apprentice, and harlot" (217). In other words, generic transformations help us to interpret shifting social values.

Alastair Fowler expands on Cohen's critique of older genre theories:

> Any successful genre theory of the future will have to be a good deal less remote than those of the past, less couched in terms of neat but undemonstrable classes. In actual literature, such categories as historical kinds, modes, and constructional types seem to overlap, change, and change places in more fluid ways than most theorists have cared to admit. [...] [T]he next phase of genre theory is likely to be less "pure," more subject to confirmation by evidence of examples [302].

This study has been an attempt to provide some such examples of generic "impurity" and to discuss their relevance to the social scenes of their appearance. I have operated on the premise that the changes to genre made by the writers I have discussed reflect changing contemporary social attitudes about such issues as nationality, politics, history, religion, gender, and sexuality: today's Western society is one where immigration and miscegenation have made it ludicrous to think of nationality and race as absolute and discrete categories; our attitudes towards history have been made more complex by our increasing awareness that absolute, reliable knowledge of the past is not attainable; in many parts of the world, religion has lost much of its power and authority, while in others it has become increasingly violent; the social divisions and inequities based on gender are, in limited areas, slowly beginning to give way to more egalitarian ideals; and, in some areas, sexuality is recognized as more varied and complex than the dominant model of heterosexuality would suggest. With these kinds of social values in flux, artistic representational conventions have similarly changed. Rushdie, Barnes, Winterson, Carter, and many of their peers alter and comment upon received genres because their work *instantiates* changes in social values just as much as it reflects them.

Another common belief about genres is that they become defunct, but this is rarely the case. New genres are arising all the time and they are usually new expressions of older genres which have had their emphases altered and/or their conventions mixed with those of other genres. Fowler comments:

> Future genre criticism should certainly be much concerned with identifying new genres. [...] But they will probably be genres that originated through familiar processes of development. In this sense, at least, there is nothing new under the generic sun. [...] [Genre] groupings are merely frivolous if they fail to come to terms with the filiations of the past. [...] A radical rewriting of genre history can only be achieved through acknowledging continuities, not by ignoring them and inventing ruptures [295, 303].

Thus, when Carter mixes and alters the conventions of fairy tales, pornography, the gothic, and science fiction, she does not create some "radical rupture" with the forms of the past; rather, she contributes to their evolution. She does not suggest that these forms are inherently sexist; she demonstrates that these forms can be used to depict progressive, feminist values about sex and gender as well. Similarly, Barnes's kind of historiography, Rushdie's magic realism and his use of the grotesque, or any of these authors' revisions of stories from scripture can be seen as continuations of older generic traditions which invest them with new concepts, values, or ideologies.

New genre groupings or new expressions of older genres, then, reflect new social conditions. Fowler provides another example: he identifies "multiperspectival" works such as Thomas Pynchon's *The Crying of Lot 49* and *Gravity's Rainbow* as "mosaic fiction," a genre that "reflects social changes characterized by increased flows of information and decreased attention span" (293). A more contemporary expression of this genre—one which reflects changes in oral and written language brought on by the increasing use of electronic forms of communication such as e-mail—might be termed "e-fiction." Examples of this genre could include: Douglas Coupland's *Microserfs*, a novel which makes liberal use of the emoticons and abbreviations familiar to those who communicate via e-mail and instant messaging; and Astro Teller's *Exegesis*, a postmodern reworking of the epistolary form in which the entire novel is presented as a series of e-mail exchanges and, further departing from the narrative conventions of traditional printed material, has no page numbers.[1] If future scholars pay attention to such newly emerging and evolving genres, and if the discussion is about changes to artistic forms and conventions as they relate to social and cultural conditions, then the study of literature and the other arts in general can lead to a new substance for humanistic study.

A Sampling of Other Generic Innovators

In focusing on the work of Rushdie, Barnes, Winterson, and Carter, I have left out of my discussion a great many other writers who are working with genre in new and interesting ways. I would like here to offer some brief observations on several other contemporary British writers in order to recognize the widespread nature of this trend and to encourage further study of generic mixing and transformation in writing. I offer these examples not as a survey of generic experimentation in contemporary British fiction, but as a sampling that could suggest possible paths for more detailed genre-based discussion of such fiction.

Some writers have altered genres in less-than-obvious ways, seeming to cling to a traditional form while actually transforming it into something else. Behind the painstaking veneer of its Victorian realist novel conventions, A. S. Byatt's *Possession*, for example, is an extraordinarily variegated novel: it uses a multitude of genres including poems, fairy tales, letters, diary entries, biographical sketches, and literary critical essays. Similar to Geoffrey Braithwaite's search for the "true" Flaubert in Barnes's *Flaubert's Parrot*, Roland Mitchell and Maud Bailey attempt to construct an authoritative history of the love affair between Randolph Ash and Christabel LaMotte, two fictional Victorian poets modeled on Robert Browning and Elizabeth Barrett Browning. *Possession* does not engage in the same kind of self-conscious or metafictional tropes as *Flaubert's Parrot*, but the message is similar: archival evidence can only give us a partial window on the past. Roland and Maud do not recognize their own role in constructing the narrative—speculating to fill in the missing pieces, organizing documents according to subjective logic, etc. It is apparent to us as readers, though, that Roland and Maud's efforts result in a fictionalized approximation of the past, thus once again highlighting that the putative authority of realist genres—of their capacity to offer a transparent and/or objective view of reality—is a product of narrative artifice.

One of the most remarkable novels of the 1990s is Martin Amis's *Time's Arrow*. The genre of Holocaust narratives, which includes memoirs such as *The Diary of Anne Frank* and Elie Wiesel's *Night* and fictionalized memoirs such as Jerzy Kosinski's *The Painted Bird*, is fittingly bleak. These are tales of fear, persecution, and inhuman violence on a scale never before witnessed. The teleology of each of these narratives is death: of a race, of the narrator and/or the narrator's family, or of the narrator's soul. *Time's Arrow* reverses the genocidal violence of the Holocaust narrative by making time run in reverse. Odilo Unverdorben, a Nazi "doctor" and perpetrator of crimes against humanity, lives his life temporally backwards and without an awareness of his life as it progressed forward in time. When he arrives at Auschwitz, all is in ruin, but he sets about the task of repairing the damage, creating life out of death. The crematoriums and mass graves at Auschwitz give birth to living humans from piles of ash and bones: Odilo and the other Nazis "dream a race" into being. They "make a people from the weather. From thunder and from lightening. With gas, with electricity, with shit, with fire" (128). They nourish these people back to health, reunite them with their families, and then ship them off to their homes. Odilo, whose strange life leaves him in utter confusion, finally is able to make sense of the world. Auschwitz, that incarnation of all that is incomprehensible in world history, becomes the one place where the world begins to have purpose. Thus, by inverting conventional narrative chronology, Amis presents us with a portrait of redemption at the site where humanity lost its soul. He changes the genre of the Holocaust narrative, but not to suggest that it can all be rationalized if only we think of it in reverse. Rather, the novel dismisses any attempt to rationally understand such titanic evil: as readers, we are aware that the idea of time running backwards is a fantasy. And because it is impossible, *Time's Arrow* suggests that the Holocaust will always remain in a sense inexplicable.

Another superb generically experimental novel that deals with the Holocaust is D. M. Thomas' *The White Hotel*. Reminiscent of Barnes's *Flaubert's Parrot*, each chapter of this novel narrates in a different genre part of the life history of a young woman. Through individual chapters that are presented variously as erotic poem, surrealistic tale, epistolary exchange, Freudian case study, traditional realism, and sheer fantasy, *The White Hotel* tells the story of Lisa Erdman-Berenstein, an opera singer who suffers a nervous breakdown, is treated by Sigmund Freud, and winds up a victim of the Nazi massacre of the Jews at Babi Yar. Like Barnes, Thomas emphasizes the impossibility of encapsulating even a single human's life by telling Lisa's tale in multiple genres that only gradually reveal a complex, though incomplete, portrait of her. And in the mass grave of Babi Yar lie thousands of similar stories untold:

> every single one of them had dreamed dreams, seen visions and had amazing experiences, even the babes in arms (perhaps especially the babes in arms). Though most of them had never lived outside the Podol slum, their lives and histories were as rich and complex as Lisa Erdman-Berenstein's. If a Sigmund Freud had been listening and taking notes from the time of Adam, he would still not fully have explored even a single group, even a single person [250].

All of these lives and the stories behind them are lost to history. But D. M. Thomas has imaginatively revived one, just as Toni Morrison set out in *Beloved* to recover the inner life of a couple of former slaves. Like so many of the novels I have discussed in this study, *The White Hotel* has a redemptive impulse. It "recuperates" the story of Lisa Erdman-Berenstein, and, in the final chapter, it presents a redeeming vision in which all of the victims of the Holocaust are gathered together in a secular afterlife where they, like those Jews who actually survived the Holocaust, rebuild a new nation of their own.

Many contemporary writers have gone the route of appropriating mass-market genres for unconventional uses. I have discussed in some detail, for example, how Winterson and Carter parody and rewrite romance and science fiction conventions, respectively, for feminist ends. In *The Innocent*, Ian McEwan transforms the spy thriller from a genre that glamorizes macho war games and displays of hyper-masculinity to one that criticizes and deflates such pursuits. The novel's unconventional protagonist is Leonard Marnham, a young and naive British postal employee who is conscripted to assemble tape recorders for a secret Cold War project in which the allies are digging a tunnel under the Berlin Wall to record the communication transmissions of the Soviets.[2] Leonard seems to be an utterly inept hero for this genre of story. Instead of being worldly, suave, assertive, competent, and "masculine," as would be expected, he is provincial, "wimpy," servile, and sexually inexperienced. Other participants in the project are, like Leonard, marked as boyish: one of the leaders of the project, John MacNamee, has only the feeble remains of his milk teeth, the adult teeth never having grown in. Thus, McEwan undermines the idea of the spy project as a masculine endeavor, suggesting that it is really an over-sized boys' game:

> [The tunnel] was a toytown, packed with boyish invention. Leonard remembered the secret camps, the tunnels through the undergrowth he used to make with friends in a scrap of woodland near his house. [...] Tunnels were stealth and safety; boys and trains crept through them, lost to sight and care, and then emerged unscathed [71–2].

But this is *not* harmless child's play, McEwan suggests. Nations in conflict conduct themselves like children amassing toy weaponry behind cardboard forts, but there are real, deadly consequences to these games when acted out by adults. This particular project is abandoned without loss of human life when one of the allies sells out to the Soviets, but McEwan suggests that the waste of time and resources as well as the perpetuation of mistrust are factors that damage human society. And at the foundation of McEwan's critique is his mockery of the "masculine" ideals that energize such "games." What Leonard is "innocent" of is the male world of violence, until his sojourn to Berlin puts him at the heart of a blatantly sexualized form of "masculine" violence: drilling into the most vulnerable spot of the enemy.[3]

As a popular male writer whose work clearly criticizes the ways in which masculinity is expressed in society, McEwan is something of an oddity. His work is full of perverse tales of masculine sexual violence which, particularly in the mid–1970s when he began publishing, have pushed the envelope of literary representations of sex. Few, if any, male British writers have been so critical of masculinity, a factor which allies him with women writers such as Carter and Winterson.

The majority of the fictional critiques of gender come from women writers who, like Carter and Winterson, have transformed genres to protest sexism, traditional gender roles, and the over-valuation of appearance. Fay Weldon's *The Life and Loves of a She-Devil*, for example, dramatizes an "unattractive" woman's suffering in a society which degrades her because of her failure to meet the social standard of beauty. Driven by her jealousy and hatred of Mary Fisher, the beautiful and rich romance novelist who is having an affair with her husband Bobbo, Ruth sets out to remake herself in Mary's image. In gothic fashion reminiscent of Mary Wollstonecraft Shelley's *Frankenstein*, Ruth's plan takes on a nightmarish tenor as she seeks out the world's best surgeons to utterly transfigure her body over the course of many years and at tremendous pain to herself so that she can literally incarnate and replace Mary Fisher. Ruth openly declares her desacralizing objective: to "[take] up arms against God Himself" (82). Weldon employs the gothic convention of putting the power of Creation into human hands in order to aggressively attack the prevalent contemporary notion that equates beauty with a particular physical form. She is not trying to suggest that looks don't count in today's society. On the contrary, Weldon demonstrates that looks—conforming to collective ideals of beauty—are so important that society encourages women to deform themselves and go through any amount of pain in order to meet those ideals.

Emma Tennant's *Faustine*—another contemporary, "feminist" gothic novel—rewrites the Faust legend with a woman as the Faust figure, and has an ideological thrust similar to Weldon's novel. Ella's grandmother, Muriel Twyman, reaching the age at which women "become invisible" in a "Centrefold world" (135), signs a contract with the Devil's representative for twenty-four years of youth, beauty, riches, and power. At first, Muriel's daughter, Anna, a feminist activist, understands and accepts Muriel's decision. Explaining to Ella, she says:

> After the first shock of your grandmother's transformation—into a woman, to put it brutally, with a future, when what was expected of her and her contemporaries was the acceptance that nothing lay ahead but memories of the past—I argued with myself that she had every right to continue enjoying her life [...] to improve the quality of her life after middle age.
>
> After all, women were programmed by nature to become grandmothers as soon as their own childbearing years were finished, and for many, after a life sacrificed to continual pregnancy, childbearing or miscarriage, this enforced old age came as a well-earned rest—a relief after the struggles that had gone before.
>
> But what of women today, who, like my mother [...] has no experiences of this kind, who want to go on living, and working and appearing youthful and attractive?
>
> Why should she be exiled to old age and redundancy just because the laws of the Victorian age laid it down [114]?

What at first seems like a gift, however, predictably turns out to be a curse: Muriel becomes a woman who "found she had no time [...] for anyone other than herself" (107). The trap of worshipping and pursuing youth, beauty, and power is that one becomes narcissistic and solipsistic. Tennant transforms the critique of male narcissism implicit in the Faust legend into a warning against the dangers of women falling prey to a Western society and culture that celebrates and rewards youth and beauty while despising agedness (i.e. if you're old you're no one). For women to "sell out" to this culture is no solution, Tennant suggests; rather, Western society must change its value system with regards to youth and old-age.

Rewriting the Faust story, like rewriting the story of Noah and the Ark or Little Red Riding Hood, automatically entails changing its genre. The Faust story has evolved from folk legend to English Renaissance play (by Christopher Marlowe), to German tragedy (by Goethe), to modern novel (by Thomas Mann), and, with Tennant's novel, to gothic feminist fable. Just as the Ballad of George Barnwell went through generic changes in response to changing social values about class, sex, and general "decorum," the Faust story has undergone generic changes so that the story correlates to the values and concerns of varying historical eras. In Mann's novel, *Doctor Faustus*, for example, the composer Adrian Leverühn makes a pact with the devil for musical creativity. His subsequent fall into madness and his eventual death allegorically parallels the collapse of Nazi Germany; thus, Mann implicates German society for the collective narcissism which brought on its own destruction. In its many variations, the Faust story has always been a cautionary tale about narcissism and defying nature, but it has always been androcentric in its focus. Tennant implies that Muriel's transformation initially takes place in the 1960s, historically situating the tale in a period which saw the birth of the modern feminist movement and was also the peak of what may be identified as the twentieth-century "cult of youth." Thus, the novel dramatizes the historical tensions between androcentric expectations with regards to women's appearance and women's desire for liberation from such expectations. Like Carter, Winterson, Weldon, and many others, Tennant suggests that Western culture continues to perpetuate very constraining notions of what it is to be a woman.

A Literature of Affirmation

Scholars have viewed postmodern literature as critical, protesting, deconstructing, demythologizing, de-naturalizing, and subversive (e.g. Hutcheon, Suleiman). It *is* all of these things, and I have added an emphasis on its characteristic irreverence, anger, and extreme frustration with social and literary conventions. Because contemporary or postmodern fiction is so often discussed in terms of what it is *against*, however, it is easy to lose sight of what it stands *for*.

The question of religion, which arises time and again in the fiction I've discussed here, is exemplary in this regard. Rushdie, Barnes, Winterson, and Carter reject religion because it has led to constraining laws and values in areas such as sexuality, gender, race, and politics. For them, religion has very often been a powerful force for repressing human individuality and diversity. But these writers also affirm human worth, life, and persistence without requiring a higher force to validate these things. Throughout this study, I have given special attention to the desacralizing gestures of the writers I have discussed, but I have also attempted to emphasize that the overall tenor of this writing is playful and, for the most part, affirmative. The combined efforts of these writers ask us to move away from faith in religion and towards faith in ourselves, both collectively and individually: not to live for the promise of a heavenly, or, as Barnes depicts it, sybaritic afterlife, but to live for the here and now. To understand this project, and not to be outraged by it, is antithetical to the kind of thinking encouraged by orthodoxy.

To turn away from looking to religion and myths for answers, as Rushdie, Barnes, Winterson, and Carter do, is not to embrace a philosophy of despair. They and many other postmodern writers and artists do not offer the message of doom that theorists of postmodern culture like Fredric Jameson and Jean Baudrillard do. Their tales represent the full range of human experience: they depict human tragedy on the personal and the society-wide levels. But their work is also full of tales of persistence, reconciliation, and triumph: Saleem Sinai's preservation of his alternative history of India; Salahuddin Chamchawalla's reconciliation with his father and his past; the woodworms' triumphant, "ennobling" survival of the flood; young Jeanette setting out for a new, more accepting life in London; Gloria Munde and her friends' attempt to survive the flood independent of God and Noah; the hinted-at reunion of Louise and the narrator in *Written on the Body*; New Eve setting out to sea to start a new world; and the remarkable, guns-blazing return of the Mother in "The Bloody Chamber" to save her daughter from the evil Marquis. To these we might add Martin Amis' redeeming portrait of Odilo Unverdorben, who undoes the horrors he has committed by re-living his life in reverse; and D. M. Thomas' redemptive view of the Holocaust — that although so many lives were, like Lisa Erdman-Berenstein's, lost, their spirits live on in those who survived to start anew.

Postmodern literature continues to struggle with making sense of human history, morality, and behavior. It is neither fundamentally utopian nor dystopian, though it sometimes takes those forms. It raises questions about the authority of received truths, the social norms of sex and gender, the abuse of power by political and religious leaders, the validity and social roles of religion, the epistemological dominance of science, purist ideals regarding race and nationality, and our capacity to know and learn from history. This literature challenges received values without proffering easy answers to the questions it poses. The questions matter; the passions matter; the desire for just social relations matter. And this literature tells us why.

Chapter Notes

Introduction. Genre and Postmodern Fiction

1. See, for example, *The Contemporary English Novel*, eds. Malcolm Bradbury and David Palmer.

2. Bernard Bergonzi's *The Situation of the Novel* (1970) is one of the more influential discussions of this facet of postwar British literature.

3. The theories of dramatists like Brecht and Artaud make the same kinds of claims for the theatre as Bakhtin does for the novel. They claim that drama is the only genre suited for comprehensive representation of human reality, and the only genre capable of growth and inspiring a true reaction from its reader/spectator (see *Brecht on Theatre* and Artaud's *The Theatre and Its Double*).

4. In today's consumer culture, an era Fredric Jameson calls "late capitalism" (*Postmodernism* 1–54), genre is primarily a means of categorizing products for the marketplace. Thus, the most popular usage of "genre" refers to the "genre fiction" of supermarket bookshelves or chain bookstores: westerns, romances, sci-fi, fantasy, spy thrillers, mysteries, etc.

5. Anne Luyat offers an interesting comparison of Ishiguro's novel to Wodehouse's Jeeves novels in her essay "Destruction of the Myth of the English Butler in Kazuo Ishiguro's *The Remains of the Day*" (Duperray 183–196).

6. Susan Suleiman shifts that emphasis by suggesting that a work's political impact depends at least as much on how it is read as what it might or might not intend (192). And it often does require some familiarity with the conventions being invoked to fully understand the critiques offered by postmodern literature.

7. This figure includes James Kelman who is technically a British citizen but "holds to an uncompromisingly nationalistic view of his [Scottish] citizenship" (Todd 79).

8. See Graham Huggan's two essays— "The Postcolonial Exotic" and "Prizing 'Otherness'"—in which he discusses the problem of the Booker serving as an imperial legitimator of literature from the former colonies.

9. Women remain proportionally underrepresented both as Booker winners and judges (see Todd 83–85).

10. For example, Ian McEwan's *Amsterdam*, which won in 1998, is widely considered to be an inferior work to his previous novel, *Enduring Love*, which wasn't even shortlisted for the prize.

One. Salman Rushdie

1. M. Keith Booker points to a number of similarities between Rushdie's *Satanic Verses* and Joyce's *Finnegans Wake*, a text he describes as encyclopedic in that "all languages, all lit-

eratures, and all cultures seem dissolved in a rich intertextual soup of signification" (191–192). Rushdie's fiction has a similar if not quite as encyclopedic scope.

2. It is commonly noted that Rushdie draws on Western sources such as Laurence Sterne, Cervantes, Italo Calvino, Gunter Grass, and Gabriel Garcia Marquez as well as Eastern sources such as *One Thousand and One Nights, The Bhagavad Gita, The Mahabharata,* and the Koran.

3. Lois Zamora and Wendy Faris suggest that the tradition extends further back—to the epic and chivalric traditions (2). Jeanne Delbaere-Garant notes that magic realism "is not exclusively a postcolonial phenomenon, but a much older one whose various offshoots require more precise and specific definitions" (Zamora, and Faris 249).

4. See, for example, *Labyrinths* (Borges), *Widows* (Dorfman), *Like Water for Chocolate* (Esquival), *One Hundred Years of Solitude* and *Love and Death in the Time of Cholera* (Marquez).

5. Roh's book is *Nach-Expressionismus, Magischer Realismus: Probleme de neuesten Europäischen Malerei* (Leipzig, Klinkhardt and Biermann, 1925). Lois Zamora and Wendy Faris provide an English translation of one of the book's chapters (15–31).

6. For example: *The Street of Crocodiles* (Schulz), *The Metamorphosis* (Kafka), and *The Book of Laughter and Forgetting* and *The Unbearable Lightness of Being* (Kundera).

7. See, for example, *The Famished Road* (Okri), *In the Skin of A Lion* (Ondaatje), and *The Infinite Rehearsal* (Harris).

8. I am indebted to Michael Gorra for his suggestion that Rushdie's fiction insists on a "literalization of metaphor" (118).

9. One of Rushdie's essays asserts that in the latter part of Mrs. Gandhi's rule her Congress party "abandoned its policy of representing the coalition of minorities, and began to transform itself into an overtly Hindu party. Not only Hindu, but Hindi: attempts to impose this language on the whole of India created much resentment" (*IH* 386). Her government, in other words, began to promote a monolithic and mono-lingual vision of India.

10. Elsewhere, Rushdie asserts that the novel narrates what he calls "memory's truth" since "reality is built on our prejudices, misconceptions and ignorance as well as on our perceptiveness and knowledge" (*IH* 25).

11. In "An Image of Africa," Chinua Achebe's famous essay on *Heart of Darkness,* Achebe points to the same passage as an example of Conrad's racist depictions of Africans (5–6).

12. In this passage, Said is specifically referring to the writings and speeches of Arthur James Balfour and Lord Cromer on the problems in Egypt, but the description is relevant for a variety of Western political and literary discourses about native non–Westerners.

13. This might explain the meaning of Kurtz's famous, ambiguous expostulation: "The horror!" (Conrad 119). Could he be referring to the "horror" of believing himself no different from the African natives?

14. Talal Asad challenges the idea that these are necessarily strengths, suggesting that it "is precisely the viewpoint of interventionist power that insists on the permeability of social groups, the unboundedness of cultural unities, and the instability of individual selves" (264). For Asad, in other words, a lack of social unity makes it easier for totalitarian forces to rule the populace. But Rushdie is not suggesting that there be *no* unifying political/ideological ideals among India's populace (Rushdie is resolutely in favor of ideals of democracy, liberty, and equality, for example), just that there be no forced erasure of what makes different groups distinct from one another culturally, ethnically, and religiously.

15. The opening of the "Circe" episode of *Ulysses* portrays a variety of grotesque figures populating Nighttown: "stunted men and women [...] [a] deaf-mute idiot [...] [a] pigmy woman [...] a gnome [...] [a] crone [...] [a] bandy child [...] a scrofulous child" (Joyce 15.5–41).

16. It is a founding assumption of both Benedict Anderson and Homi Bhabha that narratives are integral to the dissemination of a unified concept of nationhood and national identity; see Bhabha's "DissemiNation" and "Introduction: Narrating the Nation" in *Nation and Narration.*

17. I disagree with Michael Gorra's implication that the magic realist material of Rushdie's work either distances us from the horror of what is being described or detracts from its political impact. Gorra does note that Rushdie dispels his illusions to make us think critically, but remains suspicious that such a book cannot make him care about "the individual characters to whom that history happens" (147). But in *Midnight's Children,* when Saleem's home and family are destroyed during the Indo–Pakistani war, I find it an emotionally

crushing moment. It is similarly moving when he and the other children are captured and surgically deprived of their magical gifts, and in both instances the political critique of totalitarianism is evident. True, the fate of Rushdie's characters are often cartoonish, as Gorra claims, but perhaps the cartoon is a signature genre of our times: like Wile E. Coyote we seem doomed always to repeat past mistakes. Rushdie's departures from realist conventions also demand a high level of critical consciousness on the part of the reader.

18. In "'Errata': or, Unreliable Narration in *Midnight's Children*," Rushdie elaborates on this strategy: "History is always ambiguous. Facts are hard to establish, and capable of being given many meanings. Reality is built on our perceptiveness and knowledge. The reading of Saleem's unreliable narration might be, I believed, a useful analogy for the way in which we all, every day, attempt to 'read' the world" (*IH* 25).

19. Rushdie's idea of the adaptability of migrants stems back to his first novel, *Grimus* (generally considered far inferior to his subsequent work), in which the immortal pro tagonist Flapping Eagle wanders the world for seven hundred years, adopting the culture of and blending in with each society he encounters.

20. That this Imam is a satire of the Ayatollah Khomeini is ironic considering that it was then Khomeini who forced Rushdie into a living situation similar to the fictional Imam.

21. The basis of this passage comes from a comment made by Ali Shariati, one of the Iranian revolution's "main ideologues," that the revolution was a "revolt against history." Rushdie remarks that "In these three unforgettable words, history is characterized as a colossal error, and the revolution sets out quite literally to turn back the clock" (*IH* 383). Farzaneh Asari agrees that the "Obliteration of historical consciousness, i.e. history itself, [was] essential to Khomeini's revolution. His ideal of a theocratic state literally require[d] the undoing of at least five hundred years of historical development" (10).

22. "Chamcha" in Urdu means "spoon" but it is a colloquialism for a toady or sycophant.

23. Zeeny's position on "authenticity" echoes one of Rushdie's observations about Commonwealth literature: "'Authenticity' is the respectable child of old-fashioned exoticism. It demands that sources, forms, style, language, and symbol all derive from a supposedly homogeneous and unbroken tradition.

Or else. [...] One of the most absurd aspects of this quest for national authenticity is that—as far as India is concerned, anyway—it is completely fallacious to suppose that there is such a thing as a pure, unalloyed tradition from which to draw. The only people who seriously believe this are religious extremists. The rest of us understand that the very essence of Indian culture is that we possess a mixed tradition, a *mélange* of elements as disparate as ancient Mughal and contemporary Coca-Cola American. [...] Eclecticism, the ability to take from the world what seems fitting and to leave the rest, has always been a hallmark of the Indian tradition. [...] Yet eclecticism is not really a nice word in the lexicon of 'Commonwealth literature.' So the reality of the mixed tradition is replaced by the fantasy of purity" (*IH* 67–68).

24. As Julian Barnes points out, "It doesn't, of course, do any such thing" (*LL* 269).

25. Timothy Brennan calls Saladin's transformation "a grotesque imaging of racist fantasies" (155).

26. Talal Asad offers a brilliant analysis of how documents issued by John Patten, home minister responsible for race relations, on behalf of the British government during the Rushdie affair were premised on the notion that there are essential differences between British and Muslim values and that Muslim immigrants need to assimilate and accept "British" values (241–248). Asad's analysis critiques the notion that there is a monolithic ideology putatively shared by all white Britons. Asad adds that to believe in the "'authentic' English gentleman"—as Saladin does—"is to enact a racist ideology" (297). But whereas Asad critiques Rushdie for Saladin's nostalgia for a now faded "*authentic gentleman's* England" (300), the point is that Saladin is satirized and depicted as foolish precisely because he has bought into this myth. Saladin's view is that of an elitist, colonialized bourgeois and is radically different from the majority of Muslim immigrants.

27. The event parallels Rushdie's own test of his atheism when he was fifteen which he describes in his essay "In God We Trust" (*IH* 377).

28. He is also, like Barnes especially, casting doubt on the reliability of commonly accepted historical narratives by re-writing the story of the founding of Islam.

29. The recent discovery in Yemen of a gravesite of seventh- and eighth-century copies of the Koran reveals aberrations from the

standard text of the Koran, suggesting that the Koran is a text that has changed with history rather than the absolute and unchanging Word of God. The historicization of the Koran would undermine the most foundational Islamic belief (Lester).

30. In his essay "In Good Faith" Rushdie further explains that "Central to the purpose of *The Satanic Verses* is the process of reclaiming language from one's opponents" (*IH* 402).

31. This scenario and the title phrase which describe it comes from an early story of questionable authority about such "Satanic verses." Malise Ruthven provides a detailed explanation in *A Satanic Affair: Salman Rushdie and the Rage of Islam* (37–39), as does Daniel Pipes in *The Rushdie Affair* (57–59). For a Muslim perspective which argues that the incident of the "Satanic verses" is a false myth, see M. M. Ahsan, "The Orientalists' 'Satanic' Verses" (Anees 6–10).

32. "Prophet, enjoin your wives, your daughters, and the wives of true believers to draw their veils close round them. That is more proper, so that they may be recognized and not be molested" (Dawood, *Koran* 299). An important part of Rushdie's third novel, *Shame*, is to denounce this practice and its harmful effect on Muslim women and Muslim society in general.

33. *The Rushdie File* (eds. Lisa Appignanesi and Sara Maitland). Further references will be cited in text as *RF*.

34. Some critics have argued that Rushdie's characterizations of women involve patriarchal and/or sexist conventions (see, for example, Ellerby, Grewal, Kamra, Verma). While I do think there is a certain quality of androcentrism in many of Rushdie's depictions, he uses a cartoonish, comic mode of representation with practically all of his characters, female *and* male. There are women who are villains (e.g. Abu Simbel's wife Hind; the Widow in *Midnight's Children*), women who haunt men (e.g. Rekha Merchant in *The Satanic Verses*); women treated with condescension (Padma in *Midnight's Children*); and even women treated as monstrous destroyers of men (Sufiya Zinobia in *Shame*). But there are just as many, if not more, men treated at least as harshly. Further, some of his women characters, such as Zeeny Vakil, Alleluia Cone, and her mother, Alicja Cone, are clearly the most admirable personages in the novel, certainly more so that Gibreel or Saladin. And throughout Rushdie's work he demonstrates an awareness of the difficulties of women living in an androcentric society, such as when he remarks of Hind Sufyan (Sufyan's wife) that "she had sunk into the anonymity, the characterless plurality, of being merely one-of-the-women-like-her. This was history's lesson: nothing for women-like-her to do but suffer, remember, and die" (250); or when Alicja Cone tells her daughter: "So a woman's life-plans are being smothered by a man's. [...] So welcome to your gender" (348). Further, in his essay "In Good Faith," Rushdie points out that part of his reason for portraying the "Satanic verses" incident was that he "thought it was at least worth pointing out that one of the reasons for rejecting these goddesses was that *they were female*" (*IH* 399–400).

35. Like the instance of the "Satanic verses," this event has an historical basis: Malise Ruthven explains in her contribution to *The Rushdie File* that, according to an historic account, one of Muhammad's scribes lost his faith after "a deliberate mistake in his transcription of the divine text went unnoticed by the Prophet" (187).

36. In an interview, Rushdie proposes that doubt is an inescapable facet of postmodern society: "Doubt is the central condition of a human being in the 20th century. One of the things that has happened to us in the 20th century as a human race is to learn how certainty crumbles in your hand. We cannot any longer have a fixed certain view of anything" (*RF* 24).

37. Here Rushdie is again critical of androcentric values. The prostitutes turn out to be the "most old-fashioned and conventional women in Jahilia" (384). They want Baal to "Be the boss" because they have finally internalized all of the androcentric fantasies that they have spent years servicing as prostitutes: "the years of enacting the fantasies of men had finally *corrupted* their dreams, so that even in their hearts of hearts they wished to turn themselves into the oldest male fantasy of all" (384, my emphasis). While Rushdie's critique of this fantasy—of women happily enslaving themselves to a single man—is evident in his description of this arrangement as a form of corruption, it is Carter who attacks this manifestation of androcentrism most vehemently. As discussed in Chapter Four, Carter depicts a similar harem arrangement in *The Passion of New Eve* and graphically exhibits the violence to women it represents.

38. I have often thought that what those who most strongly protested the novel and its author lacked was a willingness to see the

humor of Rushdie's style. J. M. Q. Davies notes that what is often missed in discussions of the novel is attention to its "sheer zaniness [...] its affinities with say *Brazil* or Monty Python" (34). This comparison is in itself telling, as Monty Python too have provoked fundamentalist outrage—over their satirical portrait of Christ in their film *The Life of Brian*. Rushdie has a fantastic sense of humor which he uses to satirize everything from religious icons, totalitarian political leaders, and whole societies to incidental characters and himself. In reality, however, only a small minority of protesters had read the book. Instead, they had been presented with sections of the novel taken out of context and encouraged to understand them as blasphemies punishable by death rather than the masterpieces of comic satire that they are.

39. The Koran explicitly condemns imaginative writers: "Poets are followed by erring men. Behold how aimlessly they rove in every valley, preaching what they never practice" (Dawood 264). As a result, Fadia Faqir asserts, writing in Islamic countries "has never been respected and is considered by strict Muslims as an act of subversion" (*RF* 226).

40. Marquez uses butterflies in prominent magical scenes in *One Hundred Years of Solitude*.

41. The story is based on an actual event in which Naseem Fatima led thirty-eight Shi'a Muslims to their death at Hawkes Bay in Karachi in February 1983. Fatima's followers believed that the sea would open, providing them a path to the Shi'a holy city of Kerbala in Iraq (Ruthven 45–47).

42. Chapter Three discusses in detail science's displacement of religion.

43. Similarly, Daniel Pipes suggests that this part of the novel is an indictment of religious-led politics: the drowning of the villagers "is an allegory for Iran and the Islamic Revolution. The holy woman transfixing the whole population of a village, then leading them to their deaths, represents the years since 1979 in Iran" (54).

44. In an interview, Rushdie stated that "I don't believe that Mohammad had a revelation but then I don't doubt his sincerity either. Mohammad didn't make up the angel. He had that genuine mystical experience. But if you don't believe in the whole truth and you don't disbelieve him either—then what's going on? What is the nature of the mystical experience? [...] That's what I tried to write about" (*RF* 33). Like Rushdie's ideas about the adaptabil-

ity of migrants, this tension between what's real and what's mystical or fantastic stems back to his earliest work, *Grimus*. Trying to explain the reality of "supernatural" things such as immortality and dimensional travel to Flapping Eagle, Virgil Jones tells him that he "must accept that the world in which [he] lived was no simple, matter-of-fact place. [...] [The world is] what it appears to be and not what it appears to be" (61). Virgil Jones further observes that "a man is sane only to the extent that he subscribes to a previously-agreed construction of reality" (62), a comment that can be read as an explanation of a trend throughout Rushdie's later work. In *Midnight's Children*, for example, Padma questions Saleem's sanity because he proposes a view of Indian history that does not match with the consensus-reality. And in *The Satanic Verses*, the portrayal of Gibreel's sanity wavers in response to the tensions between secular and religious/mystical "construction[s] of reality."

45. It is important to note that Rushdie criticizes the dominant Western view of Islam as "not merely medieval, barbarous, repressive and hostile to Western civilization, but also united, unified, homogeneous, and therefore dangerous" (*IH* 382).

46. Ashraf also vaguely identifies the supernatural events in the text as fairy tale conventions. The fairy tale, discussed in Chapter Four, is better understood as a specific genre that evolved out of oral story-telling and is not an umbrella category for fantasy texts.

47. The most useful collection of documents concerning *The Satanic Verses* controversy from a variety of perspectives is *The Rushdie File* (eds. Lisa Appignanesi and Sara Maitland), though this collection is weighted in favor of Rushdie. *The Kiss of Judas* (ed. Munawar A. Anees) collects a variety of Muslim-authored documents and essays that are strictly anti–Rushdie in sentiment; while many of these selections provide an interesting view of Muslim perspectives on the controversy, some are juvenile in their personal vilification of Rushdie (see especially "Salman Rushdie—Professed Socialist but Keen on Money" 162–164) and others see the international defense of Rushdie as part of a Zionist anti–Muslim conspiracy (see especially Yaqub Zaki's article "Secularism at Bay" 143–145). *Sacrilege and Civility* (eds. M. M. Ahsan and A. R. Kidwai) collects a great many articles, documents, and essays about the Rushdie affair, but is also vociferously anti–Rushdie in sentiment. It

also censors statements that indicate criticisms of Muslims; the volume reprints an anti–Rushdie article by Mushahid Hussain but excises a paragraph which contains the mollifying statement that "There is little doubt that Muslims, too, are guilty of hypocrisy and double standards, particularly the majority of regimes and rulers in Muslim countries" (Hussain 13). For a collection of essays discussing the controversy from a variety of religious perspectives, see Cohn-Sherbok, *The Salman Rushdie Controversy in Interreligious Perspective*. The British monthly *Index on Censorship* devoted space to the Rushdie affair in its May 1989 (18.5) and April 1990 (19.4) issues. For detailed discussions of the "affair" as a whole, see Daniel Pipes's *The Rushdie Affair* and Malise Ruthven's *A Satanic Affair*.

48. Mushahid Hussain outrageously suggests that "Rushdie's writing *The Satanic Verses* is like a jew [sic] who tries to justify the Holocaust, who defends Hitler's extermination of millions of Jews and dismisses his crime in light hearted humour at the expense of the victims of Auschwitz" (13).

49. Daniel Pipes discusses a number of similar objections to the book (110–113) and comments that "many Muslim critics complained that Rushdie had not told the truth, as though his highly elaborated account was intended exactly to recapitulate Islamic history" (110). Pipes attempts to explain this misunderstanding as the product of a pervasive (though certainly not universal) Muslim unfamiliarity with the novel form: "The notion of the literary imagination proceeding into the hypothetical, where context shapes no less than words, remains alien to many Muslims, and fundamentalists reject this approach in its entirety" (112).

50. Daniel Pipes explains: "To doubt this is to deny the validity of Muhammad's mission and to imply that the entire Islamic faith is premised on a fraudulent base. [...] [A] Muslim may not question the authenticity of the Qur'an. To do so is to raise doubts about the validity of the faith itself, and this is usually seen as an act of apostasy" (56).

51. What Rushdie is doing is similar to what M. Keith Booker suggests Joyce did in *Finnegans Wake*: assaulting the "presumption of the sacredness and corresponding authority of *any* text" (197).

52. Rushdie lamented this irony in a letter to *The Observer*: "This is, for me, the saddest irony of all; that after working for five years to give voice and fictional flesh to the immi-

grant culture of which I am myself a member, I should see my book burned, largely unread, by the people it's about" (*RF* 62).

53. Dissenting from most Western commentators, Daniel Pipes argues that the initial *fatwa* can be ascribed more to "religious motives" which he discusses in some detail (97–104), but he also admits that Khomeini soon exploited the situation for political gain: to unite various Islamic countries against the West, to regain support from the majority Sunni branch of Islam, and to aid in the Iranian struggle against Saudi Arabia "to represent Islam internationally" (133–136). I am not suggesting that religious motivations weren't important to the protest, but that Khomeini's interest was obviously more than merely religious.

54. The linking of Rushdie to American imperialism is ironic and ridiculous in the extreme considering Rushdie's history of harshly criticizing America: in *The Jaguar Smile: A Nicaraguan Journey*, he takes America to task for its policy with regard to the Sandanistas; he criticizes American values in various essays in *Imaginary Homelands* (see, for example, "In God We Trust" 389–392); and he mocks American politics, culture, and economic imperialism throughout his fiction, including *The Satanic Verses* which contains a derogatory reference to the "Coca-Colonization of the planet" (406).

55. Similarly, Rushdie claims that "whereas religion seeks to privilege one language above all others, one set of values above all others, one text above all others, the novel has always been *about* the way in which different languages, values and narratives quarrel, and about the shifting relations between them, which are the relations of power. The novel does not seek to establish a privileged language, but it insists upon the freedom to portray and analyse the struggle between the different contestants for such privileges" (*IH* 420). Speaking more specifically of *The Satanic Verses*, Rushdie asserts, correctly I think, that it "dissents most clearly from imposed orthodoxies *of all types*, from the view that the world is quite clearly This and not That. It dissents from the end of debate, of dispute, of dissent" (396).

Two. Julian Barnes

1. In addition to Hutcheon's influential studies of postmodern fiction, there have been

a number of other important discussions of how recent fiction has drawn attention to the affiliations between fictive and historical forms of writing, including Barbara Foley's *Telling the Truth: The Theory and Practice of Documentary Fiction*, Steven Connor's *The English Novel in History 1950–1995*, Andrzej Gasiorek's *Post-War British Fiction*, Alison Lee's *Realism and Power*, and Patricia Waugh's *Metafiction*.

2. As Susana Onega points out, this way of viewing history was prevalent during the Renaissance—giving rise to hybrid genres such as "the 'mirror', the 'history play', and the historical poem" (9)—and lasted as late as the eighteenth century. With the Enlightenment, however, history as a form of disciplinary inquiry was expected to be objective or "scientific." New Historicists such as White have in a sense brought back the Renaissance idea of history as a literary genre, but with more of an emphasis on the structural and linguistic conventions shared by both.

3. Angela Carter's portrait of the community of professors in *Heroes and Villains* (see Chapter Four) suggests that the masculinist pursuit of objectivity can have a petrifying effect on its adherents. Carter's professors are an updated portrait of Swift's Houynynms: they may embody rationality but they lack the vitality of the Yahoo-esque Barbarians.

4. Similarly, Paul Veyne notes that history and literature share the following common conventions: "selection, organization, diegesis, anecdote, temporal pacing, and emplotment" (see Hutcheon, *Poetics* 111).

5. See, for example, Gasiorek 159; Higdon 180; Kotte 108, 127; Scott 58, 64–65; Todd 273.

6. Graham Hendrick, the historian protagonist of Barnes's *Before She Met Me* who becomes obsessed with his wife's sexual past, is very similar; and most of the narrators of the various episodes in *A History of the World* are incapable of anything approaching "objectivity." This kind of protagonist—who is unable to separate his or her own life from wider historical events, and who feels victimized by history—is actually one of the more common conventions in historiographic metafiction. Such characters as Braithwaite, or Rushdie's Saleem Sinai, or Graham Swift's Tom Crick (*Waterland*) exemplify the dilemma of the disoriented "postmodern" individual unable to make sense of modern history.

7. In his review of Barnes's fictions from *Metroland* through *Flaubert's Parrot*, Frank Kermode notes that Barnes seems to be "obsessed with obsessions."

8. They include *Duffy*, *Fiddle City*, *Putting the Boot In*, and *Going to the Dogs*.

9. Similarly, Louise Colet has two competing entries in Braithwaite's "Dictionary of Accepted Ideas" about Flaubert: one as a "Tedious, importunate, promiscuous woman, lacking talent of her own" (153) and the other as a "Brave, passionate, deeply misunderstood woman crucified by her love for the heartless, impossible, provincial Flaubert" (154).

10. It seems reasonable to assume that Braithwaite is at least in part referring to Fowles's *The French Lieutenant's Woman*, an extremely influential postmodern novel which offers both a conventional ending in which hero and heroine are happily reunited after separation and long suffering, and an unconventional one in which they meet and then go their separate ways, the heroine asserting her independence in a proto-feminist refusal to play into the prescribed social convention of marriage.

11. The comparison with Flaubert's Charles Bovary—also a medical doctor—is an obvious one. Andrzej Gasiorek further suggests that Braithwaite's biography is a Freudian cliché of impotence (161).

12. Del Ivan Janik is more pessimistic about the motivation of his quest: for Braithwaite, he writes, "confrontation with the past provides neither resolution, escape, nor consolation, but at least it forces an acknowledgement of one's inner reality [...] what Flaubert called 'the religion of despair'" (169–170).

13. Gasiorek suggests yet another layer to this game of hypothesizing about people's lives: "The reader is urged to construct a biography of Braithwaite while the latter constructs one of Flaubert. But Braithwaite remains as unknowable as his subject" (160–61).

14. Another is Hemingway's *Nick Adams Stories*.

15. See *The Dialogic Imagination*, especially the "Epic and Novel" essay (3–40).

16. Gasiorek asserts that, as a "cyclical collage," the novel "expunges teleology and totality" and the writer is forced to acknowledge that "he is condemned to traffic in scraps and fragments" (159).

17. The danger of historical revisionism underlies most of Barnes's work. The case of the woodworm is comic, but Barnes is more serious about it in *The Porcupine*, a novel that demonstrates how history is shaped to suit popular opinion by depicting the "show trial" of Stoyo Petkanov, the deposed leader of a former Soviet republic who is modeled on

Bulgaria's Todor Zhivkov. Faced with his ongoing failure to convict Petkanov on the kinds of charges he deserves, the prosecutor, Peter Solinsky, contemplates the possibility that Petkanov will one day be rehabilitated or forgiven by history: "Whether or not such revisionism occurred would partly depend on how he performed in the final week of the trial" (103). To prevent this from happening, Solinsky ironically resorts to a form of historical revisionism of his own—using falsified evidence to accuse Petkanov of having murdered his own daughter.

18. Stuart, the cast-aside husband of Barnes's 1991 novel *Talking It Over*, typifies and gives voice to the twentieth-century obsession with money and material goods, finding in wealth a "consolation" for the wrongs he has suffered: "I'm a materialist. What else is there to be, if you're not a Buddhist monk? The two great creeds that have ruled the world this century—capitalism and communism—are both materialist; one's just better at it than the other, as recent events have proved. Man likes consumer goods, always has, always will. We may as well get used to it" (231–32).

19. Originally published in *The New Yorker* as "The Maggie Years" (15 November 1993: 82–89).

20. Thatcher ignored her Foreign Secretary's advice to attempt a diplomatic resolution. Steven Berkoff hilariously satirized the event in his mock–Shakespearean play *Sink the Belgrano!* (which was widely panned because of its inflammatory nature). The Thatcher persona (called Maggot in the play) responds to "Pimp's" (the Foreign Secretary) suggestion with:

> Oh bloody bollacks compromise you mean
> And wait in turn for others to redeem our
>   wealth
> And sit in calm compliance while we hope
> For others to present to us a deal,
> While whispering give up old colonial ties
> As they in turn make profits with their trade
> Their greed to capture markets far and wide
> Will sugar every bloody thing they say
> And in the end we'll give the bloody lot
>   away!
> By the way Pimp ... where is the Falklands??
> (5)

21. In another essay, Barnes remarks that it was Thatcher's habit to take "History by the lapels and [slap] it around the face in case it was planning to give her less than her due" (*LL* 70).

Three. Jeanette Winterson

1. Following Yahweh, all of the members of Noah's family are arch-capitalists. Noah's son Ham recruits Gloria's mother, Mrs. Munde, to cook in a new chain of restaurants to be built in God's name. Their God is not a socialist, he assures her; he is "YAHWEH the Omnipotent Stockbroker and YAHWEH the Omniscient Lawyer" (30). Indeed, when Yahweh first confronts Noah about the planned film, his protest is a materialistic one—he complains that he doesn't have a contract (90). Winterson's comic portrayal of God as a money-hungry stockbroker and financial guru allies him with the selfish and exploitative ideologies of capitalism. The base, material concerns of capitalism are antithetical to the announced ideologies of Christianity, and yet, Winterson hints, Christian ideals have been compromised in part by such things as the financial exploitation of church congregations by many religious leaders (especially those of the Evangelical communities). Ham's revelation of God as "the Omnipotent Stockbroker" and "Omniscient Lawyer" contributes to Winterson's secularizing portrait of the figurehead of what is to her an oppressive religious institution.

2. See Chapter Four which discusses Carter's views on the consolatory function myths.

3. Moreover, marriage always precedes sex in Bunny's novels so as to mitigate the taboo of sex—the idea that, as Angela Carter puts it in *The Sadeian Woman*, "sex is sanctified only in the service of reproduction" (76)—and therefore not generate guilt in the reader.

4. See Mary Midgley's excellent *Science as Salvation*, a thorough analysis of the history of the human drive to create salvation myths and science's displacement of religion in this regard.

5. Winterson dramatizes this in *Gut Symmetries* when Jove lectures the passengers of the QE2 on time-travel theory. His audience takes it as a given that science will eventually provide a "cure" for aging: "Every morning [Jove] had to explain to elderly gentlemen why they would not be able to regain their hairline by stepping into a time machine. [...] Everyone wanted to know when they would be able to extend their lives indefinitely by living them backwards" (15). Exasperated by their assumptions, he comments to his mistress, Alice: "How many more of them will ask me whether or not they should be refrigerated at death

until science can defrost them into the warmth of perpetual youth?" (18)

6. *Frankenstein*, it is important to note, portrays this ambivalently. Shelley suggests that the resurrection is a crime of science against nature, but she depicts the "Creature" sympathetically. He has a soul, but he cannot find acceptance in a society that considers him "unnatural"; his exile becomes necessary to retain the order of the natural world.

7. Elizabeth Grosz also argues that male dominance has been historically justified by the construction of women's bodies as frail, unpredictable, and unreliable (13).

8. For other feminist critiques of male-biased scientific discourse, see: Lowe and Hubbard; Hubbard, Henifen, and Fried; Birke and Hubbard; Hubbard; Bleier; and Martin (*Woman in the Body*).

9. These last three refer to sexual identities discussed by Julia Cream as not fitting the dominant male/female dichotomy.

10. Hubbard enumerates and criticizes these myths (*Women's Biology*, especially 25–28).

11. See Ute Kauer, "Narration and Gender: The Role of the First-Person Narrator in Jeanette Winterson's *Written on the Body*" (Grice and Woods 41–51).

12. Several other scholars have, like Kauer, come to the conclusion that the narrator is a woman. See, for example: Patricia Duncker, "Jeanette Winterson and the Aftermath of Feminism" (Grice and Woods 77–88); Cath Stowers, "The Erupting Lesbian Body: Reading *Written on the Body* as a Lesbian Text" (Grice and Woods 89–101); and Carolyn Allen, *Following Djuna: Women Lovers and the Erotics of Loss*, who reads the narrator as a woman to support her idea that *Written on the Body* progressively revises the genre of "lesbian popular romance in which the girl loses the girl back to the husband" (71).

13. The ease with which positivist philosophy lends itself to misogynist ideas about femininity is nowhere more clear than in Villiers de L'Isle Adam's *L'Eve Future*. In this novel, Thomas Edison (a fictional portrayal of the historical personage who represents the embodiment of positivism) constructs an automaton to take the place of Alicia, a woman whose "soul" is considered to be "vulgar" by the passion-struck Lord Ewald because she possesses reason and does not exhibit the "saintly stupidity" (43) which is to be expected and desired in a woman. In convincing the reticent Ewald that a machine can easily take the place of a woman, Edison declares that, utilizing the "formidable present-day resources of science," he can "seize the very grace of her gesture, the plentitude of her body, the fragrance of her flesh, the timbre of her voice, the suppleness of her figure, the light of her eyes, the distinctive features in her movements and walk, the personality of her glance" (72), etc. In a text littered with vicious misogyny, perhaps the most striking example of the sexism of Edison's plan is his limitation of the automaton to approximately "seventy general movements [...] the usual repertory of a well-bred woman" (150). These movements are to be utterly controlled by Ewald by pressing on one of her ten rings or the pearls of her necklace. Similarly, Edison's proposal to produce the automaton's voice via recordings held on two internal phonograph records is aimed at limiting her utterances to those consistent with "the first hours of love" (154). *L'Eve Future* revels in lengthy, detailed passages about how women can be reduced to predictable, mechanical processes that can be reproduced through technology.

14. In *Gut Symmetries*, Winterson quotes Robert Oppenheimer: "If we ask whether the position of the electron remains the same we must say no. If we ask whether the electron's position changes with time, we must say no. If we ask whether the electron is at rest we must say no. If we ask whether it is in motion we must say no" (84).

15. See also Baudrillard's *Simulations*, in which he argues that the whole of reality has become simulacral—that "reality" has become "hyperreal" or, in other words, is now characterized by the complete substitution of "signs of the real for the real itself" (4).

16. Scott Bukatman discusses William Gibson's cyberpunk fiction in this respect, demonstrating how Case, the protagonist of *Neuromancer*, is only fully himself when he is "jacked in" to cyberspace (204–208). Paradoxically, to achieve substantiality and empowerment in cyberspace requires insubstantiality and disempowerment in "real" space (195).

17. In *Orlando*—which, given its androgynous protagonist, its subject matter, and Winterson's stylistic homage to Woolf, is an important intertext for *Written on the Body*—Woolf makes her ambivalence to modernity clear: "what more terrifying revelation can there be than that it is the present moment? That we survive the shock at all is only possible because the past shelters us on one side,

the future on another" (298). Winterson acknowledges her debt to Woolf in *Art Objects*, especially in the essays "A Gift of Wings" (61–77) and "A Veil of Words" (79–99).

18. This section of the novel is, as Christy Burns (299), M. Daphne Kutzer (143), and Patricia Duncker ("Jeanette Winterson and the Aftermath of Feminism," Grice and Woods 77–88) have noted, evocative of Monique Wittig's *The Lesbian Body*, another text that seeks to poetically re-imagine the female body by using anatomical and scientific vocabulary.

19. Ruth Hubbard observes that "Scientific language helps to lend science an aura of depersonalized authority. [...] [I]t is usual for that language to delete the agent. [...] [It] implicitly denies the relevance of time, place, social context, authorship, and personal responsibility" (*Women's Biology* 12–13). Ruth Bleier is particularly critical of this convention, associating science's mask of "neutrality" with the fascism of the Ku Klux Klan: "It is the lab coat, literally and symbolically, that wraps the scientist in the robe of innocence—of a pristine and aseptic neutrality—and gives him, like the klansman, a faceless authority that his audience can't challenge. From the sheeted figure comes a powerful, mysterious, impenetrable, coercive, anonymous male voice" (62).

20. Hubbard argues that "The acceptance of science as the only proper way to learn about the natural world, including ourselves, locks us into seeing the world as the sum of those relationships and juxtapositions of objects and events that scientists can comprehend and analyze" (15).

21. Such metaphors have been used to justify abhorrent political actions. Nazi propaganda, for example, frequently portrayed the Jews as a cancer, "legitimating" a radical "treatment": excision, as of a tumor (Sontag 83–84).

22. Christy Burns relates this strategy to the fantastic and argues that throughout Winterson's work she uses fantastic language "to bridge the gap between harsh reality and a more hopeful construction of the social imaginary [...] to open up a space for alternative lifestyles (alternatives to family, to heterosexuality, to society, to postmodern media)" (304).

23. Similarly, Elizabeth Grosz contends that "the guiding assumptions and prevailing methods used by [medical, biological, chemical] disciplines (indeed, by any disciplines) have tangible effects on the bodies studied. Bodies are not inert; they function interactively and productively. They act and react" (xi).

24. Similarly, in Richard Hernnstein's infamous *The Bell Curve*, he employed supposedly scientific methods and criteria to support his claim that black people are less intelligent than white people. As Ruth Bleier would no doubt comment, in defending his conclusions as the result of "scientific" analysis, he attempted to hide behind the mask of scientific "neutrality."

25. Stacy D'Erasmo observes that Winterson depicts Louise's body as "weapon, flora, fauna, weather, animal, geography, prison, food, light, nest, jagged edge: it is the body as a whole world" (85); and Leigh Allison Wilson notes that "At times Louise disappears into abstraction, her personality more on the order of a nebula than an individual" (6).

26. See Lyn Pykett, "A New Way With Words? Jeanette Winterson's Post-Modernism" (Grice and Woods 53–60).

27. Flax enumerates such key Enlightenment-derived beliefs in "Postmodernism and Gender Relations in Feminist Theory" (41–42).

28. Carolyn Allen comments that "The ending makes a definitive closure impossible, even as it invites readers driven by romance conventions [among the most important of which is the happy ending] to conclude that Louise has returned" (72)

29. See "Grand (Dis)Unified Theories? Dislocated Discourses in *Gut Symmetries*" (Grice and Woods 117–126).

Four. Angela Carter

1. Only Doris Lessing comes to mind as an "experimental" British woman writer to have preceded Carter.

2. See "'A Room of One's Own, or a Bloody Chamber?': Angela Carter and Political Correctness" (Sage, *Flesh* 308–320).

3. Cranny-Francis offers the example of George Eliot's *Middlemarch*, in which the conventional heterosexual marriage is offered but the reader is left in doubt as to whether it will succeed (94).

4. See, for example: Lee's *Red as Blood*, Sexton's *Transformations*, Tepper's *Beauty*, Byatt's *The Djinn in the Nightingale's Eyes: Five Fairy Stories*, and Atwood's *Bluebeard's Egg and Other Stories*. Jack Zipes collects a number of excellent feminist fairy tales in *Don't Bet on the Prince*.

5. Though, as Angela Carter points out in

her introduction to *The Virago Book of Fairy Tales*, "since there is no such thing as pure pleasure, there is always more going on than meets the eye" (xii).

6. Given the nationalistic project of the Grimm brothers, their fairy tales constitute one of the discourses which Benedict Anderson suggests contribute to the process of "imagining" a "political community." See also Zipes, *The Brothers Grimm*.

7. Zipes is referring to Propp's *Morphology of the Folk Tale*.

8. There is an English translation of this collection by Carter entitled *The Fairy Tales of Charles Perrault*.

9. The conduct book was a popular genre of the time which was aimed at controlling the social and sexual deportment of young women

10. See, for example, Bettelheim's *The Uses of Enchantment*. For an excellent overview of psychoanalytical interpretations of fairy tales, see Dundes.

11. Mary Kaiser argues that Carter's "recyclings" carry their revisionary ideological import especially in their historical and cultural specificity. That is, Carter takes fairy tales out of the timeless frame offered by the "Once upon a time" formula and "link[s] each tale to the zeitgeist of its moment [...] to call attention to the literary fairy tale as a product, not of a collective unconscious, but of specific cultural, political, and economic positions. [...] Carter deconstructs the underlying assumptions of the 'official' fairy tale: that fairy tales are universal, timeless myths, that fairy tales are meant exclusively for an audience of children, and that fairy tales present an idealized, fantastic world unrelated to the contingencies of real life. Instead, Carter [...] presents them as studies in the history of imagining sexuality and gender" (35).

12. In *The Sadeian Woman*, Carter strikingly suggests that sexual relationships are inevitably commodified and that marriage is a form of "legalised prostitution" (59).

13. In "The Popularity of Pornography," Andrew Ross chronicles in detail the split between antiporn feminists and what he terms the "anti-antiporn feminists."

14. See Elizabeth Wilson, "Feminist Fundamentalism: The Shifting Politics of Sex and Censorship" (Segal and McIntosh 15–28: 16).

15. See, for example: Dworkin's *Pornography: Men Possessing Women* and *Letters from a War Zone*; MacKinnon's *Only Words*. See also Kappeler, Griffin, and Brownmiller.

16. Snitow's essay is "Retrenchment vs. Transformation: The Politics of the Antipornography Movement" (Ellis 10–17).

17. Carter, as Elaine Jordan implies (27), was frequently contentious for the sake of unsettling our assumptions.

18. In "(Male) Desire and (Female) Disgust: Reading *Hustler*," Laura Kipnis appreciates similarly iconoclastic strategies at the heart of one of today's most infamous products of pornography: *Hustler* magazine. Though an intensely misogynistic publication, Kipnis, similar to Carter's appraisal of Sade, notes that *Hustler* presents irreverent images that attack the ideologies of a reactionary, theistic, and morally hypocritical society.

19. See especially pages 84–85. Carter, in turn, has confided to Elaine Jordan that "if I can get up [...] the Dworkin proboscis, then my living has not been in vain" (Sage, *Flesh* 332, n5).

20. Also in that essay—"Biological Superiority: The World's Most Dangerous and Deadly Idea"—Dworkin criticizes some feminists who believe in the biological superiority of women.

21. Naomi Morgenstern discusses *Mercy* as a text whose foremost generic traits are derived from pornographic and gothic fiction—two of the genres most used by Carter. Harriet Gilbert, in "So Long as It's not Sex and Violence: Andrea Dworkin's *Mercy*" (Segal and McIntosh 216–229), finds numerous parallels in *Mercy*'s story line to that of Sade's *Justine*. While not wanting to establish that the novel is "pornographic," Gilbert makes it clear that it would be very easy for a legal authority to do so. Gilbert's argument was prophetic as, ironically, one of the censorship laws inspired by MacKinnon and Dworkin's antipornography ordinance resulted in the seizure of Dworkin's books *Woman Hating* and *Pornography: Men Possessing Women* by Canadian customs officials (see Strossen 158, 205–6).

22. There have been many arguments that there is no evidence for such a causal relationship (see, for example, Goldstein and Kant; McNair 60–71). By the same token, a view of fantasy as utterly divorced from reality is naive. Certainly, pornographic depictions can be a part of the construction of real-life sexuality, though Goldstein has suggested that, if anything, it is the withholding of pornographic materials and other sources of information about sex in adolescence that can contribute to the development of criminal sexual behavior. But what Carter wants to convince us of

is that pornography can also be scripted and/ or perceived in such a way as to critique the power relations between the sexes.

23. Mackinnon, like Kappeler, makes an over-simplistic equation between pornographic representations and sexual reality: "Pornography is not imagery in some relation to a reality elsewhere constructed. It is not a distortion, reflection, projection, expression, fantasy, representation, or symbol either. It is sexual reality" (*Feminism Unmodified* 149).

24. Nor do I mean to uncritically endorse all of Carter's ideas on the subject. I find some of the details of Carter's analysis of Sade unconvincing and misguided. For all of her glorification of Juliette's transgressions of taboo, Carter does, as Kappeler points out, relish the representation of woman as inflictor of suffering—a role that has historically been exercised exclusively by men. While this does represent an upheaval of gender power dynamics, it is not, to say the least, the most humanitarian attitude towards gender role reformation. Fortunately, Carter does qualify her celebration of this impulse (*SW* 111).

25. Linda Williams critiques Dworkin's appeal to the archetype of the "suffering woman" to broker an alliance with the conservative, male-dominated Meese Commission on Pornography: "only by casting her archetypal 'suffering woman' in the role of the absolute victim of history can Dworkin utter her appeal to the compassionate man who will save her" (21).

26. This is one of Judith Butler's arguments in *Gender Trouble*, but Carter had conceived and, more importantly, dramatized the idea of gender as performance years beforehand.

27. Susan Rubin Suleiman notes that Carter derives elements of this scene from the Surrealist writer Robert Desnos's *La Liberté ou l'amour!* (see Suleiman 137).

28. Other sexually explicit scenes in Carter's fiction similarly demonstrate how the conventions of pornography highlight sexuality devoid of humanity, as when Desiderio, the protagonist of *The Infernal Desire Machines of Doctor Hoffman*, accompanies the Sadeian Count to the "House of Anonymity": they don costumes which are "unaesthetic, priapic and totally obliterated our faces and our self-respect; the garb grossly emphasized our manhoods while utterly denying our humanity" (130).

29. Robert Clark is notorious for having done so. His arguments against Carter have been more than adequately debated in Elaine Jordan's article "Enthralment: Angela Carter's Speculative Fictions" and elsewhere.

30. Gerardine Meaney contrasts Carter's critique of the maternal archetype to Cixous and Kristeva's ideas (98–100).

31. Marianne Warner writes that the kind of "double drag" Carter performs here—"a woman speaking through a man disguised as a woman"—was her favored stratagem for questioning how sexual identity is attained; see "Angela Carter: Bottle Blonde, Double Drag" (Sage, *Flesh* 243–256: 251).

32. Irigaray is implicitly responding to Lacan's exclusion of women from the symbolic in his model of psycho-linguistic development (see "The Mirror Stage"). Given the numerous allusions to Lacan in this part of *New Eve*, it is reasonable to assume that Zero is intentionally a parody of Lacan.

33. In *The Sadeian Woman*, Carter suggests that Justine relocates her virginity from her hymen to her frigidity: as long as she represses all possibility of experiencing pleasure, she is still "pure" (48–49). Similarly, each sexual encounter between Eve and Zero is "a renewed defloration, as if his violence perpetually refreshed my virginity" (*PNE* 101).

34. Or, as Alison Lee notes, "Both Eve and Tristessa learn to *perform* their genders, and the very act of performance suggests a liminality that would seem to argue against an original essence" ("Angela" 246).

35. According to Kabbalistic tradition, Lilith was the first wife of Adam who was destroyed by God for insisting on sexual equality.

36. It is also important to note that the text does warn of the persistence of archetypes: Mother has "retired" but only "for the duration of the hostilities" (*PNE* 174). And the text ends with Eve at sea, ironically praying to the ocean as mother: "Ocean, ocean, mother of mysteries, bear me to the place of birth" (191).

37. Williams derives this idea from Jameson's analysis of the medieval romance in *The Political Unconscious* (Williams 129).

38. "Speculative-fiction" is often a preferred term for categorizing a group of closely affiliated genres such as science fiction, fantasy, dystopian fiction, the fantastic, etc.

39. Mary E. Bradley Lane's *Mizora: A Prophecy* (1890) was another important early feminist utopia.

40. See, for example: Lessing's *Memoirs of a Survivor*; Tiptree's "The Girl Who Was Plugged In"; Atwood's *The Handmaid's Tale*; Charnas's *Motherlines*; Le Guin's *The Left Hand*

of Darkness and *The Dispossessed*; Russ's *The Female Man*; Piercy's *Women on the Edge of Time*.

41. See, for example: Butler's *Dawn* and *The Parable of the Sower*; Sargent's *The Shore of Women*; Tuttle's *A Spaceship Built of Stone and Other Stories*; Tepper's *The Gate to Women's Country*; Cadigan's *Synners*; Elgin's *Native Tongue*; Weldon's *The Cloning of Joanna May*; Dorsey's *Machine Sex and Other Stories*. A good introduction to some of the best recent feminist science fiction is Pamela Sargent's anthology *Women of Wonder: The Contemporary Years*.

42. Roz Kaveney, in "New New World Dreams: Angela Carter and Science Fiction" (Sage, *Flesh* 171–188), describes some of Carter's influences in the SF genre and discusses her importance to contemporary SF fans and authors.

43. In an interview with Olga Kenyon, Carter declared that her novel was in part inspired by one of the earliest examples of this genre: Richard Jeffries's 1885 "apocalyptic, back-to-nature" novel, *After London* (Kenyon 30).

44. Gorman Beauchamp, for example, writes that the dystopian novel "warns against the growing potentialities of modern technology" (53). Occasionally, however, the genre served as propaganda for America's nuclear armament policy. For an excellent historical discussion of fictional depictions of nuclear armageddon, see H. Bruce Franklin's *War Stars*, especially chapters 8–14.

45. This idea was later given extensive academic attention by Michel Foucault in *Discipline and Punish*.

46. Gerardine Meaney notes that Carter modeled Jewel in part on *Wuthering Heights*'s Heathcliff (91).

Five. Failing to Observe Decorum

1. Thanks to Jeanne Rose for sharing her ideas and work on this contemporary genre of fiction.

2. The scenario, McEwan reveals in an author's note at the end of the novel, is based on an actual spy project executed jointly by the CIA and MI6 from 1955 to 1956.

3. McEwan is similarly incisive in his critique of masculine ideals in *The Comfort of Strangers*, a novel which employs conventions of the travel fiction genre but which plays out as a tale that critiques and warns of the link between masculine, patriarchal violence and sado-masochistic sexual violence.

Works Cited

Achebe, Chinua. "An Image of Africa." *Hopes and Impediments: Selected Essays*. New York: Anchor Books, 1989. 1–20.

Afzal-Khan, Fawzia. *Cultural Imperialism and the Indo-English Novel: Genre and Ideology in R. K. Narayan, Anita Desai, Kamala Markandaya, and Salman Rushdie*. University Park, PA: Penn State UP, 1993.

Ahmad, Aijaz. *In Theory: Classes, Nations, Literatures*. London: Verso, 1992.

Ahsan, M. M., and A. R. Kidwai, eds. *Sacrilege versus Civility: Muslim Perspectives on* The Satanic Verses *Affair*. 1991. Revised ed. Leicester, U.K.: The Islamic Foundation, 1993.

Allen, Carolyn. *Following Djuna: Women Lovers and the Erotics of Loss*. Bloomington: Indiana UP, 1996.

Amis, Martin. *The Information*. 1995. New York: Vintage, 1996.

_____. *London Fields*. 1989. New York: Vintage, 1991.

_____. *Time's Arrow*. 1991. London: Penguin, 1992.

Anderson, Benedict. *Imagined Communities: Reflections on the Origin and Spread of Nationalism*. 1983. London: Verso, 1991.

Anees, Munawar A. *The Kiss of Judas: Affairs of a Brown Sahib*. Kuala Lumpur, Malaysia: Quill, 1989.

Annan, Gabriele. "Devil in the Flesh." Rev. of *Written on the Body*, by Jeanette Winterson. *New York Review of Books* 4 March, 1993: 22–23.

Appignanesi, Lisa. Interview with Angela Carter. *Writers Talk, Ideas of Our Time*. Videocassette. ICA Guardian Conversations (Tape 20). London: ICA Video, 1989.

Appignanesi, Lisa, and Sara Maitland, eds. *The Rushdie File*. Syracuse: Syracuse UP, 1990.

Artaud, Antonin. *The Theatre and Its Double*. Trans. Mary Caroline Richards. New York: Grove, 1958.

Asad, Talal. *Genealogies of Religion: Discipline and Reasons of Power in Christianity and Islam*. Baltimore: Johns Hopkins UP, 1993.

Asari, Farzaneh. "Iran in the British Media." *Index on Censorship* 18.5 (May 1989): 9–13.

Atwood, Margaret. *The Handmaid's Tale*. 1985. New York: Ballantine, 1987.

_____. *Bluebeard's Egg and Other Stories*. 1983. Boston: Houghton Mifflin, 1986.

Bakhtin, Mikhail. *The Dialogic Imagination*. Ed. Michael Holquist. Trans. Caryl Emerson and Michael Holquist. Austin: U of Texas P, 1981.

_____. "The Problem of Speech Genres." *Speech Genres and Other Late Essays*. Trans. Vern W. McGee. Eds. Caryl Emerson and Michael Holquist. Austin: U of Texas P, 1986.

Barnes, Julian. *Before She Met Me*. 1982. London: Picador, 1986.

_____. *Flaubert's Parrot*. 1984. London: Picador, 1985.

_____. *A History of the World in 10 1/2 Chapters*. London: Picador, 1989.

_____. *Letters from London*. New York: Vintage, 1995.

_____. *Metroland*. 1980. London: Picador, 1990.

_____. *The Porcupine*. 1992. London: Picador, 1993.

_____. *Staring at the Sun*. London: Picador, 1986.

_____. *Talking It Over*. 1991. London: Picador, 1992.

Barr, Helen. "Face to Face: A Conversation Between Jeanette Winterson and Helen Barr." *English Review* 2 (1991): 30–33.

Baudrillard, Jean. "The Ecstasy of Communication." *The Anti-Aesthetic: Essays on Postmodern Culture*. Ed. Hal Foster. Seattle: Bay Press, 1983. 126–34.

_____. *Simulations*. Trans. Paul Foss, Paul Patton, Philip Beitchman. New York: Semiotext[e], 1983.

Bayley, John. "Fighting for the Crown." *The New York Review of Books*. 23 April 1992. 9–11.

Beauchamp, Gorman. "Technology in the Dystopian Novel." *Modern Fiction Studies* 32.1 (1996): 53–63.

Beebee, Thomas O. *The Ideology of Genre: A Comparative Study of Generic Instability*. University Park, PA: Penn State UP, 1994.

Bergonzi, Bernard. *The Situation of the Novel*. 1970. Rev. ed.: London: Macmillan, 1979.

Berkoff, Steven. *Sink the Belgrano! and Massage*. London: Faber, 1987.

Bettelheim, Bruno. *The Uses of Enchantment: The Meaning and Importance of Fairy Tales*. New York: Knopf, 1996.

Bhabha, Homi K., ed. *Nation and Narration*. London: Routledge, 1990.

Birke, Lynda, and Ruth Hubbard, eds. *Reinventing Biology: Respect for Life and the Creation of Knowledge*. Bloomington: Indiana UP, 1995.

Bleich, David. *Know and Tell: A Writing Pedagogy of Disclosure, Genre, and Membership*. Portsmouth, NH: Boynton/Cook, 1998.

Bleier, Ruth. "Lab Coat: Robe of Innocence or Klansman's Sheet?" *Feminist Studies/ Critical Studies*. Ed. Teresa de Lauretis. Bloomington: Indiana UP, 1986. 54–66.

Bono, Paula. "The Passion for Sexual Difference: On (Re)Reading Angela Carter's *The Passion of New Eve*. *Tessera* 11 (Winter 1991): 31–46.

Booker, M. Keith. "*Finnegans Wake* and *The Satanic Verses*: Two Modern Myths of the Fall." *Critique: Studies in Contemporary Fiction* 32.3 (Spring 1991): 190–207.

Borges, Jorge Luis. *Labyrinths: Selected Stories and Other Writings*. 1962. New York: New Directions, 1964.

Bradbury, Malcolm, and David Palmer, eds. *The Contemporary English Novel*. London: Edward Arnold, 1979.

Brecht, Bertolt. *Brecht on Theatre: The Development of an Aesthetic*. Ed. and Trans. John Willett. New York: Hill and Wang, 1964.

Brennan, Timothy. *Salman Rushdie and the Third World: Myths of the Nation*. New York: Saint Martin's, 1989.

Brownmiller, Susan. *Against Our will: Men, Women, and Rape.* New York: Simon and Schuster, 1975.

Bukatman, Scott. *Terminal Identity: The Virtual Subject in Postmodern Science Fiction.* Durham, North Carolina: Duke UP, 1993.

Burgess, Anthony. *A Clockwork Orange.* 1962. New York: Norton, 1986.

Burns, Christy. "Fantastic Language: Jeanette Winterson's Recovery of the Postmodern Word." *Contemporary Literature* 37.2 (1996): 278–306.

Butler, Judith. *Gender Trouble: Feminism and the Subversion of Identity.* New York: Routledge, 1990.

Butler, Octavia. *Dawn.* New York: Warner, 1987.

_____. *The Parable of the Sower.* New York: Warner, 1993.

Byatt, A. S. *The Djinn in the Nightingale's Eyes: Five Fairy Stories.* New York: Random House, 1997.

_____. "A New Body of Writing: Darwin and Recent British Fiction." *New Writing 4: An Anthology.* Eds. A. S. Byatt and Alan Hollinghurst. London: Vintage 1995. 439–448.

_____. *Possession: A Romance.* 1990. New York: Vintage, 1991.

Cadigan, Pat. *Synners.* New York: Bantam, 1991.

Carter, Angela. *The Bloody Chamber and Other Stories.* London: Virago, 1979.

_____. *Fireworks.* 1974. London: Virago, 1988.

_____. *Heroes and Villains.* 1969. London: Penguin, 1981.

_____. *The Infernal Desire Machines of Doctor Hoffman.* 1972. London: Penguin, 1982.

_____. "The Language of Sisterhood." *The Fate of the Language.* Eds. L. Michaels and C. Ricks. Berkeley: U of California P, 1980.

_____. *The Magic Toyshop.* 1967. London: Virago, 1981.

_____. *Nights at the Circus.* 1994. London: Penguin, 1986.

_____. "Notes from the Front Line." *On Gender and Writing.* Ed. Michelene Wandor. London: Pandora, 1983. 69–77.

_____. *Nothing Sacred.* London: Virago, 1982.

_____. *The Passion of New Eve.* 1977. London: Virago, 1982.

_____. *The Sadeian Woman and the Ideology of Pornography.* New York: Pantheon, 1978.

_____. *Shadow Dance.* 1966. London: Virago: 1994.

_____. *Wise Children.* 1991. London: Penguin, 1993.

_____, ed. *The Virago Book of Fairy Tales.* London: Virago, 1990. ix–xxii.

Charnas, Suzy McKee. *Motherlines.* Hastings-on-Hudson: Ultramarine Publishing, 1978.

Chaudhuri, Una. "Imaginative Maps: Excerpts from a Conversation with Salman Rushdie." *Turnstile* 2.1 (1990): 36–47.

Chodorow, Nancy. *The Reproduction of Mothering: Psychoanalysis and the Sociology of Gender.* Berkeley: U of California P, 1978.

Cixous, Helene. "The Laugh of the Medusa." Trans. K. and P. Cohen. *Signs* 1(1): 875–99.

Clark, Robert. "Angela Carter's Desire Machines." *Women's Studies* 14 (1987): 147–161.

Cohen, Ralph. "Afterword: The Problems of Generic Transformation." *Romance: Generic Transformation from Chretien de Troyes to Cervantes.* Eds. Kevin Brownlee and Marina Scordilis Brownlee. Hanover: UP of New England, 1985. 265–280.

_____. "Do Postmodern Genres Exist?" *Postmodern Genres.* Ed. Marjorie Perloff. Norman: U of Oklahoma P, 1989. 10–27.

_____. "History and Genre." *New Literary History: A Journal of Theory and Interpretation* 17.2 (1986): 203–18.

Cohn-Sherbok, Dan, ed. *The Salman Rushdie Controversy in Interreligious Perspective.* Lewiston, NY: Edwin Meelen, 1990.

Comte, August. *Cours de Philosophie Positive.* 6 vols. Paris: J. B. Bailliaere, 1869.

Connor, Steven. *The English Novel In History 1950–1995.* London: Routledge, 1996.

Conrad, Joseph. *Heart of Darkness and The Secret Sharer.* New York: Bantam, 1981.

Coupland, Douglas. *Microserfs.* New York: ReganBooks 1995.

Cranny-Francis, Anne. "Gender and Genre: Feminist Subversion of Genre Fiction and Its Implications for Critical Literacy." *The Powers of Literacy: A Genre Approach to Teaching Writing.* Eds. Bill Cope and Mary Kalantzis. Pittsburgh, PA: U of Pittsburgh P, 1993.

Cream, Julia. "Re-solving Riddles: The Sexed Body." *Mapping Desire: Geographies of Sexualities.* Eds. David Bell and Gill Valentine. London: Routledge, 1995. 31–40.

D'Erasmo, Stacy. "A Lover's Discourse: Jeanette Winterson's Body of Evidence." Rev. of *Written on the Body*, by Jeanette Winterson. *Village Voice Literary Supplement* 23 February, 1993: 85.

Davies, J. M. Q. "Aspects of the Grotesque in Rushdie's *The Satanic Verses.*" *AUMLA: Journal of the Australasian Universities Language and Literature Association* 85 (May 1996): 29–37.

Dawood, N. J., trans. *The Koran.* 1956. London: Penguin, 1995.

DeLillo, Don. *White Noise.* New York: Viking, 1985.

Doan, Laura. "Jeanette Winterson's Sexing the Postmodern." *The Lesbian Postmodern.* Ed. Laura Doan. New York: Columbia UP, 1994. 137–155.

Dorfman, Ariel. *Widows.* Trans. Stephen Kessler. New York: Penguin, 1983.

Dorsey, Candas Jane. *Machine Sex and Other Stories.* London: Women's Press, 1988.

Doyle, Roddy. *Paddy Clarke Ha Ha Ha.* 1994. New York: Viking 1995.

Dundes, Alan. "Interpreting 'Little Red Riding Hood' Psychoanalytically." *Little Red Riding Hood: A Casebook.* Ed. Alan Dundes. Madison: U of Wisconsin P, 1989. 192–236.

Duperray, Max, ed. *Historicité et Metafiction dans le Roman Contemporain des Iles Britanniques.* Aix-en-Provence, France: U of Provence P, 1994.

Dworkin, Andrea. *Letters from a War Zone.* Brooklyn, NY: Lawrence Hill, 1993.

_____. *Mercy.* New York: Four Walls Eight Windows, 1991.

_____. *Pornography: Men Possessing Women.* New York: Putnam, 1979.

Elgin, Suzette. *Native Tongue.* New York: DAW, 1984.

Ellerby, Janet Mason. "Narrative Imperialism in *The Satanic Verses.*" *Multicultural Literatures through Feminist/Poststructuralist Lenses.* Ed. Barbara Frey Waxman. Knoxville: U of Tennessee P, 1993. 173–89.

Ellis, Kate, et al., eds. *Caught Looking: Feminism, Pornography, and Censorship.* East Haven, CT: Long River Books, 1986.

Esquivel, Laura. *Like Water for Chocolate: A Novel in Monthly Installments, with Recipes, Romances, and Home Remedies.* Trans. Carol and Thomas Christensen. New York: Doubleday, 1992.

Flax, Jane. "The End of Innocence." *Feminists Theorize the Political.* Eds. Judith Butler and Joan W. Scott. New York: Routledge, 1992. 445–463.

_____. "Postmodernism and Gender Relations in Feminist Theory." *Feminism/ Postmodernism.* Ed. Linda J. Nicholson. New York: Routledge, 1990. 39–62.

Foley, Barbara. *Telling the Truth: The Theory and Practice of Documentary Fiction.* Ithaca, NY: Cornell UP, 1986.

Foucault, Michel. *Discipline and Punish: The Birth of the Prison.* 1975. Trans. Alan Sheridan. New York: Vintage, 1979.

Fowles, John. *The French Lieutenant's Woman.* 1969. Boston: Signet, 1970.

Fowler, Alastair. "The Future of Genre Theory: Functions and Constructional Types." *The Future of Literary Theory.* Ed. Ralph Cohen. New York: Routledge, 1989. 291–303.

Franklin, H. Bruce. *War Stars: The Superweapon and the American Imagination.* New York: Oxford UP, 1988.

Freedman, Diane P. *An Alchemy of Genres: Cross-Genre Writing by American Feminist Poet-Critics.* Charlottesville, VA: U of Virginia P, 1992.

French, Jana L. *Fantastic Histories: A Dialogic Approach to a Narrative Hybrid.* Unpublished Dissertation. University of Wisconsin-Madison, 1996.

Frye, Northrop. *Anatomy of Criticism: Four Essays.* 1957. Princeton: Princeton UP, 1971.

Gasiorek, Andrzej. *Post-War British Fiction: Realism and After.* London: Edward Arnold, 1995.

Gibson, William. *Neuromancer.* New York: Ace, 1984.

Gilman, Charlotte Perkins. *Herland.* 1915. New York: Pantheon, 1979.

Goldstein, Michael J., and Harold Sanford Kant. *Pornography and Sexual Deviance.* Berkeley: U of California P, 1973.

Goldsworthy, Kerryn. Interview with Angela Carter. *Meanjin* 44.1 (March 1985): 4–13.

Gorra, Michael. *After Empire: Scott, Naipaul, Rushdie.* Chicago: U of Chicago P, 1997.

Greene, Graham. *The Heart of the Matter.* 1948. London: Penguin, 1968.

_____. *The Power and the Glory.* 1940. London: Penguin, 1962.

Grewal, Inderpal. "Salman Rushdie: Marginality, Women, and Shame." *Genders* 3 (Fall 1988): 24–42.

Grice, Helena, and Tim Woods, eds. *'I'm telling your stories': Jeanette Winterson and the Politics of Reading.* Amsterdam: Rodopi, 1998.

Griffin, Susan. *Pornography and Silence: Culture's Revenge Against Nature.* New York: Harper & Row, 1981.

Grosz, Elizabeth. *Volatile Bodies: Toward a Corporeal Feminism.* Bloomington: Indiana UP, 1994.

Haggard, H. Rider. *Three Adventure Novels.* New York: Dover, 1951.

Hampden, John. *The Beggar's Opera and other Eighteenth-Century Plays.* London: Dent (Everyman's Library), 1975.

Harris, Wilson. *The Infinite Rehearsal.* London: Faber, 1987.

Hemingway, Ernest. *The Nick Adams Stories.* New York: Scribner, 1972.

Herrnstein, Richard. *The Bell Curve: Intelligence and Class Structure in American Life.* New York: Free Press, 1994.

Higdon, David Leon. "'Unconfessed Confessions': the Narrators of Graham Swift and Julian Barnes." *The British and Irish Novel Since 1960.* Ed. James Acheson. New York: St. Martin's, 1991.

Hubbard, Ruth. *The Politics of Women's Biology.* New Brunswick: Rutgers UP, 1990.

Hubbard, Ruth, Mary Sue Henifen, and Barbara Fried, eds. *Women Look at Biology Looking at Women: A Collection of Feminist Critiques.* Cambridge, Mass.: Schenkman, 1979.

Huggan, Graham. "The Postcolonial Exotic: Salman Rushdie and the Booker of Bookers." *Transition* 64: 22–29.

_____. "Prizing 'Otherness': A Short History of the Booker." *Studies in the Novel* 29.3 (Fall 1997): 412–433.

Hulme, Keri. *The Bone People.* 1984. New York: Penguin, 1986.

Hussain, Mushahid. "A Muslim's Perspective." *Index on Censorship* 19.4 (April 1990): 12–13.

Hutcheon, Linda. *A Poetics of Postmodernism: History, Theory, Fiction.* New York: Routledge, 1988.

_____. *The Politics of Postmodernism*. London: Routledge, 1989.

Irigaray, Luce. *This Sex Which Is Not One*. Trans. Catherine Porter. Ithaca: Cornell UP, 1985.

Ishiguro, Kazuo. *The Remains of the Day*. London: Faber, 1989.

Jackson, Rosemary. *Fantasy: The Literature of Subversion*. 1981. London: Routledge, 1988.

Jameson, Fredric. "Magical Narratives: Romance as Genre." *New Literary History* 7.1 (1986): 135–163.

_____. "Modernism and Imperialism." *Nationalism, Colonialism, and Literature*. Eds. Fredric Jameson, et al. Minneapolis: U of Minnesota P, 1990. 43–66.

_____. *The Political Unconscious*. Ithaca: Cornell UP, 1981.

_____. *Postmodernism, or, The Cultural Logic of Late Capitalism*. Durham, NC: Duke UP, 1991.

Janik, Del Ivan. "No End of History: Evidence from the Contemporary English Novel." *Twentieth Century Literature* 41.2 (Summer 1995): 160–89.

Jeffries, Richard. *After London, or, Wild England*. 1885. North Stratford: Ayer, 1975.

Jordan, Elaine. "Enthrallment: Angela Carter's Speculative Fictions." *Plotting Change: Contemporary Women's Fiction*. Ed. Linda Anderson. London: Edward Arnold, 1990. 19–40.

Jordan, June. "Nobody Mean More to Me Than You and the Future Life of Willie Jordan." *On Call: Political Essays*. Boston: South End Press, 1985. 123–139.

Joyce, James. *Ulysses*. Ed. Hans Walter Gabler. New York: Vintage, 1986.

Kafka, Franz. *The Metamorphosis, The Penal Colony, and Other Stories*. Trans. Willa and Edwin Muir. New York: Schocken, 1948.

Kaiser, Mary. "Fairy Tales as Sexual Allegory: Intertextuality in Angela Carter's *The Bloody Chamber*." *The Review of Contemporary Fiction* 14.3 (Fall 1994): 30–36.

Kamra, Sukeshi. "Replacing the Colonial Gaze: Gender as Strategy in Salman Rushdie's Fiction." *Between the Lines: South Asians and Post-Coloniality*. Eds. Deepika Bahri and Mary Vasudeva. Philadelphia, PA: Temple UP, 1996. 237–49.

Kappeler, Susanne. *The Pornography of Representation*. Cambridge, U.K.: Polity Press, 1986.

Katsavos, Anna. "An Interview with Angela Carter." *The Review of Contemporary Fiction* 14.3 (Fall 1994): 11–17.

Kavanagh, Dan [Julian Barnes]. *Duffy*. London: Jonathan Cape, 1980.

_____. *Fiddle City*. London: Jonathan Cape, 1981.

_____. *Going to the Dogs*. London: Jonathan Cape, 1987.

_____. *Putting the Boot In*. London: Jonathan Cape, 1985.

Kendrick, Walter. "Fiction in Review." Rev. of *Written on the Body*, by Jeanette Winterson. *The Yale Review* 81 (1993): 131–33.

Kenyon, Olga. *The Writer's Imagination: Interviews with Major International Women Novelists*. Bradford: U of Bradford P, 1992.

Kermode, Frank. "Obsessed with Obsession." *The Uses of Error*. Cambridge, MA: Harvard UP, 1991: 362–68.

Kipnis, Laura. "(Male) Desire and (Female) Disgust: Reading *Hustler*." *Cultural Studies*. Eds. Lawrence Grossberg, Cary Nelson, Paula Treichler. New York: Routledge, 1992. 373–391.

Kirk, John Van. "Fiction Chronicle." Rev. of *Written on the Body*, by Jeanette Winterson. *Hudson Review* 46 (Autumn 1993): 600–604.

Kotte, Claudia. "Random Patterns? Orderly Disorder in Julian Barnes's *A History of the World in 10½ Chapters*." *Arbeiten aus Anglistik und Amerikanistik* 22.1 (1997): 107–128.

Kristeva, Julia. "Women's Time." Trans. Alice Jardine and Harry Blake. *The Kristeva Reader*. Ed. Toril Moi. New York: Columbia UP, 1986.

Kundera, Milan. *The Book of Laughter and Forgetting*. 1979. Trans. Michael Henry Heim. New York: Penguin, 1981.

_____. *The Unbearable Lightness of Being*. 1984. Trans. Michael Henry Heim. New York: Harper & Row, 1985.

Kureishi, Hanif. *The Buddha of Suburbia*. London: Faber, 1990.

Kutzer, M. Daphne. "The Cartography of Passion: Cixous, Wittig, and Winterson." *Re-Naming the Landscape*. Eds. Jürgen Kleist and Bruce A. Butterfield. New York: Peter Lang, 1994.

Lacan, Jacques. "The Mirror Stage." *Écrits: A Selection*. Trans. Alan Sheridan. New York: Norton, 1977. 1–7.

Lane, Mary E. Bradley. *Mizora: A Prophecy*. New York: G. W. Dillingham, 1890.

Lauter, Estella, and Carol Schreier Rupprecht, eds. *Feminist Archetypal Theory: Interdisciplinary Re-visions of Jungian Thought*. Knoxville, TE: U of Tennessee P, 1985.

Le Guin, Ursula. *The Dispossessed*. 1974. New York: Avon, 1975.

_____. *The Left Hand of Darkness*. 1969. London: Futura, 1981.

Lee, Alison. "Angela Carter's New Eve(lyn): De/En-Gendering Narrative." *Ambiguous Discourse: Feminist Narratology & British Women Writers*. Ed. Kathy Mezei. Chapel Hill: U of North Carolina P, 1996: 238–49.

_____. *Realism and Power: Postmodern British Fiction*. London: Routledge, 1990.

Lee, Tanith. *Red as Blood*. New York: DAW, 1983.

Lefanu, Sarah. *In the Chinks of the World Machine: Feminism and Science Fiction*. Bloomington: Indiana UP, 1989.

Lessing, Doris. *Memoirs of a Survivor*. 1974. New York: Vintage, 1988.

Lester, Toby. "What is the Koran?" *The Atlantic Monthly* 283.1 (January 1999): 43–56.

Lowe, Marian, and Ruth Hubbard, eds. *Woman's Nature: Rationalizations of Inequality*. New York: Pergamon, 1983.

Lyotard, Jean-François. *The Postmodern Condition: A Report on Knowledge*. Trans. Geoff Bennington and Brian Massumi. Minneapolis: U of Minnesota P, 1984.

MacKinnon, Catherine. *Feminism Unmodified: Discourses on Life and Law*. Cambridge, MA: 1986.

_____. *Only Words*. Cambridge, MA: Harvard UP, 1993.

Mann, Thomas. *Doctor Faustus: The Life of the German Composer, Adrian Leverkühn*. 1947. Trans. H. T. Lowe-Porter. New York, Knopf, 1948.

Márquez, Gabriel Garcia. *Love in the Time of Cholera*. 1981. New York: Knopf, 1989.

_____. *One Hundred Years of Solitude*. Trans. Gregory Rabassa. 1967. London: Picador, 1978.

Martin, Emily. "Body Narratives, Body Boundaries." *Cultural Studies*. Eds. Lawrence Grossberg, Cary Nelson, Paula A. Treichler. New York: Routledge, 1992. 409–419.

_____. *The Woman in the Body: A Cultural Analysis of Reproduction*. Boston: Beacon Press, 1987.

Massa, Ann, and Alistair Stead, eds. *Forked Tongues? Comparing Twentieth-Century British and American Literature*. London: Longman, 1994.

McEwan, Ian. *Amsterdam*. New York: Nan A. Talese, 1999.

_____. *The Child In Time*. 1987. London: Picador, 1988.

_____. *The Comfort of Strangers*. 1981. London: Picador, 1992.

_____. *Enduring Love*. New York: Nan A. Talese, 1998.

_____. *First Love, Last Rites*. 1975. London: Picador, 1976.

_____. *The Innocent*. London: Picador, 1990.

McNair, Brian. *Mediated Sex: Pornography and Postmodern Culture*. London: Arnold, 1996.

Meaney, Gerardine. *(Un)like Subjects: Women, Theory, Fiction*. London: Routledge, 1993.

Midgley, Mary. *Science as Salvation: A Modern Myth and Its Meaning*. London: Routledge, 1992.

Miner, Valerie. "At Her Wit's End." Rev. of *Written on the Body*, by Jeanette Winterson. *Women's Review of Books* 10 (May 1993): 21.

Mo, Timothy. *Sour Sweet*. New York: Random House, 1985.

Morgenstern, Naomi. "'There is Nothing Else Like This': Sex and Citation in Pornogothic Feminism." *Genders 25: Sex Positives? The Cultural Politics of Dissident Sexualities*. Eds. Thomas Foster, Carol Siegel, and Ellen E. Berry. New York: New York UP. 39–67.

Morrison, Toni. *Beloved*. 1987. London: Picador, 1988.

Mulvey, Laura. "Visual Pleasure and Narrative Cinema." *Visual and Other Pleasures*. Bloomington: Indiana UP, 1989. 14–26.

Natarajan, Nalini. "Woman, Nation, and Narration in *Midnight's Children*." *Scattered Hegemonies: Postmodernity and Transnational Feminist Practices*. Eds. Inderpal Grewal and Caren Kaplan. Minnesota: U of Minnesota P, 1994.

Nicoll, Allardyce. *British Drama*. Sixth ed. Rev. J. C. Trewin. New York: Harper & Row, 1978.

Noble, David F. *A World Without Women: The Christian Clerical Culture of Western Science*. New York: Oxford UP, 1992.

Okri, Ben. *The Famished Road*. 1991. London: Vintage, 1992.

Ondaatje, Michael. *The English Patient*. 1992. New York: Vintage, 1993.

_____. *In the Skin of a Lion*. New York: Penguin, 1987.

Onega, Susana. "'A Knack for Yarns': The Narrativization of History and the End of History." *Telling Histories: Narrativizing History, Historicizing Literature*. Ed. Susana Onega. Amsterdam: Rodopi, 1995.

Perloff, Marjorie, ed. *Postmodern Genres*. Norman, OK: U of Oklahoma P, 1989.

Perrault, Charles. *The Fairy Tales of Charles Perrault*. Trans. Angela Carter. London: Gollancz, 1977.

Piercy, Marge. *Women on the Edge of Time*. Greenwich, Conn.: Fawcett Crest, 1976.

Pipes, Daniel. *The Rushdie Affair: The Novel, the Ayatollah, and the West*. New York: Carol, 1990.

Propp, Vladimir. *Morphology of the Folktale*. 2nd ed. Austin: U of Texas P, 1968.

Radway, Janice. *Reading the Romance: Women, Patriarchy and Popular Literature*. 1984. Chapel Hill, NC: U of North Carolina P, 1991.

Ross, Andrew. "The Popularity of Pornography." *No Respect: Intellectuals and Popular Culture*. New York: Routledge, 1989. 171–208.

Roy, Arundhati. *The God of Small Things*. 1997. New York: HarperCollins, 1998.

Rushdie, Salman. *East, West*. 1994. New York: Vintage, 1995.

_____. *Grimus*. 1975. Woodstock, NY: Overlook Press, 1982.

_____. *Imaginary Homelands: Essays and Criticism 1981–1991*. London: Granta, 1991.

_____. "*Midnight's Children* and *Shame*." *Kunapipi* 7.1 (1985): 1–19.

_____. *Midnight's Children*. 1981. London: Picador, 1982.

_____. *Shame*. 1983. New York: Vintage, 1989.

_____. *The Jaguar Smile: A Nicaraguan Journey*. London: Picador, 1987.

_____. *The Satanic Verses*. 1988. New York: Viking, 1989.

Russ, Joanna. *The Female Man*. 1975. Boston: Beacon Press, 1986.

Ruthven, Malise. *A Satanic Affair: Salman Rushdie and the Rage of Islam*. London: Chatto and Windus, 1990.

Sage, Lorna. Interview with Angela Carter. *New Writing*. Eds. Malcolm Bradbury and Judy Cooke. London: Minerva, 1992. 185–193.

_____, ed. *Flesh and the Mirror: Essays on the Art of Angela Carter*. London: Virago, 1994.

Said, Edward. *Culture and Imperialism*. New York: Knopf, 1994.

_____. *Orientalism*. New York: Vintage, 1979.

Sargent, Pamela. *The Shore of Women*. New York: Crown, 1986.

_____, ed. *Women of Wonder: The Contemporary Years*. Sand Diego: Harvest, 1995.

Saunders, Kate. "From Flaubert's Parrot to Noah's Woodworm." *The Sunday Times* (18 June 1989): G9.

Savigny, Jean Baptiste Henri, and Alexandre Corréard. 1818. *Narrative of A Voyage to Senegal in 1816*. London: Dawsons, 1968.

Schulz, Bruno. *The Street of Crocodiles*. Trans. Celina Wieniewska. 1934. New York: Penguin, 1977.

Scott, James B. "Parrot as Paradigms: Infinite Deferral of Meaning in 'Flaubert's Parrot.'" *ARIEL* 21.3 (July 1990): 57–68.

Segal, Lynn, and Mary McIntosh, eds. *Sex Exposed: Sexuality and the Pornography Debate*. New Brunswick, NJ: Rutgers UP, 1993.

Sexton, Anne. *Transformations*. Boston: Houghton Mifflin, 1972.

Sheehan, Aurelie Jane. Rev. of *Written on the Body*, by Jeanette Winterson. *Review of Contemporary Fiction* 13 (Fall 1993): 208–209.

Sheets, Robin Ann. "Pornography, Fairy Tales, and Feminism: Angela Carter's 'The Bloody Chamber.'" *Journal of the History of Sexuality* 1.4 (1991): 633–657.

Shelley, Mary Wollstonecraft. *Frankenstein*. 1818. London: Penguin, 1992.

Smith, Amanda. Interview with Julian Barnes. *Publisher's Weekly*. 3 November 1989. 73–74.

Sontag, Susan. *Illness as Metaphor*. 1977. New York: Farrar, Straus, and Giroux, 1978.

Strandley, Arline Reilein. *Auguste Comte*. Boston: Twayne, 1981.

Strossen, Nadine. *Defending Pornography: Free Speech, Sex, and the Fight for Women's Rights*. New York: Scribner, 1995.

Stuart, Andrea. "Terms of Endearment." Rev. of *Written on the Body*, by Jeanette Winterson. *New Statesman and Society* 18 September, 1992: 37–38.

Suleiman, Susan Rubin. *Subversive Intent: Gender, Politics, and the Avant-Garde*. Cambridge, Mass.: Harvard UP, 1990.

Suleri, Sara. *The Rhetoric of English India*. Chicago: U of Chicago P, 1992.

Sutherland, John. "On the Salieri Express." Rev. of *Written on the Body*, by Jeanette Winterson. *London Review of Books* 24 September, 1992: 18–20.

Swift, Graham. *Waterland*. 1983. London: Picador, 1984.

Teller, Astro. *Exegesis*. New York: Vintage, 1997.

Tennant, Emma. *Faustine*. London: Faber, 1992.

Tepper, Sheri. *Beauty*. 1991. New York: Bantam, 1992.

_____. *The Gate to Women's Country*. New York: Bantam, 1988.

Thomas, D. M. *The White Hotel*. 1981. New York: Penguin, 1993.

Thatcher, Margaret. *The Downing Street Years*. London: Harper Collins, 1993.

Tiptree, James, Jr. [Alice Sheldon]. "The Girl Who Was Plugged In." *Cybersex*. Ed. Richard Glyn Jones. New York: Carroll and Graf, 1996: 187–213.

Todd, Richard. *Consuming Fictions: The Booker Prize and Fiction in Britain Today*. London: Bloomsbury, 1996.

Tuttle, Lisa. *A Spaceship Built of Stone and Other Stories*. London: Women's Press, 1987.

Veeser, H. Aram, ed. *The New Historicism*. New York: Routledge, 1989.

Verman, Charu. "Padma's Tragedy: A Feminist Deconstruction of Midnight's Children." *Panjab University Research Bulletin (Arts)* 20.2 (Oct. 1989): 59–65.

Villiers de L'Isle-Adam, Auguste, comte de. *Eve of the Future Eden* (*L'Eve Future*). Trans. Marilyn Gaddis Rose. Lawrence, Kansas: Coronado Press: 1981.

Waugh, Patricia. *Metafiction: The Theory and Practice of Self-Conscious Fiction.* London: Routledge, 1984.

Weldon, Fay. *The Cloning of Joanna May.* 1989. New York: Viking, 1990.

_____. *The Life and Loves of a She-Devil.* 1983. Reading, England: Coronet, 1984.

White, Hayden. "The Fictions of Factual Representations." *The Literature of Fact: Selected Papers From the English Institute.* New York: Columbia UP, 1976. 21–44.

_____. "The Historical Text as Literary Artefact." *The Writing of History: Literary Form and Historical Understanding.* Eds. Robert H. Canary and Henry Kozicki. Madison: U of Wisconsin P, 1978. 41–62.

Wilde, Oscar, *The Complete Works of Oscar Wilde.* Leicester, U.K.: Blitz Editions, 1990.

Williams, Linda. *Hard Core.* Berkeley: U of California P, 1989.

Wilson, Leigh Allison. "Getting Physical." Rev. of *Written on the Body*, by Jeanette Winterson. *Washington Post Book World* 14 February, 1993: 6.

Winterson, Jeanette. "All Teeth 'N' Smiles." *New Statesman and Society* 2.81 (December 1989): 32–33.

_____. *Art and Lies.* 1994. New York: Vintage, 1996.

_____. *Art Objects: Essays on Ecstasy and Effrontery.* Toronto: Vintage Canada, 1996.

_____. *Boating For Beginners.* London: Methuen, 1985.

_____. *Gut Symmetries.* New York: Knopf, 1997.

_____. *Oranges are Not the Only Fruit.* 1985. New York: Atlantic Monthly Press, 1987.

_____. *Sexing the Cherry.* 1989. London: Vintage, 1990.

_____. *The Passion.* 1987. London: Penguin, 1988.

_____. *Written on the Body.* 1993. New York: Vintage, 1994.

Wittig, Monique. *The Lesbian Body.* Trans. David Le Vay. New York: William Morrow, 1975.

Woolf, Virginia. *Orlando: A Biography.* New York: Harcourt Brace, 1928.

_____. *Three Guineas.* New York: Harcourt Brace, 1938.

Zamora, Lois Parkinson, and Wendy B. Faris, eds. *Magical Realism: Theory, History, and Community.* Durham, NC: Duke UP, 1995.

Zipes, Jack. *The Brothers Grimm: From Enchanted Forests to the Modern World.* New York: Routledge, 1988.

_____. *Fairy Tale as Myth / Myth as Fairy Tale.* Lexington, Kentucky: UP Kentucky, 1994.

_____. *Fairy Tales and the Art of Subversion: The Classical Genre for Children and the Process of Civilization.* 1983. New York: Methuen, 1988.

_____. "Introduction." *Beauties, Beasts, and Enchantment: Classic French Fairy Tales.* Markham, Ontario: Nal Books, 1989.

_____, ed. *Don't Bet on the Prince: Contemporary Feminist Fairy Tales in North America and England.* New York: Methuen, 1986.

Index

Afzal-Khan, Fawzia 29–30, 37
Ahmed, Aijaz 24–25
Akhtar, Shabbir 73, 75–76
Al-Azmeh, Aziz 75
An Alchemy of Genres 24
Allen, Carolyn 122, 130
Amis, Kingsley 11, 147
Amis, Martin 10, 12, 27, 107, 187, 192, 197
Anatomy of Criticism 14
Anderson, Benedict 29–30, 36, 182
Anderson, Sherwood 94
Androcentrism 13, 61, 97–98, 111, 113–116, 121, 125, 145–146, 147, 149–154, 157, 159, 165–168, 170–171, 174, 182, 185, 196
Appignanesi, Lisa 177
Argentina 108
Aristotle 14, 188
Arnold, Matthew 180
Art 99–102, 139–140, 146
Art and Lies 120–121, 126, 142–143
Art criticism 99
Art Objects 10, 92, 134, 139, 140, 146
Asad, Talal 54
Ashraf, Syed Ali 59, 68–69
Atwood, Margaret 150, 175–176
Auden, W. H. 89
Auschwitz 192
Ayatollah Khomeini 45, 57, 65, 71–73, 75–76

Bacon, Francis 126
Bakhtin, Mikhail 14–15, 16, 74, 94
Baldick, Chris 179

Bangladesh 41
Banville, John 21
Barnes, Julian 9, 12–13, 21, 23, 26–27, 41, 53, 54, 70, 76, 77–109, 110–111, 116, 117, 119, 121, 128, 139, 141, 147, 149, 172, 174, 188, 190, 191, 193, 197
Barnwell 189
Barth, John 10
Bataille, Georges 184
Baudrillard, Jean 133, 142, 197
Bay of Pigs 176
Bayley, John 147–148
Beebee, Thomas 15, 20, 150
Before She Met Me 106
The Beggar's Opera 7–8, 14, 116, 188
Belgrano 108
Beloved 22, 193
Bettelheim, Bruno 152
Bible 53, 72, 95–96, 112–113, 115–121, 124, 125, 167; and women 119
Bildungsroman 29, 42, 101, 112, 115
Biography 81–86, 90–92
The Black Album 26
Blake, William 22
Bleich, David 16–17, 19, 45
The Bloody Chamber and Other Stories 150, 152–155, 161, 175
Boating for Beginners 87, 111, 115–125, 141, 174
The Bone People 26
Book of Common Prayer 183
Booker Prize 24–26
Borges, Jorge Luis 32

Brennan, Timothy 52, 66
British fiction 24–27; contemporary 9–10; post–World War II 10; realism in 10–11
Browning, Elizabeth Barrett 191
Browning, Robert 14, 191
Brownmiller, Susan 157
The Buddha of Suburbia 26
Burgess, Anthony 12, 147
Butler, Judith 170
Butler, Octavia 175
Byatt, A. S. 27, 78, 81, 107, 150, 191

Cadigan, Pat 175
Carter, Angela 8–9, 10, 12–13, 16, 18, 21, 23, 24, 32, 54, 55, 59, 64, 76, 77, 110–111, 116, 119, 122, 125, 147–186, 188, 190, 191, 193, 194, 196, 197
Charnas, Suzy McKee 175
Chaudhuri, Una 39
The Child in Time 10, 107
Christianity 81, 111, 112–116, 120, 124, 126, 155, 164, 171, 180
Cixous, Helene 165
Clarissa 20, 23
Class, representations of 8
Classism 110
A Clockwork Orange 12
Cohen, Ralph 15–16, 18–19, 21, 22–23, 31, 38, 150, 153, 158, 188–189
Cold War 176, 193
Commonwealth literature 24–27
Comte, Auguste 125–127
Connor, Steven 10
Conrad, Joseph 37–38
Corréard, Alexandre 99
Coupland, Douglas 191
Cours de Philosophie Positive 125
Cranny-Francis, Anne 149–150
Cream, Julia 129
The Crying of Lot 49 191
Culture and Imperialism 41

DeLillo, Don 78
Desacralization 13–14, 53, 55–56, 61, 71–72, 95, 111, 114, 116–119, 140, 143, 157, 166, 167, 172–173, 181, 188, 195, 197
Detective fiction 83
Dhondy, Farrukh 75
Diary of Anne Frank 192
Doan, Laura 114
Doctor Faustus 196
Don Quixote 32
Dorfman, Ariel 32

Dorsey, Candas Jane 175
The Downing Street Years 108–109
Doyle, Roddy 25
Drabble, Margaret 10, 11
Dubliners 94
Duncker, Patricia 138
Dworkin, Andrea 155, 157–159

Elgin, Suzette 175
The English Patient 25
Enlightenment 13, 58, 78–79, 125–127, 139, 140, 146, 176, 179
Esquival, Laura 32
Eugenics 40
Exegesis 191

Fables 23, 29, 118, 196
Fabulation 98–99, 101, 104–105, 107, 119
Fairy Tale as Myth 151, 160
Fairy Tales 16, 23, 29, 68, 116, 118, 125, 148, 149–155, 158, 159, 160; and pornography 153–154, 175–177, 181–183, 185–186, 190, 191
Fairy Tales and the Art of Subversion 151
Falklands War 9, 39, 47, 75, 108–109
The Famished Road 25
Fanon, Frantz 62
Fantastic 32, 33, 36, 40, 43, 48, 51, 58, 59, 60, 63, 66–68, 71
Fantasy 16, 33, 43, 60, 68, 69–71, 118, 175
Farce 116
Faris, Wendy 32–33
Faustine 195–196
Feminism 98, 118, 124, 149, 164, 167, 172, 195–196; and pornography 148, 149, 153–160; and postmodernism 112, 116, 140, 149; and psychoanalysis 165, 172
Feminist Archetypal Theory 160
Fielder, Leslie 178
Fielding, Henry 8, 19–20, 116
Flaubert, Gustave 81–93
Flaubert's Parrot 81–93, 95, 101–102, 103, 105, 109, 191–192
Flax, Jane 140
Fowler, Alastair 14, 189–191
Fowles, John 12, 78, 147
Frankenstein 116, 126, 194
Freedman, Diane 24, 26
The French Lieutenant's Woman 12, 78
Freud, Sigmund 152, 165, 172, 193
Freund, Charles Paul 74
Fromm, Erich 152
Frye, Northrop 15, 188
Fuentes, Carlos 72, 74, 76

Fundamentalism 40, 155, 176, 178; and gender 75–76, 110–111, 112–115, 141; religious 35, 38, 55, 59, 65, 72–76, 95, 110–111, 112–115, 117, 119, 124, 167, 171

Gandhi, Indira 35–36, 40–41
Gandhi, Sanjay 40
Gasiorek, Andrzej 11, 105
Gay, John 7–8, 14, 19, 116, 188
Gender 110–111, 123, 128–130, 137, 145, 147, 159–161, 172, 194; archetypes of 159–161, 163, 166–169, 173–175, 183–184, 186, 190, 197; as performance 170–173
Genre 14–23, 69, 85, 106, 148, 150, 153, 159, 165, 174, 188–196; and feminism 24, 149–150, 190, 193; and ideology 19–23, 151, 158, 181; and language 16–17; mixing of 8, 13, 14–19, 23, 24, 26, 54, 60, 73, 81, 84, 94, 101, 109, 115–116, 118, 136–137, 140–141, 153, 176, 190–191; use-value of 15, 23, 151
Géricault, Theodore 99–101, 103
Gilman, Charlotte Perkins 175
The God of Small Things 25
Gothic fiction 116–117, 125, 148, 149, 175–186, 190, 194–196
Grafton, Sue 83
Gravity's Rainbow 191
Greene, Graham 11–12, 107
Grice, Helena 145
Griffin, Susan 157
Grimm brothers 151
Grosz, Elizabeth 137
Grotesque 36–39, 43, 48–52, 111, 138, 162, 164–166, 182, 188, 190
Gut Symmetries 142–146

Haggard, H. Rider 37–38
Hammett, Dashiel 83
The Handmaid's Tale 176
Harris, Wilson 32
Heart of Darkness 37
The Heart of the Matter 11–12, 107
Heller, Joseph 10
Herland 175
Heroes and Villains 176–186
Hinduism, and women 110
Hiroshima 176
Histoires ou contes du temps perdu 151–152
Historical fiction 78
The Historical Register 19
Historical revisionism 69, 105
Historiographic metafiction 20–21, 78, 86, 93, 97

Historiography 29, 41–42, 78–105, 117, 190
A History of the World in 10½ Chapters 70, 77, 81, 94–109, 111, 139, 174
Hollywood 160, 161, 166, 167, 169, 173
Holocaust 69, 99, 120; narratives of 192–193, 197
Homosexuality 113–114, 120–121, 129
Horace 14
Howe, Geoffrey 48
Hubbard, Ruth 127–128, 136
Hulme, Keri 26
Hutcheon, Linda 13, 20, 21, 78–79, 90, 159, 196
Hybrid identity 43–47, 50–51, 63, 73

Illness as Metaphor 136
Imagined Communities 29
Imperialism 35, 39, 41
In Theory 24–25
India 33–43, 44, 59, 64
The Infernal Desire Machines of Doctor Hoffman 176
The Information 187
The Innocent 107, 193–194
Iran 72
Irigaray, Luce 160, 163, 168
Ishiguro, Kazuo 10, 12, 17–18, 26, 27, 107
Islam 53–57, 64–65, 69–75; and women 55, 110
Israeli-Arab conflict 97

Jackson, Rosemary 33
Jameson, Fredric 20, 23, 37, 142, 197
Jane Eyre 115
Jordan, June 17
Jouve, Nicole Ward 161, 173
Joyce, James 14, 39, 94
Judaism 164, 180
Jung, Carl 152, 160

Kafka, Franz 32, 49
Kappeler, Susanne 157, 159
Kauer, Uta 130
Kavanagh, Dan 83
King Solomon's Mines 37
Kingston, Maxine Hong 21
Kipling, Rudyard 37–38, 49
Know and Tell 16–17
Koran 53–57, 61, 70–73
Kosinski, Jerzy 192
Kotte, Claudia 99, 104
Kristeva, Julia 165
Kundera, Milan 32
Kureishi, Hanif 26

Language: idioms 17–18, 45; language use 16–17, 44–45; of science/medicine 134–136
Language genres 44–45, 136, 141
Larkin, Philip 103
Leavis, Q. D. 9, 10, 24
Lee, Alison 84, 93
Lee, Hermione 148
Lee, Tanith 150
Lefanu, Sarah 175
Le Guin, Ursula 175
Lessing, Doris 175
Letters from London 9, 108–109
Lewis, C. S. 68
The Life and Loves of a She-Devil 194–195
Lillo, George 189
Literary criticism 87–88, 91, 191
Lively, Penelope 27, 78
London Fields 10
The London Merchant 189
Longinus 14
Lorde, Audre 24
Louis XIV 151
Love and Death in the American Novel 178
Lyotard, Jean-François 67, 81, 140–141

MacKinnon, Catherine 155, 158–159
Madame Bovary 90
Magic realism 29, 31–71, 148, 190
The Magic Toyshop 183, 184
Mann, Thomas 196
Marlowe, Christopher 196
Marquez, Gabriel Garcia 32, 57
Martin, Emily 127–128, 140
Marxism 81
Master narratives (also grand narratives, metanarratives) 67, 81, 105
McEwan, Ian 10, 12, 27, 107, 193–194
Mecca 57–59, 66
Mercy 158
Metafiction 20, 61, 81, 86, 99, 102
The Metamorphosis 32, 33, 49
Metroland 101–102
Michener, James 78
Microserfs 191
Midnight's Children 10, 26, 31, 33–43, 45, 92
Migrancy 50–51
Mo Timothy 26
Modernism 10–12, 20, 134
Monty Python 8
Moore, C. L. 175
Morrison, Toni 22, 32, 193
Muhammad 53–54, 57

Mullen, Peter 70–71
Mulvey, Laura 169
Munro, Alice 21
Murdoch, Iris 11, 12
Myth (and myths) 29, 118, 119, 149, 156–157, 159, 160, 167, 171, 173–176, 180–181, 184, 186, 197

Naipaul, V. S. 27
Narrative of a Voyage to Senegal in 1816 99
Nationalism 30, 39, 48, 109, 110, 198
New Historicism 78–80, 93
New Statesman and Society 114
New York Review of Books 147
The New Yorker 108
Newton, Isaac 126
Night 192
Nights at the Circus 10, 161, 185
Noble, David 126
Nothing Sacred 148

Okri, Ben 25, 32
Old Testament 70–71, 95–96, 110, 116–120, 166, 167
Ondaatje, Michael 21, 25, 32, 78
Opera 8, 188
Oranges Are Not the Only Fruit 112–115, 120, 124, 125, 146
Orientalism 37–38

Paddy Clarke Ha Ha Ha 25
The Painted Bird 192
Pakistan 59, 72
Pamela 20, 23
Pantomime 8–9, 115–116
Parekh, Bhikhu 71
Paretsky, Sarah 83
Pasquin 19
The Passion 10
The Passion of New Eve 33, 122, 161–175, 183, 184, 185
Percy, Bishop 189
Perloff, Marjorie 21–22
Perrault, Charles 151–152, 156, 159, 181
The Picture of Dorian Gray 89
Piercy, Marge 24, 175
Plato 14, 186
Pornography 15, 16, 23, 148, 149, 153–163, 166, 167–170, 173–174, 184, 190
Pornography: Men Possessing Women 158
Positivism 125–127, 130, 133, 139, 140, 145–146
Possession 191–192

Postcolonialism 29, 45, 74
The Postmodern Condition 140
Postmodern era (also postmodern culture) 133, 139–140, 142, 197
Postmodern fiction/literature 13, 19–23, 63, 71, 78–81, 84, 86, 90–91, 115, 127, 142, 147, 148, 150, 167, 177, 188, 196–198; and genre 19–23, 115; and irreverence 13; and profanity 12–14
The Power and the Glory 107
Propp, Vladimir 151
Psychoanalysis 149, 155, 160, 161, 164–167, 172
Purity, cultural 45–46, 55, 74
Pykett, Lyn 139, 148
Pynchon, Thomas 10, 191

Rabelais, François 38
Racism 13, 110, 198
Radway, Janice 15, 121–122
Rank, Otto 152
Reading the Romance 15
Realism (also realist representation) 10–12, 43, 60, 68, 69–70, 90–91, 100–101, 112, 142, 147, 149–150, 158, 191–192
Religion 13, 52–77, 94–97, 102, 107, 111, 115, 125 126, 139, 140, 143–144, 149, 160, 161, 172–173, 180–181, 183, 196–198; and gender/women 55, 110–111, 113–114, 182–183
Religious texts 13, 53–56, 71–73, 95, 110, 113, 115–116, 121, 125, 190; and morality 63–64
The Remains of the Day 10, 17–18, 26, 107
Richardson, Samuel 20
Roh, Franz 32
Romance 15, 115–116, 121–123, 125, 129–130, 181–183, 188, 193
Roy, Arundhati 25
Rushdie, Salman 10, 12–13, 18, 20, 21, 23, 26, 29–76, 77, 92, 95, 97, 110–111, 113, 117, 121, 128, 141, 147, 148, 149, 171, 172, 188, 190, 191, 197; and Commonwealth literature 24–26; and the *fatwa* 65, 69–76
Russ, Joanna 175
Rutherford, Edward 78

Sade, Marquis de 153–154, 156–157, 160, 163, 165, 169, 171, 173, 184, 188
The Sadeian Woman 153–161, 164, 165, 172, 180
Sage, Lorna 10
Said, Edward 37–38, 41, 74

Sargent, Pamela 175
Satanic verses 53–54
The Satanic Verses 10, 20, 26, 43–76, 111, 117
Savigny, Jean Baptiste Henri 99
Schulz, Bruno 32
Science (also scientific discourse) 58, 79, 125–130, 134–137, 139–146, 198; and androcentrism 126–128, 145; and gender 127–128, 137; and love 131–132; and medicine 133–137; and postmodern era/culture 127, 132–134, 143
Science fiction *see* Speculative-fiction
Scott, James 81
Scripture *see* Religious texts
Self, Will 12, 27
Sexing the Cherry 125, 143
Sexism 111, 121, 194; *see also* Androcentrism
Sexton, Anne 150
Shadow Dance 185
Shahabuddin, Syed 73
Shame 72
Shamela 20
Sheehan, Aurelie Jane 129
Sheldon, Alice 175
Shelley, Mary Wollstonecraft 116, 126, 194
Slave narratives 22–23
Snitow, Ann 155
Sontag, Susan 136
Sour Sweet 26
Spark, Muriel 11, 12
Speculative-fiction 15, 16, 148, 149, 175, 181, 186, 190, 193; and cyberpunk 16; feminist uses of 16, 175
The Spice Girls 9
Spy thriller genre 193–194
Staring at the Sun 106
Sterne, Laurence 8, 19
Suez Canal crisis 10
Suleiman, Susan 21, 124, 196
Suleri, Sara 64
Surr, Thomas Skinner 189
Sutherland, John 129
Swift, Graham 12, 27, 78, 92, 107
Swift, Jonathan 8, 19, 38

Taheri, Amir 75
Talking It Over 103
Technology *see* Science
Teller, Astro 191
Tennant, Emma 195–196
Tepper, Sheri 150, 175

Thatcher, Margaret 75, 108–109
Thatcherism 9
Thomas, D. M. 14, 192–193, 197
The Thousand and One Nights 32
Time's Arrow 107, 192
Tiptree, James, Jr. (a.k.a. Alice Sheldon)
  175
Todd, Richard 24, 26
Tom Jones 20, 116
Torah 72
Tory Party 9, 109
Totalitarianism 35, 38–39, 41
Tristam Shandy 19
Tuttle, Lisa 175

Ulysses 14, 33

Vader, Darth 9
The Virago Book of Fairy Tales 151, 153
Vonnegut, Kurt 10

Walpole, Sir Robert 19
Warner, Marina 55
Waterland 92, 107
Weldon, Fay 175, 194–195, 196

Westerns 15
White, Hayden 78–80, 86, 93, 101
The White Hotel 14, 192–193
Wiesel, Elie 192
Wilde, Oscar 89
Williams, Linda 174
Wilson, Angus 10, 11, 12
Wilson, Elizabeth 155
Winesburg, Ohio 94
Winterson, Jeanette 10, 13, 21, 23, 24, 32,
  53, 54, 55, 64, 76, 77, 87, 92, 102, 103,
  110–111, 112–146, 147, 148, 149, 170, 171,
  172, 174, 188, 190, 191, 193, 194, 196,
  197; and realism 10–12
Wise Children 161
Wodehouse, P. G. 17–18
Women's Biology 127
Woods, Tim 145
Woolf, Virginia 133
A World Without Women 126
Written on the Body 115, 128–142, 143, 197

Zamora, Lois 32–33
Zipes, Jack 151–152, 160